TORT

TORT
FOURTH EDITION

Carl Price

This edition published 2024 by
The University of Law
2 Bunhill Row
London EC1Y 8HQ

© The University of Law 2024

All rights reserved. No part of this publication may be reproduced, stored in a retrieval system, or transmitted, in any form or by any means, without the prior written permission of the copyright holder, application for which should be addressed to the publisher.

Contains public sector information licensed under the Open Government Licence v3.0

British Library Cataloguing in Publication Data

A catalogue record for this book is available from the British Library.

ISBN 978 1 80502 121 6

Preface

This book is part of a series of Study Manuals that have been specially designed to support the reader to achieve the SQE1 Assessment Specification in relation to Functioning Legal Knowledge. Each Study Manual aims to provide the reader with a solid knowledge and understanding of fundamental legal principles and rules, including how those principles and rules might be applied in practice.

This Study Manual covers the Solicitors Regulation Authority's syllabus for the SQE1 assessment for Tort in a concise and tightly focused manner. The Manual provides a clear statement of relevant legal rules and a well-defined road map through examinable law and practice. The Manual aims to bring the law and practice to life through the use of example scenarios based on realistic client-based problems and allows the reader to test their knowledge and understanding through single best answer questions that have been modelled on the SRA's sample assessment questions.

For those readers who are students at the University of Law, the Study Manual is used alongside other learning resources and the University's assessment bank to best prepare students not only for the SQE1 assessments, but also for a future life in professional legal practice.

We hope that you find the Study Manual supportive of your preparation for SQE1 and we wish you every success.

The legal principles and rules contained within this Manual are stated as at 1 May 2024.

Author acknowledgements
Wendy Laws and Ruth Rutter.

Contents

Preface		v
Table of Cases		xv
Table of Statutes		xix

Chapter 1   Negligence: Duty of Care   1

SQE1 syllabus		1
Learning outcomes		1
1.1	Introduction	2
1.2	Duty of care	3
	1.2.1 Established duty situations	3
	1.2.2 Novel duty situations	4
1.3	Liability for omissions to act	7
	1.3.1 The general rule: no liability for omissions	7
	1.3.2 Exceptions to the general rule of no liability for omissions	8
Summary		9
Summary flowchart		10
Sample questions		10

Chapter 2   Negligence: Breach of Duty   15

SQE1 syllabus		15
Learning outcomes		15
2.1	Introduction	16
2.2	The standard of care	16
	2.2.1 The nature of the 'reasonable person' test	16
	2.2.2 Special standards: the skilled defendant	17
	2.2.3 Special standards: the under-skilled defendant	18
	2.2.4 Special standards: children	19
2.3	Relevant factors in determining whether defendant has achieved the required standard of care	19
	2.3.1 Magnitude of the risk	20
	2.3.2 Cost and practicability of precautions	21
	2.3.3 Defendant's purpose	22
	2.3.4 Common practice	22
	2.3.5 The current state of knowledge	22
2.4	Proving breach of duty	23
	2.4.1 *Res ipsa loquitur*	23
	2.4.2 The Civil Evidence Act 1968	24

Contents

Summary	24
Summary flowchart	25
Sample questions	26

Chapter 3 Negligence: Causation 29

SQE1 syllabus		29
Learning outcomes		29
3.1	Introduction	30
3.2	Causation in fact	31
	3.2.1 The 'but for' test	31
	3.2.2 Proof of factual causation: the 'all or nothing' approach	31
	3.2.3 Proof of factual causation: the material contribution approach	32
	3.2.4 Factual causation: material increase in risk?	33
	3.2.5 Factual causation: what if a claimant is injured more than once?	33
3.3	Divisible injury: proportionate damages	34
3.4	Indivisible injury: contribution between tortfeasors	34
3.5	Breaking the chain of causation: intervening acts	35
	3.5.1 Breaking the chain of causation: intervening acts; the actions of a third party	36
	3.5.2 Breaking the chain of causation: intervening acts; the actions of the claimant	37
3.6	Remoteness of damage	37
	3.6.1 Remoteness of damage: the basic rule	37
	3.6.2 Remoteness of damage: the 'similar in type' rule	39
	3.6.3 Remoteness of damage: the 'egg-shell skull' rule	39
Summary		40
Summary flowchart		41
Sample questions		42

Chapter 4 Negligence: Pure Economic Loss 45

SQE1 syllabus		45
Learning outcomes		45
4.1	Introduction	46
4.2	Economic loss caused by acquiring a defective item of property	47
4.3	Economic loss unconnected to personal injury to the claimant or physical damage to the claimant's property	49
	4.3.1 Economic loss caused by damage to the property of a third party	50
	4.3.2 Economic loss caused where there is no personal injury to the claimant or physical damage to the claimant's property	51
4.4	Pure economic loss: breach of duty and causation of damage	55
4.5	Exclusion of liability	56
Summary		57

		Summary flowchart	58
		Sample questions	59
Chapter 5		**Negligence: Pure Psychiatric Harm**	**63**
	SQE1 syllabus		63
	Learning outcomes		63
	5.1	Introduction	64
	5.2	Pure psychiatric harm: limiting factors for duty of care	65
	5.3	Pure psychiatric harm: different types of victim	66
	5.4	Primary victims	67
	5.5	Secondary victims	68
		5.5.1 Secondary victims: foreseeability of psychiatric harm	69
		5.5.2 Secondary victims: proximity of relationship	69
		5.5.3 Secondary victims: proximity in time and space and proximity of perception	70
	5.6	Rescuers	71
	5.7	Pure psychiatric harm: breach of duty and causation of damage	72
	Summary		73
	Summary flowchart		74
	Sample questions		75
Chapter 6		**Negligence: Employers' Liability**	**79**
	SQE1 syllabus		79
	Learning outcomes		79
	6.1	Introduction	80
	6.2	Employer's common law duty	80
		6.2.1 Competent staff	81
		6.2.2 Adequate plant and equipment	82
		6.2.3 Safe system of work	82
		6.2.4 Safe workplace	83
		6.2.5 Stress at work	83
	6.3	Breach of duty	84
	6.4	Causation	85
	6.5	Defences	86
	Summary		86
	Summary flowchart		86
	Sample questions		87
Chapter 7		**Defences**	**91**
	SQE1 syllabus		91
	Learning outcomes		91

	7.1	Introduction		92
	7.2	Consent (voluntary assumption of risk)		92
		7.2.1	Claimant's knowledge of the risk	92
		7.2.2	Claimant's consent	92
		7.2.3	Consent and employees	93
		7.2.4	Consent and rescuers	93
	7.3	Contributory negligence		94
		7.3.1	The effect of a finding of contributory negligence	94
		7.3.2	Examples of contributory negligence	95
		7.3.3	The kind of behaviour that may amount to contributory negligence	96
	7.4	Illegality (*ex turpi causa non oritur actio*)		98
	7.5	Excluding liability		99
	Summary			99
	Summary flowchart			100
	Sample questions			100

Chapter 8 Principles of Remedies for Personal Injury and Death Claims — 103

	SQE1 syllabus			103
	Learning outcomes			103
	8.1	Introduction		104
	8.2	Compensatory damages: general principles		105
		8.2.1	The measure of damages	105
		8.2.2	Mitigation of loss	105
		8.2.3	The one action rule	105
		8.2.4	General and special damages	105
	8.3	Damages for personal injury		106
		8.3.1	Non-pecuniary losses	106
		8.3.2	Quantification of non-pecuniary damages	107
		8.3.3	Pecuniary losses	108
		8.3.4	Provisional damages and periodic payments	114
	8.4	Damages on death		115
		8.4.1	The Law Reform (Miscellaneous Provisions) Act 1934	115
		8.4.2	The Fatal Accidents Act 1976	117
	Summary			120
	Summary flowchart			120
	Sample questions			122

Chapter 9 Vicarious Liability — 125

	SQE1 syllabus		125
	Learning outcomes		125
	9.1	Introduction	126

	9.2	Requirements for vicarious liability	126
		9.2.1 Who is an employee?	126
		9.2.2 Employee must act 'in the course of employment'	127
		9.2.3 Acts expressly prohibited by the employer	128
		9.2.4 Intentional torts	129
		9.2.5 'Frolic' cases	129
	9.3	Employer's indemnity	130
	Summary		130
	Summary flowchart		131
	Sample questions		132
Chapter 10	**Occupiers' Liability**		**135**
	SQE1 syllabus		135
	Learning outcomes		135
	10.1	Introduction	136
	10.2	Liability of occupiers to visitors	136
		10.2.1 Who is an occupier?	136
		10.2.2 Who is a 'visitor'?	137
		10.2.3 Premises	138
		10.2.4 The common duty of care	138
		10.2.5 Breach of the common duty of care	138
		10.2.6 Causation and remoteness of damage	142
		10.2.7 Defences	142
	10.3	Liability of occupiers to trespassers	144
		10.3.1 To whom is the duty owed?	144
		10.3.2 Existence of the duty	145
		10.3.3 Scope of the 1984 Act duty	145
		10.3.4 Breach of duty	146
		10.3.5 Causation and remoteness	147
		10.3.6 Defences	147
	Summary		147
	Summary flowcharts		148
	Sample questions		150
Chapter 11	**Product Liability**		**153**
	SQE1 syllabus		153
	Learning outcomes		153
	11.1	Introduction	154
	11.2	Negligence	154
		11.2.1 Duty of care: the narrow rule in *Donoghue v Stevenson*	154
		11.2.2 Who is a 'manufacturer'?	154
		11.2.3 What is a 'product'?	155

		11.2.4	Who is a 'consumer'?	155
		11.2.5	Intermediate examination	155
		11.2.6	Scope of the duty owed under the narrow rule	156
		11.2.7	Breach of duty	157
		11.2.8	Proof of breach	157
		11.2.9	Causation and remoteness	158
		11.2.10	Defences	158
	11.3	Consumer Protection Act 1987		158
		11.3.1	Who can sue?	158
		11.3.2	'Damage'	159
		11.3.3	'Caused by'	159
		11.3.4	'Defect'	160
		11.3.5	'Product'	160
		11.3.6	Who is liable?	160
		11.3.7	Nature of liability	161
		11.3.8	Defences	161
	Summary			163
	Summary flowcharts			163
	Sample questions			164
Chapter 12	**Nuisance**			**169**
	SQE1 syllabus			169
	Learning outcomes			169
	12.1	Introduction		170
	12.2	Private nuisance		170
		12.2.1	Definition of private nuisance	170
		12.2.2	Interferences	170
		12.2.3	Unlawful interference	171
		12.2.4	Relevant factors	171
		12.2.5	Abnormal sensitivity	173
		12.2.6	Who can sue in private nuisance?	174
		12.2.7	Who is liable in private nuisance?	174
		12.2.8	Damage	176
		12.2.9	Defences	176
		12.2.10	Remedies	179
		12.2.11	Differences between private nuisance and negligence	182
	12.3	The rule in *Rylands v Fletcher*		183
		12.3.1	The defendant brings onto their land for their own purposes something likely to do mischief	183
		12.3.2	Escape	184
		12.3.3	Non-natural use of land	184
		12.3.4	Causes foreseeable damage of the relevant type	184
		12.3.5	Defences	184

12.4	Public nuisance	185
	12.4.1 Unreasonable conduct that materially affects the reasonable comfort and convenience of a 'class of His Majesty's subjects'	185
	12.4.2 The claimant has suffered particular harm	185
	12.4.3 Differences between public nuisance and private nuisance	186

Summary	186
Summary flowcharts	187
Sample questions	189

Index	193

Table of Cases

A
A v National Blood Authority [2001] 3 All ER 289	160-1
Adams v Ursell [1913] 1 Ch 269	173
Alcock v Chief Constable of South Yorkshire Police [1991] 4 All ER 907	68-72, 74, 76
Aldred's Case (1610) 9 Co Rep 57b	171
Allen v Gulf Oil Refining Ltd [1981] AC 1001	177
Andrews v Hopkinson [1957] 1 QB 229	154, 155
Ashton v Turner [1981] QB 137	99

B
Baker v TE Hopkins & Son Ltd [1959] 3 All ER 225	3-4, 97
Barber v Somerset County Council [2004] 2 All ER 385	83
Barnett v Chelsea and Kensington Hospital Management Committee [1969] 1 QB 428	31
Blyth v Birmingham Waterworks (1856) 11 Ex 781	16
Bolam v Friern Hospital Management Committee [1957] 2 All ER 118	17, 22
Bolitho v City and Hackney Health Authority [1997] 4 All ER 771	18
Bolton v Stone [1951] AC 850	20
Bonnington Castings Ltd v Wardlaw [1956] AC 613	32, 33
Bourhill v Young [1943] AC 92	5

C
Cambridge Water Co Ltd v Eastern Counties Leather plc [1994] 2 AC 264	176, 184
Caparo Industries plc v Dickman [1990] 1 All ER 568	4, 5-7, 11, 12, 52-3, 54, 59
Capps v Miller [1989] 2 All ER 333	96
Carmarthenshire CC v Lewis [1955] AC 549	20
Carroll v Fearon [1998] PIQR P416	157
Castle v St Augustine's Links (1922) 38 TLR 615	185
Caswell v Powell Duffryn Associated Collieries Ltd [1940] AC 152	98
Century Insurance v NI Road Transport Board [1942] 1 All ER 491	128
Chadwick v British Railways Board [1967] 2 All ER 945	72
Chaudhry v Prabhakar [1989] 1 WLR 29	53, 61
Coventry v Lawrence [2014] UKSC 13	172, 178, 179, 181

D
Daniels v R White & Sons [1938] 4 All ER 258	157
Dann v Hamilton [1939] 1 KB 509	92
Donoghue v Stevenson [1932] AC 562, [1932] All ER Rep 1	4, 5, 7, 154-7, 161, 163, 167
Dulieu v White & Sons [1901] 2 KB 669	67

E
East Suffolk Rivers Catchment Board v Kent and another [1940] 4 All ER 527	8
Evans v Triplex Safety Glass Co Ltd [1936] 1 All ER 283	158

F
Fardon v Harcourt-Rivington [1932] All ER Rep 81	20
Froom v Butcher [1975] 3 All ER 520	95-6

G

General Cleaning Contractors v Christmas [1953] AC 180	83
Gillingham BC v Medway Docks Co Ltd [1992] 3 WLR 449	179
Glasgow Corporation v Taylor [1922] 1 AC 44	139, 146
Gough v Thorne [1966] 3 All ER 398	96
Grant v Australian Knitting Mills [1936] AC 85	157

H

Halsey v Esso Petroleum Co [1961] 1 WLR 683	179
Harrison v Michelin Tyre Co Ltd [1985] 1 All ER 918	128
Haseldine v Daw & Son Ltd [1941] 3 All ER 156	142, 154
Hatton v Sutherland [2002] 2 All ER 1	83
Haynes v Harwood [1935] 1 KB 146	94
Hedley Byrne v Heller & Partners Ltd [1964] AC 465	52, 54, 59, 61
Henderson v Merrett Syndicates Ltd [1994] 3 All ER 506	55
Herald of Free Enterprise, The, Re (1987) Independent, 18 December	22
Hill v Chief Constable of West Yorkshire [1989] AC 53	3, 6
Hollywood Silver Fox Farm v Emmett [1936] 2 KB 468	173
Holtby v Brigham and Cowan (Hull) Ltd [2000] 3 All ER 421	33, 34, 35
Home Office v Dorset Yacht Co Ltd [1970] AC 1004	9, 13
Hotson v East Berkshire Area Health Authority [1987] 2 All ER 909	31
Housecroft v Burnett [1986] 1 All ER 332	113
Hudson v Ridge Manufacturing Co Ltd [1957] 2 QB 348	81, 88
Hughes v Lord Advocate [1963] 1 All ER 705	39
Hunter v Canary Wharf [1997] AC 655, [1997] 2 All ER 426	170-1, 174, 176, 180, 182

J

James McNaughton Papers Group Ltd v Hicks Anderson & Co (a firm) [1991] 1 All ER 134	53
Jones v Boyce [1814-23] All ER Rep 570	98

K

Knightley v Johns [1982] 1 WLR 349	36
Kubach v Hollands [1937] 3 All ER 907	156-7

L

Lamb v Camden London Borough Council [1981] QB 625	36
Latimer v AEC Ltd [1953] AC 643, [1953] 2 All ER 449	21, 80, 83
Lister and others v Hesley Hall Ltd [2001] 2 All ER 769	129
Lister v Romford Ice & Cold Storage Co Ltd [1957] 1 All ER 125	131
Lloyd v Grace, Smith & Co [1912] AC 716	129

M

McGhee v National Coal Board [1973] 1 WLR 1	33
McKew v Holland & Hannen & Cubitts (Scotland) Ltd [1969] 3 All ER 1621	37
McKinnon Industries v Walker [1951] 3 DLR 577	173
McLoughlin v O'Brian [1982] 2 All ER 298	70-1
Mohamud v WM Morrison Supermarkets plc [2016] UKSC 11	129
Morgan Crucible Co plc v Hill Samuel Bank Ltd [1991] 1 All ER 148	53
Morris v Murray [1990] 3 All ER 801	93
Mullin v Richards [1998] 1 All ER 920	19
Murphy v Brentwood DC [1990] 2 All ER 908	48, 51, 156

N	Nettleship v Weston [1971] 3 All ER 58	18

O	Overseas Tankship (UK) Ltd v Morts Dock and Engineering Co Ltd, The Wagon Mound (No 1) [1961] 1 All ER 404	38, 39, 40, 43, 158, 160, 176
	Owens v Brimmell [1997] QB 859	96

P	Page v Smith [1995] 2 All ER 736	67, 73
	Paris v Stepney Borough Council [1951] AC 367, [1951] 1 All ER 42	20, 85
	Performance Cars v Abraham [1962] 1 QB 33	33
	Phipps v Rochester Corporation [1955] 1 QB 450	139, 147
	Pickett v British Rail Engineering [1980] AC 136	112
	Pitts v Hunt [1990] 3 All ER 344	99
	Poland v Parr [1926] All ER Rep 177	127
	Polemis, Re [1921] All ER 40	160

R	Ratcliff v McConnell and another [1999] 1 WLR 670	147
	Reeves v Metropolitan Police Commissioner [1999] 3 All ER 897	95
	Revill v Newbery [1996] 2 WLR 239	146, 147
	Robinson v Kilvert (1889) LR 41 Ch D 88	173
	Robinson v Post Office [1974] 1 WLR 1176	39
	Roe v Ministry of Health [1954] 2 QB 66	22
	Rose v Plenty [1976] 1 All ER 97	128
	Rouse v Squires [1973] QB 889	36
	Rylands v Fletcher (1868) LR 3 HL 330	169–70, 183–6, 188, 190–2

S	Sayers v Harlow UDC [1958] 1 WLR 623	98
	Schneider v Eisovitch [1960] 2 QB 430	112
	Scott v London and St Katherine Docks Co (1865)	23
	Scott v Shepherd (1773) 2 Wm Bl 892	36
	Sedleigh-Denfield v O'Callaghan [1940] 3 All ER 349	171, 175
	Shelfer v City of London Electric Lighting Co [1895] 1 Ch 287	181
	Sienkiewicz v Greif (UK) Ltd [2011] UKSC 10	33
	Smith v Baker [1891] AC 325	93
	Smith v Eric S Bush; Harris v Wyre Forest District Council [1989] 2 All ER 514	56–7, 144
	Smith v Manchester Corporation (1974) 17 KIR 1	113
	Southport Corporation v Esso Petroleum [1956] AC 218	178
	Spartan Steel & Alloys Ltd v Martin & Co (Contractors) Ltd [1973] QB 27	50, 51
	Spring v Guardian Assurance plc [1994] 3 WLR 354	54
	Stannard (t/a Wyvern Tyres) v Gore [2012] EWCA Civ 1248	184
	Stansbie v Troman [1948] 1 All ER 599	36
	Stennett v Hancock [1939] 2 All ER 578	154
	Stovin v Wise [1996] AC 923	7
	Sturges v Bridgman (1879) 11 Ch D 852	177

T	Tetley v Chitty [1986] 1 All ER 663	175
	Tomlinson v Congleton Borough Council [2003] 3 All ER 1122	145
	Transco v Stockport Metropolitan Borough Council [2003] UKHL 61	183–4

Table of Cases

	Tremain v Pike [1969] 3 All ER 1303	39
	Twine v Bean's Express (1946) 202 LT 9	128
V	Various Claimants v Catholic Child Welfare Society and Others [2012] UKSC 56	127
W	Walker v Northumberland County Council [1995] 1 All ER 737	83
	Walter v Selfe (1851) 4 De G & Sm 315	171
	Warren v Henleys Ltd [1948] 2 All ER 935	127
	Waters v Commissioner of Police for the Metropolis [2002] 1 WLR 1607	81
	Watt v Hertfordshire County Council [1954] 1 WLR 835	22
	Weller & Co v Foot and Mouth Disease Research Institute [1966] 1 QB 569	51
	Wells v Cooper [1958] 2 QB 265	18, 19
	West v Shephard [1964] AC 326	107
	Wheat v E Lacon & Co Ltd [1966] 1 All ER 582	136
	Wheeler v Saunders [1995] 2 All ER 697	179
	White v Chief Constable of the South Yorkshire Police [1999] 1 All ER 1	71
	White v Jones [1995] 1 All ER 691	54, 55
	Wieland v Cyril Lord Carpets Ltd [1969] 3 All ER 1006	37
	Wilsher v Essex Area Health Authority [1987] QB 730	18
	Wilsher v Essex Area Health Authority [1988] AC 1074	32
	Wilsons & Clyde Coal Co Ltd, The v English [1937] 3 All ER 628	80, 82
	Wise v Kaye [1962] 1 QB 638	107
	Woodward v The Mayor of Hastings [1945] KB 174	142

Table of Statutes

A

Administration of Justice Act 1982
    s 1(1)(b) — 107

C

Civil Evidence Act 1968 — 25
    s 11 — 24
Civil Liability (Contribution) Act 1978 — 35, 36, 40, 97, 101, 130
    s 1(1) — 34
    s 2(1) — 34
Consumer Protection Act 1987 — 153–4, 158–64, 166–8
Consumer Rights Act 2015 — 143–4, 147, 150, 158, 165
    s 62 — 56
    s 65(1) — 56, 57, 58
Contract (Rights of Third Parties) Act 1999 — 47, 154
Countryside and Rights of Way Act 2000 — 145

D

Damages Act 1996 — 110
    s 2 — 115

E

Employer's Liability (Defective Equipment) Act 1969
    s 1(1) — 82
Employers' Liability (Compulsory Insurance) Act 1969 — 80

F

Fatal Accidents Act 1976 — 116, 117, 119–21, 123

H

Health and Safety at Work etc Act 1974 — 85, 87
    s 47 — 85
Highways Act 1980 — 145

L

Law Reform (Contributory Negligence) Act 1945
    s 1(1) — 94
Law Reform (Miscellaneous Provisions) Act 1934 — 115–16, 119, 120, 121
    s 1(1) — 116
Law Reform (Personal Injuries) Act 1948
    s 2(4) — 109

N

National Parks and Access to the Countryside Act 1949 — 144

O

Occupiers' Liability Act 1957 — 99, 135–9, 141–4, 145–8, 150, 151
    s 2(4)(b) — 83
Occupiers' Liability Act 1984 — 135, 136–8, 144, 145–9, 152

R

Road Traffic Act 1988
    s 149   93, 102

S

Senior Courts Act 1981
    s 32A   114
Social Security (Recovery of Benefits) Act 1997   114

U

Unfair Contract Terms Act 1977   58, 143–4, 147, 158
    s 1(1)(b)   56
    s 2   56
    s 2(1)   56
    s 2(2)   56
    s 11   56
    s 11(3)   56

1 Negligence: Duty of Care

1.1	Introduction	2
1.2	Duty of care	3
1.3	Liability for omissions to act	7

SQE1 syllabus

This chapter will enable you to achieve the SQE1 Assessment Specification in relation to Functioning Legal Knowledge concerned with the core principles of tort on negligence and when a duty of care will be owed between a defendant and a claimant in a claim for damages in negligence.

Note that for SQE1, candidates are not usually required to recall specific case names or cite statutory or regulatory authorities. Cases are provided for illustrative purposes only.

Learning outcomes

By the end of this chapter you will be able to apply relevant core legal principles and rules appropriately and effectively, at the level of a competent newly qualified solicitor in practice, to realistic client-based and ethical problems and situations in the following areas:

- negligence and established duty situations;
- negligence and novel duty situations.

Tort

1.1 Introduction

The word 'tort' means 'wrong'. A tort involves the infringement of a legal right (or breach of a legal duty) and it gives rise to a claim in the civil courts. A person who commits a tort is called 'a tortfeasor' and their liability is described as tortious.

The law of tort is the body of civil law which governs what happens when one person sues another person because of what that other person has done. The person bringing the case is known as the 'claimant' (prior to 1999 such a person was called a 'plaintiff' and this term is used in cases before this date). The person against whom the case is brought is the 'defendant'.

The tort of negligence can provide compensation for harm caused to a claimant by the carelessness of a defendant. This tort is the most important tort in practice as more claims are brought in negligence than any other tort. However, not all careless or neglectful behaviour will lead to a successful claim in the tort of negligence. It is necessary to distinguish between negligence in the everyday sense of the word and negligence in the legal sense. It is essential to start with a legal definition of the tort being considered and the tort of negligence may be defined as: 'A breach of a legal duty of care owed to a claimant that results in harm to the claimant, undesired by the defendant.'

The courts deal with the question of how to determine whether or not a defendant should be held responsible to an injured claimant for his carelessness by first asking whether or not the defendant owed the claimant a *legal* duty to take care.

The purpose of this first chapter on negligence is to consider this first question. However, before this is considered in detail, it will help to outline the other elements of the tort of negligence which the claimant must also prove if they are to receive compensation.

Whenever a possible claim in the tort of negligence is considered, the following elements are examined, in this order:

Figure 1.1 Elements of the tort of negligence flowchart

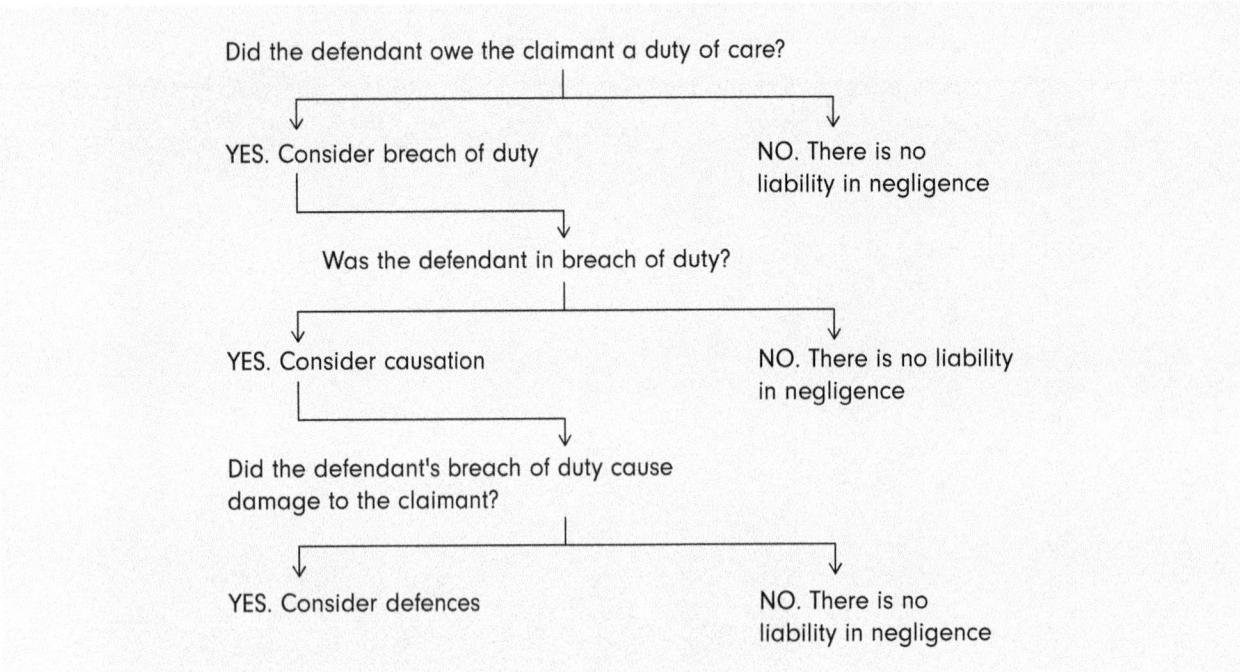

Each of these elements are considered in the following chapters.

It is important to note that negligence is a common law tort, which means the law governing it is made by the courts and case law forms the basis of the tort of negligence. It is not contained in an Act of Parliament.

1.2 Duty of care

Not all careless acts give rise to liability in negligence even if a defendant is at fault and this causes damage to the claimant. A defendant will be liable in negligence only if they are under a legal duty to take care for the person who is injured. Thus, the essential first element which a claimant has to prove is that the defendant owed them a legal duty of care.

1.2.1 Established duty situations

It is necessary to know whether or not a particular relationship between claimant and defendant will give rise to a duty of care. The rules of negligence are established by case law. Once the courts have decided that a duty of care does exist in a given situation, this establishes a precedent. The court can, however, establish that a duty of care is *not* owed. For example, there is no established general duty owed by the police to a suspect regarding the way in which the police conduct their investigation. This is considered in the case of *Hill v Chief Constable of West Yorkshire* [1989] AC 53 below.

There are a number of situations in which it is already clear from case law that a duty of care is owed. These are described as established duty situations.

It should be noted that these duties can *only* be relied upon by a claimant when they have suffered physical damage – either personal injury or damage to property. They *cannot* be relied upon where the damage suffered is classed as pure economic loss or pure psychiatric harm. The special rules governing whether a duty of care may be owed for these types of damage are considered in **Chapters 4** and **5**.

There are many established duty situations. The most common are:

- one road user to another: this would include driver to other drivers; driver to passenger; driver to pedestrian; cyclist to driver; cyclist to pedestrian
- doctor to patient
- employer to employee
- manufacturer to consumer
- tutor to tutee, teacher to pupil

⭐ Example

Brian drove his car carelessly along a road and caused an accident in which Harry's car went off the road and down a steep bank. Morris saw the accident and climbed down the bank to rescue Harry from the car. In doing so Morris was himself injured. The accident was entirely Brian's fault and both Harry and Morris were acting carefully. Brian owes a duty of care to other road users such as Harry under the established duty of care between one road user to another. This established duty does not apply to Morris because he was not a road user at the time of his injury.

However, Brian does owe a duty of care to Morris as a rescuer. Where a defendant's actions have created a dangerous situation so that it is reasonably foreseeable that someone may attempt a rescue, the defendant owes a duty of care to the rescuer

(Baker v TE Hopkins & Son Ltd [1959] 3 All ER 225). This is another duty situation that can be added to the list of established duties.

1.2.2 Novel duty situations

Although there are very many established duties, they still do not cover every eventuality. New or novel situations do come before the courts in which they are asked to decide for the first time whether or not a particular relationship, or set of facts, would give rise to a duty of care.

It should be noted that these novel duties can only be relied upon by a claimant when they have suffered physical damage – either personal injury or damage to property. They cannot be relied upon where the damage suffered is classed as pure economic loss or pure psychiatric harm.

The modern test which the courts apply to determine whether or not a duty of care should be imposed in a novel situation was handed down in the case of *Caparo*. However, it is necessary to consider the earlier case of *Donoghue v Stevenson* as *Caparo* builds upon the 'neighbour principle' considered below.

1.2.2.1 The neighbour principle

In the case of *Donoghue v Stevenson* [1932] AC 562, Lord Macmillan said, 'The categories of negligence are never closed'. This landmark case provided the original test for whether a duty should be owed in any given new or novel situation.

 *In Donoghue v Stevenson [1932] the claimant went to a cafe with a friend. The friend bought her a bottle of ginger beer. The bottle was opaque and when she poured out the drink a partly decomposed snail came out. She suffered shock and gastro-enteritis. The problem for the claimant was that she did not buy the ginger beer so she could not make a claim in contract. However, the court held that a duty was owed in negligence. The manufacturer owed her a duty of care. (This is considered in **Chapter 11**.)*

At its narrowest, this case just added one more to the list of established duties: manufacturer to consumer. More importantly, the case established the 'neighbour principle', which was used to determine whether or not the defendant owed a duty of care in any novel situation which came before a court.

The passage from Lord Atkin's judgment which is of most importance is the one which sets out this neighbour principle: 'You must take reasonable care to avoid acts or omissions which you can reasonably foresee would be likely to injure your neighbour.'

He then goes on to define your neighbour: 'Who then, in law, is my neighbour? The answer seems to be persons who are so closely and directly affected by my act that I ought reasonably to have them in my contemplation as being so affected when I am directing my mind to the acts or omissions which are called in question.'

The test is one of close relationship or proximity. This does not mean proximity in the physical sense but in the sense of having the other person in mind when you do a certain act. The criterion for establishing the duty is whether this particular defendant ought reasonably to have foreseen the likelihood of injury to this claimant.

This 'neighbour' test formulated by Lord Atkin was accepted by the courts as the test to be applied to determine whether or not a given novel situation gives rise to a legal duty of care.

When applying this test the courts have produced a new duty whenever they have considered it right to do so, particularly where personal injury or other physical damage occurs.

In other areas, though, the courts have been wary of imposing new duty situations. The following are all examples of areas in which the courts have been wary of imposing a duty of care. These are considered in more detail below.

- a negligent police investigation;
- a careless omission to act by a local authority;
- a negligent statement by a journalist causing economic loss; and
- psychiatric injuries caused by a major train crash.

The test for when a duty may be imposed in new or novel situations was later discussed in the case of *Caparo*. This case re-defined the neighbour principle and handed down the *Caparo* test that is now used to determine when a duty of care will be owed in novel situations.

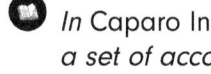 *In* Caparo Industries plc v Dickman *[1990] 1 All ER 568 the defendant auditors prepared a set of accounts to value a company. They were negligent as the accounts showed the company was worth a lot more money than it really was. Relying on this valuation the claimant purchased more shares in the company but lost money because the company was overvalued. The problem for the claimant was that the accounts were not prepared for the claimant, but for a statutory audit. The House of Lords held that the auditors did not owe a duty of care to the claimant.*

In *Caparo* the House of Lords set out a three-part test that is now used to determine whether a duty is owed in any novel situation. The three questions to be considered are:

- reasonable foresight of harm to the claimant;
- sufficient proximity of relationship between the claimant and defendant; and
- that it is fair, just and reasonable to impose a duty.

The first two parts of the *Caparo* test, foreseeability of harm to the claimant and proximity of relationship between claimant and defendant, are simply a different way of expressing the neighbour principle.

However, the third part of the test and the requirement that it must be fair, just and reasonable to impose a duty of care allow the court to reach a conclusion based on policy matters. This allows the courts to limit the very wide scope of the original test for duty from *Donoghue v Stevenson*.

Lord Bridge in *Caparo* also stated that, when considering novel duty situations, the law should only develop incrementally and by analogy with established authority.

Set out below are some illustrations:

Foreseeability

The first requirement is reasonable foresight of harm to the claimant. The question is: is it reasonably foreseeable that the defendant's actions will affect this particular claimant?

 Bourhill v Young *[1943] AC 92 is an example where harm to the particular claimant who suffered injury was not reasonably foreseeable. The claimant heard a collision between a motorcycle and a car, and walked to the scene. She saw blood on the roadway and claimed she suffered shock and a miscarriage as a result. She claimed damages against the estate of the dead motorcyclist whose negligence had caused the accident. Did the motorcyclist owe a duty of care to her? It is clear that the motorcyclist would owe a duty to the driver of the car involved in the accident, because damage to the driver of another vehicle on the road was foreseeable. However, the claimant was not a foreseeable victim of the motorcyclist's negligence, so no duty of care was owed to her. Therefore, her claim for damages failed.*

Tort

Proximity

The second requirement in the *Caparo* test is proximity. Proximity relates to the relationship between the claimant and the defendant. The facts and decision of *Caparo* itself are both very relevant here. In *Caparo* the claim for damages failed because the relationship between the claimant and the defendant was not sufficiently close. This is considered in more detail in **Chapter 4**.

Lack of proximity between the parties may be regarded as the basis for special limitations upon the duty of care owed in certain types of cases. Thus the duty of care may be limited in the case of:

- omissions, such as the failure of the local authority to improve a road junction;
- pure economic loss, such as the loss of investments caused by the journalist;
- pure psychiatric harm, such as that suffered by the victims of the train crash.

Fair, just and reasonable

The final requirement – whether it is fair, just and reasonable to impose a duty is demonstrated by the following case.

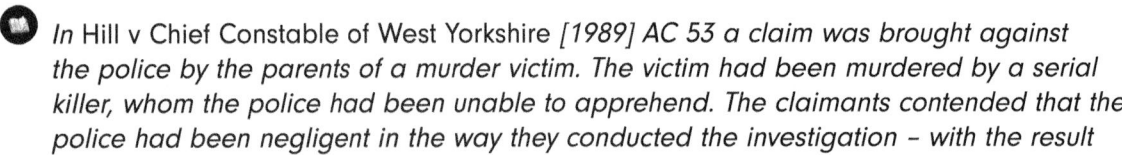

In Hill v Chief Constable of West Yorkshire [1989] AC 53 a claim was brought against the police by the parents of a murder victim. The victim had been murdered by a serial killer, whom the police had been unable to apprehend. The claimants contended that the police had been negligent in the way they conducted the investigation – with the result that the killer was not caught before he killed this victim.

In Hill, the police were exonerated from liability, on the basis that they did not owe a duty of care to any individual, as their duty is to the public at large. This was a decision based on policy and whether it was fair, just and reasonable to impose a duty of care on the police. If a duty had been imposed on the police in the case of Hill, the duty owed to the public would be too wide and too onerous.

1.2.2.2 The duty of care and policy

There are many factors which the court might take into account in determining whether it is 'fair, just and reasonable' to impose a duty of care on a defendant in a novel duty situation which could be considered to be policy factors. These include:

- *The 'floodgates' argument* – ie if one case is allowed to succeed, the floodgates will open to admit hundreds of other similar cases.
- *Deterrence* of a certain type of behaviour may be a consideration – the courts may feel that in order to deter others from acting in a way they consider wrong or anti-social, they should rule in favour of the claimant.
- *Resources* – the courts know that when a claimant succeeds against a defendant, money will pass from one to the other. The courts are also aware that in the majority of cases it is not the defendant, personally, who will pay the compensation awarded but the defendant's insurers, or his employer's insurers. The cost of this payment is then met by an overall increase in premiums, funded by society in general. Equally, the court will consider a decision very carefully if the defendant has no insurance to meet an award of compensation.
- *Public benefit* – the court may take into account any benefit to the public as a result of its decision, eg increased public safety.
- *Upholding the law* – on occasions, adhering strictly to the rules of law may produce a result which appears to be unjust in the eyes of the public. Nevertheless, it must be part

of the court's policy to uphold those legal rules, despite public criticism, or the law would lose its power.

1.2.2.3 The test for duty in novel situations: conclusions

A distinction is drawn between established duty situations (eg road users) and novel duty situations. If it is clear that there is an established duty situation, it is not necessary to go further and consider the *Caparo* test. It is necessary to apply the *Caparo* test when it is not clear that there is an existing established duty which is applicable on the facts.

Thus, having looked at the test established in *Donoghue v Stevenson* and *Caparo*, it is possible to give the following broad conclusions in relation to duty of care in novel situations.

A duty of care will *usually* be owed whenever harm is caused by one individual to another by a positive act of wrongdoing and that harm is foreseeable physical injury to the person or physical damage to property. This because the *Caparo* criteria of foreseeability, proximity, and fair, just and reasonable are very likely to be satisfied in cases of this kind.

By contrast, there *may not* be a duty of care where:

- harm is caused by a public body, such as a local authority or the police (as opposed to an individual); or
- harm is caused by an omission to act (as opposed to a positive act of wrongdoing); or
- the harm caused is pure psychiatric injury (as opposed to physical injury); or
- the harm caused is pure economic loss (as opposed to physical damage to property).

The *Caparo* criteria are less likely to be satisfied in this kind of case. For example, it may not be fair, just and reasonable to impose a duty of care on a public body such as the police.

Case law has established special rules in relation to omissions to act, pure psychiatric harm and pure economic loss. Each of these might be seen as instances where there is insufficient proximity between claimant and defendant, as required by the *Caparo* criteria. Omissions to act are considered in the next section. Pure psychiatric harm and pure economic loss will be dealt with in **Chapters 4** and **5**.

1.3 Liability for omissions to act

1.3.1 The general rule: no liability for omissions

The general rule is that a duty of care is not owed for omissions, ie failing to act to prevent harm to the claimant.

 The authority for this general rule is the case of Stovin v Wise *[1996] AC 923. In this case the highway authority knew that a road junction was dangerous but failed to exercise its powers to reduce the danger. An accident occurred at the junction and it was alleged that the highway authority should contribute towards compensating the injured party. However, it was held that the authority owed no duty of care to road users to alleviate the danger.*

⭐ *Example*

John sees a stranger drowning in a canal and fails to do anything about it. John cannot be sued in negligence as he does not owe the stranger a duty to act positively on his behalf. However, there are exceptions to this general rule that are considered below. For example, even though there is no legal duty to act positively to save someone,

John might feel compelled morally to act, and the implications of that decision are considered below.

1.3.2 Exceptions to the general rule of no liability for omissions

1.3.2.1 The duty not to make the situation worse

In general there is no duty to act positively for the benefit of others. However, if someone decides to act, they have a duty not to make the situation worse.

 In East Suffolk Rivers Catchment Board v Kent and another [1940] 4 All ER 527 land belonging to the claimant was flooded when a sea wall was breached. The defendant had no duty to repair the wall but it did have a statutory power to do so. The defendant did decide to repair the wall. However, it took a long time to do so, during which the claimant's land remained flooded.

The House of Lords said that there was no liability in tort for the Board's omission to act. Their Lordships said that, if a defendant does not owe a duty to act but nevertheless decides to intervene, there is no liability in negligence even if the defendant does act carelessly, unless *they make matters worse.*

 Example

John sees a stranger (Adrian) drowning in a canal and decides to jump in the canal to help them. Unfortunately, John gets into difficulties himself and causes injuries to Adrian while they are being helped by Jameel. John could be liable in negligence to Adrian because he owes a duty of care not to make the situation worse.

1.3.2.2 Occasions when there is a duty to act positively

There is a duty to act positively in tort if a person has some sort of power or control over the other person or object. This special relationship of control could arise in several different ways, eg:

- employer and employee;
- schools and children;
- parents and children;
- instructors and pupils.

 Example

Martina is a passenger in Nisha's car. There is generally no liability if a passenger fails to take some steps to prevent an accident as no duty is owed. There is no duty in such a situation as the passenger has no control over either the car or the driver. Martina would, of course, be liable if she opened the door of the car and hit a passing pedestrian or cyclist. Martina would also have a positive duty to act if she had control over Nisha, eg Martina is a driving instructor (professional or not).

The list of special relationships is endless, as each case could produce a new scenario.

Where there is a special relationship, one party may have a duty to take positive action to safeguard the other. For example, the duty owed by the lifeguard to save the drowning swimmer, or the duty of a teacher to look after pupils so that they do not injure themselves.

Also, where one person has a relationship of control over another, they may have a duty to take positive action to prevent harm being caused to third parties. For example, the duty of an instructor to make sure that a learner driver does not cause an accident, or the duty of a teacher to prevent a pupil running into the road and causing a danger to drivers.

The leading case on the principle is considered below.

 In Home Office v Dorset Yacht Co Ltd *[1970] AC 1004 a group of young offenders who were incarcerated in a young offender institution were taken on a work party at a local harbour. During the day they were working on a repair project within the harbour. At night the officers in charge of the young men went to bed and left them unsupervised. The boys 'escaped' and boarded a yacht which they set in motion. This yacht collided with the claimant's yacht and caused extensive damage. The claimant sued the officers' employer for their negligence.*

The House of Lords decided that there was a duty of care owed to the claimant by the Home Office which was liable for the negligent acts of its employees. (The Home Office's liability for the negligent acts of its employees was based on the concept of vicarious liability. This is considered in detail in **Chapter 9**.*) This duty was owed by the officers because they should have foreseen the harm to the claimant's yacht when they failed to supervise the boys, who all had criminal records. The damage which occurred to the claimant's yacht was due to an omission to act, for which ordinarily no duty would be owed. In this case, however, a duty was imposed because the officers had control over the boys.*

Summary

- The claimant must show that the defendant owes them a duty of care.
- This may be a duty already established by case law, eg doctors owe their patients a duty of care.
- If the duty is not already established then this is a novel situation and the claimant needs to apply the three-part test in *Caparo* to show that a duty is owed, ie
    - reasonable foresight of harm to the claimant.
    - sufficient proximity of relationship between the claimant and defendant.
    - that it is fair, just and reasonable to impose a duty.
- Generally there is no duty with omissions to act. There are exceptions to this, ie
    - the duty not to make the situation worse
    - the duty to act positively in tort if a person has some sort of power or control over the other person or object.

Tort

Summary flowchart

Figure 1.2 Negligence: duty of care flowchart

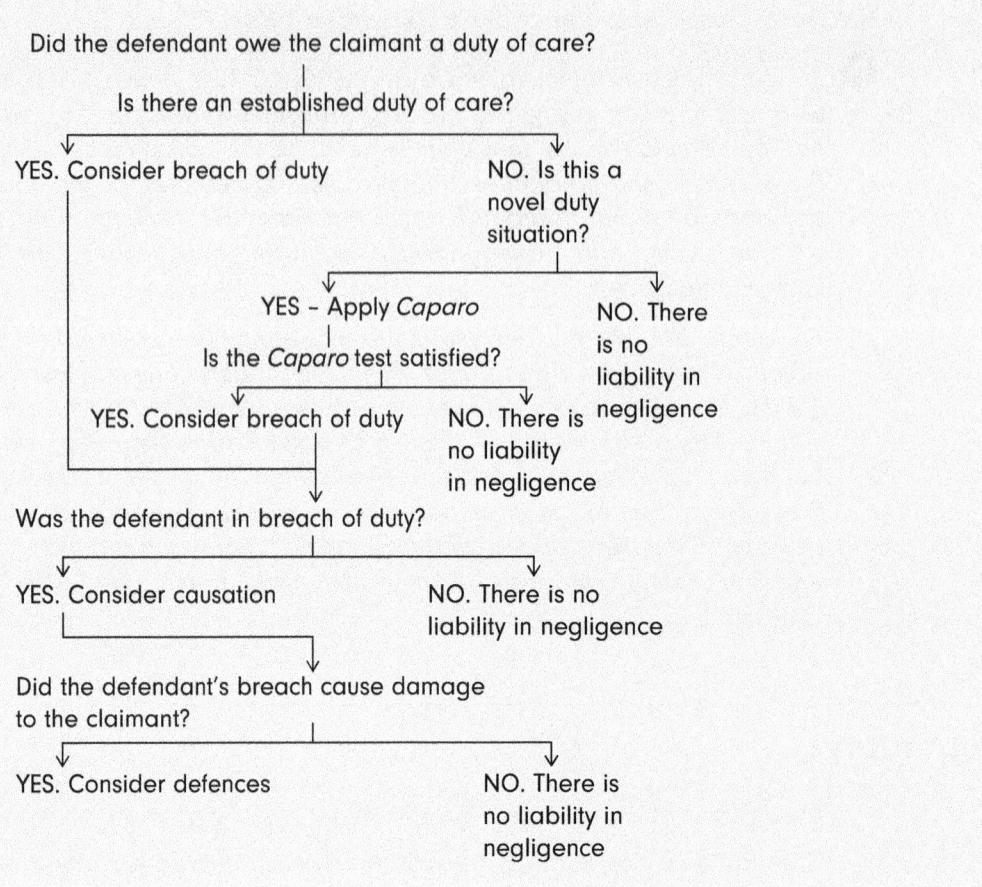

Sample questions

Question 1

A claimant is employed by a hospital as a research biochemist. One afternoon, while conducting an experiment in the hospital laboratory, they lit a gas Bunsen burner and there was a small explosion. As a result of the explosion the claimant sustained burns to their hand.

The hospital have had the Bunsen burner inspected by an expert who has reported that they cannot find anything wrong with it.

Which statement best explains whether the claimant will be owed a duty of care by the hospital?

A Yes, because the type of harm was foreseeable, the claimant and the hospital were in a proximate relationship and it is fair, just and reasonable to impose a duty of care on the hospital.

B Yes, because there is an established duty between the claimant and the hospital as the type of harm was foreseeable, the claimant and the hospital were in a proximate relationship and it is fair, just and reasonable to impose a duty of care on the hospital.

10

C Yes, because there is an established duty between the claimant and the hospital.

D No, because the expert evidence suggests that it would not be fair, just or reasonable to impose a duty of care on the hospital.

E No, because the expert evidence suggests that the harm suffered by the claimant was unforeseeable.

Answer

Option C is correct as the claimant can rely upon the established duty of care between an employer and its employees.

Option A is wrong because, while the foreseeability, proximity and fairness would seem to be satisfied, this is not why a duty of care would be owed in this case. The *Caparo* test (from *Caparo Industries plc v Dickman* [1990] 1 All ER 568) is only relied upon in novel (new) duty situations. If the claimant falls within an established duty situation then they will not be required to satisfy the *Caparo* test.

Option B is wrong because, while it does correctly state that this is an established duty situation, it does not depend upon this claimant having to satisfy the *Caparo* test.

Option D is wrong because it is confusing the issue of whether a duty of care is owed with whether the defendant may be in breach of its duty.

Option E is wrong for the same reason as option D.

Question 2

A claimant was severely injured while canoeing on a river on their own. They had previously purchased a guidebook published by the defendant and chose a stretch of the river because it was described in the defendant's guidebook as 'a pleasant paddle on the river'. The description was in fact grossly inaccurate and the defendant has now changed their description in their new edition of the guidebook to read 'this part of the river is dangerous and should not be attempted'.

There is no previous case law that establishes whether the defendant owes the potential claimant a duty of care in negligence. The defendant is a registered charity and all proceeds of the sale of their guidebook are used to promote their charitable purpose.

Which of the following statements best describes whether the defendant owes the claimant a duty of care in negligence?

A Yes, because the claimant is a foreseeable victim. It seems likely that any lack of care by the defendant in advising on the safety of the river could cause harm to the claimant.

B Yes, because the claimant is a foreseeable victim and there was a relationship of sufficient proximity between the claimant and the defendant to justify imposition of a duty of care. The fact that the claimant had purchased the guidebook would determine the issue.

C Yes, because the defendant chose to publish the guidebook and the defendant was also clearly at fault. It is only fair, just and reasonable therefore that the claimant should be owed a duty of care.

D No, because while the claimant is a foreseeable victim, the court will be reluctant to find that the defendant undertook any responsibility towards the claimant. The court may also consider policy issues and determine that it would be unfair for a charity to be liable to the public in these circumstances.

E No, because while the claimant is a foreseeable victim, there was not a relationship of sufficient proximity between the claimant and the defendant to justify imposition of a duty of care. However, the court will not consider any policy issues as that is beyond their remit.

Answer

Option D is correct – it considers (and applies correctly) all three limbs of the *Caparo* test.

Option A is wrong because, while the injury to the claimant is foreseeable, this is not the only criteria that the court would consider to determine whether a duty of care is owed in a novel situation. The court would also consider the proximity of relationship between the parties and whether it would be fair, just and reasonable to impose a duty of care.

Option B is wrong because the court would consider whether it would be fair, just and reasonable to impose a duty and the fact that the claimant had purchased the guidebook would not determine the issue.

Option C is wrong because the fact that the defendant may have been at fault does not determine the issue of whether a duty of care is owed. Option C also fails to consider the first two limbs of the *Caparo* test.

Option E is wrong because the courts can consider policy issues under the third limb of the *Caparo* test.

Question 3

The claimant owns and occupies property which is next to a cinema. The cinema is being redeveloped by the defendants. The defendants have commenced work, but leave the building locked and unattended at night. Vandals have broken in on a few occasions and started small fires. The defendants did not have any knowledge of these fires as they were extinguished by passers-by. However, on the last occasion the vandals broke in and started a large fire which spread and caused extensive damage to the claimant's property. The claimant is seeking advice as to whether it should sue the defendants in negligence for the damage caused.

Which of the following statements best describes why the defendants do not owe the claimant a duty of care in negligence?

A Because the general rule is that there is no duty of care owed for omissions.

B Because the duty on an occupier would be too wide if it was held responsible for damage caused to neighbouring property by third parties entering the occupier's property.

C Because the claimant's damage was caused by the defendants' failure to act and the defendants had no knowledge of, or control over, the vandals.

D Because the defendants are not at fault as they did not start the fire.

E Because there is never a duty of care owed by a defendant to a claimant for the actions of third parties.

Answer

Option C is correct – defendants can be liable for their omissions if they have a positive duty to exercise control over third parties but this principle does not apply to the facts of the claimant's case. The defendants were not in a special (proximate) relationship with the vandals and would not be expected to exercise control over them.

Option A is only partially correct because, while the general rule is that there is no duty of care owed for omission, there are exceptions to this general rule.

Option B is also only partially correct because, while the courts can consider the wider ramifications of their decision (ie policy), this is not in itself cause of an exception to the general rule that there is no duty for omission.

Option D is wrong as, while the defendants may or may not have been at fault, this is not an issue that determines whether a duty of care is owed (it is, however, relevant to breach).

Option E is wrong as the statement is too absolute, ie there are exceptions (eg *Home Office v Dorset Yacht Co Ltd* [1970] AC 1004), but this exception does not apply to the claimant's facts.

2 Negligence: Breach of Duty

2.1	Introduction	16
2.2	The standard of care	16
2.3	Relevant factors in determining whether defendant has achieved the required standard of care	19
2.4	Proving breach of duty	23

SQE1 syllabus

This chapter will enable you to achieve the SQE1 Assessment Specification in relation to Functioning Legal Knowledge concerned with the core principles of tort on negligence and the breach of a defendant's duty of care.

Note that for SQE1, candidates are not usually required to recall specific case names or cite statutory or regulatory authorities. Cases are provided for illustrative purposes only.

Learning outcomes

By the end of this chapter you will be able to apply relevant core legal principles and rules appropriately and effectively, at the level of a competent newly qualified solicitor in practice, to realistic client-based and ethical problems and situations in the following areas:

- the standard of reasonable care in negligence;
- the factors which the courts apply to determine whether a defendant has either met that standard or has breached their duty of care in negligence.

2.1 Introduction

For a defendant to be liable in the tort of negligence, they must not only owe the claimant a duty of care, but they must also be in breach of that duty. This means that the defendant must be at fault by failing to come up to the standard required by law for fulfilling the duty.

> **Example**
>
> *A road accident occurs when two cars collide. A duty of care can be established since this is a recognised duty situation (road users). However, before liability in the tort of negligence can exist, a breach of that duty must be established on the part of one of the drivers, ie one driver must have been at fault (eg driving too fast). This would not be the case if the driver had suffered a sudden and unexpected disabling illness, resulting in the driver totally losing control of the car.*

Whether a defendant has breached a duty of care is a question of fact for the judge to decide. The issue of breach involves the application of a two-stage test:

- The court first assesses how the defendant ought, in the circumstances, to have behaved, ie what standard of care the defendant should have exercised (a question of law).
- The court then decides whether the defendant's conduct fell below the required standard (a question of fact).

In practice, this second stage – establishing a breach on the facts of the case – is often the most difficult element for a claimant to satisfy in a negligence claim. The facts are not always clear and undisputed. There may be no independent witnesses, or, if there are, their evidence may conflict.

There are some rules which may assist the claimant in proving a breach of duty on the facts, and these are considered at **2.4** below.

The next section considers the first stage of the test for breach of duty: what standard of care is the defendant required to meet?

2.2 The standard of care

The defendant's conduct will be measured against the required standard of care in determining whether there is a breach of the duty of care.

In *Blyth v Birmingham Waterworks* (1856) 11 Ex 781, Alderson B stated that 'negligence is the omission to do something which a reasonable man... would do, or doing something which a prudent and reasonable man would not do'.

The defendant must meet the standard of 'the reasonable man'. (The more up-to-date term 'reasonable person' is used below). The defendant is required to take as much care as would be taken by a reasonable person. It is necessary, therefore, to assess what the reasonable person might be expected to do in any given situation.

2.2.1 The nature of the 'reasonable person' test

The reasonable person has been described as 'the man on the Clapham omnibus', or 'the man on the street'. The reasonable person, therefore, is the average person. That is, someone who is neither very intelligent nor very stupid; neither overly cautious nor unduly optimistic, etc. Thus, the defendant must meet the standard of care which would be expected of a reasonable person.

The test is an objective one; the courts do not take into account the personal attributes of each defendant. The test is also impersonal. The issue to be decided is not 'What did this defendant foresee?' but 'What would a reasonable person have foreseen in the particular circumstances?' Similarly, it is not a question of whether the defendant did their best, but whether they came up to the standard of the reasonable person.

⭐ Example

An illustration of the fact that the duty is only to do what is reasonable is to consider the position of a defendant who suffers from an unexpected disability. A defendant driver may suddenly suffer from some impairment of consciousness, being previously unaware that they suffered from such a condition. In those circumstances the driver will not be in breach if they have met the standard of the reasonable driver who is unaware of this condition. Similarly, a driver suffering a sudden unexpected heart attack will not be in breach. However, a defendant who did know that they were adversely affected by a medical condition could be liable if they unreasonably undertook an activity, and caused harm, because their performance was impaired.

In some situations the courts have set special standards, having recognised that it would be inappropriate in these circumstances to apply the normal reasonable person test. In cases like these the courts do still apply the 'reasonable person' test but they set special standards by modifying the test. The standard of care required is that of a reasonable person in the defendant's position. These situations are considered below.

2.2.2 Special standards: the skilled defendant

In Bolam v Friern Hospital Management Committee *[1957] 2 All ER 118, the claimant was undergoing electro convulsive therapy as treatment for his mental illness. The doctor did not give any relaxant drugs and the claimant suffered a serious fracture. There was divided opinion amongst professionals as to whether relaxant drugs should be given. If they were given there was a very small risk of death, if they were not given there was a small risk of fractures. The claimant argued that the doctor was in breach of duty by not using the relaxant drug. It was true that some doctors would not have carried out the treatment in the same way as the defendant. However, there was also a body of professional opinion which did approve of the treatment.*

The House of Lords held that a doctor must show a greater degree of skill and care than the reasonable person in the street. A doctor must show the same degree of skill as a reasonable doctor. Doctors must meet the standard of their profession. The Court also held that a defendant would not be in breach of their duty provided they had acted in accordance with a practice accepted as proper by a responsible body of doctors skilled in that particular art.

The principle established in *Bolam* does not just apply to doctors. It applies to anyone who exercises a special skill. So, where a person exercises a special skill, that person is not judged according to the standard of the reasonable person in the street – because the reasonable person does not profess to have that skill. Instead, they will be judged according to the degree of skill or competence to be expected from a person who has that special skill.

The other principle from *Bolam* is that, as long as a defendant's actions are supported by a reasonable body of professional opinion, they should not be judged to be negligent. However, without more, this could lead to a situation in which members of the relevant profession were the judges of negligence rather than the court itself. Therefore, case law has recognised that it is always for the court finally to decide whether or not a skilled defendant has acted reasonably.

This was established in the case of *Bolitho v City and Hackney Health Authority* [1997] 4 All ER 771. In *Bolitho* the court acknowledged that in some cases it cannot be demonstrated that the body of opinion relied on by the defendant is reasonable or responsible. Thus, in a particular case a claimant might be able to demonstrate that the professional opinion relied on by the defendant is not capable of withstanding logical analysis. In that situation, the court would be able to find the defendant in breach of duty (notwithstanding that they could point to some opinion in his support).

2.2.3 Special standards: the under-skilled defendant

In Nettleship v Weston *[1971] 3 All ER 58, the claimant, an experienced driver, agreed to give a friend's wife some driving lessons in her husband's car. On the third occasion, when she was holding the steering wheel and controlling the pedals and he was moving the gear lever and handbrake, she failed to straighten out after turning left, and panicked. This caused the car to crash and to injure the claimant.*

The Court of Appeal held that the duty of care owed by the learner driver to the passenger instructor was the same objective and impersonal standard as that owed by every driver. That standard was not affected or reduced by reason of the instructor's knowledge of the learner's lack of skill and experience. Accordingly, where the learner had driven without due care and attention, she was in breach of her duty to the claimant and was liable in damages.

A learner driver, even on their first drive, is expected to reach the standard of the reasonably competent driver. The decision in *Nettleship* may seem harsh on the learner driver, but this is mitigated by the fact that liability insurance is compulsory. The additional risk that a learner driver creates for other road users by venturing on to the road will be spread via the insurance company. There is therefore an element of policy in this decision.

In *Wilsher v Essex Area Health Authority* [1987] QB 730, the Court of Appeal decided that no allowance should be made for the inexperience of a junior doctor. A junior doctor is expected to show the level of competence befitting a doctor holding the same post.

The effect of the Court of Appeal's decision in *Wilsher* is that a junior hospital doctor on their first day on the wards must come up to the standard of a hypothetical competent doctor in that post. A patient's legitimate expectations of competent treatment cannot vary according to the experience (or inexperience) of the particular doctor. The standard is tailored to the task or post, therefore, not to the doctor's individual level of experience. An inexperienced doctor is expected to call on more expert assistance when they feel out of their depth.

The case of *Wells v Cooper* [1958] 2 QB 265 is authority for the fact that even where odd jobs are done around the house, the courts are prepared to demand a certain level of skill from a defendant householder, ie that of the reasonably competent amateur carpenter, etc.

Furthermore, if an amateur tackles, unaided, a job which far exceeds their capability and which is normally done by a professional, the householder is likely to be judged to have been negligent in attempting it in the first place.

In summary, the position on defendants who hold special skills and those who lack skill or experience is as follows:

- The test for the standard of care in negligence is an objective, impersonal one. In each case the court will determine the standard required for the activity or task in question. The defendant must meet that standard and no allowance will be made for his lack of qualification, skill, or experience.

- It is relevant to look at whether the defendant has held themselves out as possessing a particular level of skill.

If a defendant presents themselves as a specialist, eg a consultant surgeon rather than a general practitioner, then they will be expected to meet that higher standard.

By undertaking a task which requires a particular level of professional skill, a defendant holds themselves out as having the necessary expertise and must meet the standard required for the task they have undertaken to perform.

- If a defendant does not profess to have a particular professional skill (as in *Wells v Cooper*), they may not be required to meet a higher professional standard. However, they must still meet the minimum standard required by the task undertaken. Moreover, if they undertake a task which requires a special skill which they do not possess, that in itself is likely to be negligent.

2.2.4 Special standards: children

In Mullin v Richards *[1998] 1 All ER 920, the claimant and the defendant, both 15-year-old schoolgirls, engaged in a mock sword fight using plastic rulers while sitting at their desk in class, a common game at the school. One of the rulers snapped and a fragment of plastic entered the claimant's right eye, causing her to lose all useful sight in that eye. The claimant sued the defendant and the education authority for damages for negligence.*

The Court of Appeal held that the standard of care is adjusted only for the child's age. According to Hutchinson LJ: '... the question for the judge is not whether the actions of the defendant were such as an ordinary prudent and reasonable adult in the defendant's situation would have realised gave rise to a risk of injury, it is whether an ordinary, prudent and reasonable 15-year-old schoolgirl in the defendant's situation would have realised as much.' On this basis, the defendant was found not to have breached their duty of care.

A child defendant will, therefore, be expected to show such care as can reasonably be expected of an ordinary child of the same age.

While there is no fixed age below which it can be said that a child cannot be liable in negligence, very young children are rarely found liable. The younger a child is, the less likely the child is able to foresee harm to others.

As regards a child's ability to be sued, a child under 18 cannot be sued (or sue) unless he has an adult to represent him. This adult is known as a litigation friend. In most cases this will be one of the child's parents. A decision needs to be made whether it is worthwhile suing a child if they have no money with which to pay the judgment.

2.3 Relevant factors in determining whether defendant has achieved the required standard of care

The standard against which the defendant's conduct will be measured is that of the reasonable person. In determining the degree of care to be expected of a reasonable person, the courts will take into account all the circumstances of the case.

In general terms, in assessing whether or not a defendant has fallen below a reasonable standard of care, the court needs to weigh up:

- the risk created by the defendant's activities; and
- the precautions which the defendant ought to reasonably have taken in response to that risk.

There are some factors which will always be relevant, and they can be regarded as guidelines to enable the courts to decide the issue of fault. These factors are considered below.

2.3.1 Magnitude of the risk

This factor involves considering two elements:

- How likely was it that the defendant's actions could cause an injury?
- If an injury was caused, how serious was it likely to be?

2.3.1.1 The likelihood of an injury occurring

The greater the chances of the defendant's activity causing injury to the claimant, the more precautions the defendant must take.

> *In* Bolton v Stone *[1951] AC 850, the claimant was injured by a ball hit out of a cricket ground and sued the cricket club. The claimant was standing in the street outside the ground. The ball had travelled 100 yards, and cleared the boundary fence which was seven feet high. The ball had only been hit out of the ground six times in the previous 30 years. The court held that the defendants were not in breach of their duty of care. Although an accident of this sort was foreseeable, it was very unlikely to happen, so taking such a small risk was not a breach.*

The decision in *Bolton v Stone* recognised that it is justifiable not to take steps to eliminate a real risk if the risk of injury is small and if the circumstances are such that a reasonable person would think it right to neglect it.

However, the case should not be regarded as authority for the view that it is always reasonable to ignore a small risk. The risk must be measured against other factors which are considered below – in particular, the purpose of the defendant's activity and the practicability of precautions.

An illustration of the fact that the duty is only to do what is reasonable is that a defendant's duty is to guard against 'reasonable probabilities not fantastic possibilities'. This is taken from the case of *Fardon v Harcourt-Rivington* [1932] All ER Rep 81. In this case the defendant left his dog in a parked car. The dog broke a window. The claimant passer-by was blinded by a splinter of glass. This was a fantastic possibility and the defendant was not liable.

However, a rare event is not necessarily a 'fantastic possibility'. In *Carmarthenshire CC v Lewis* [1955] AC 549, a 4-year-old child strayed from a school playground, causing a lorry to swerve. The driver was killed. Despite its uniqueness, this was a reasonable possibility.

2.3.1.2 The risk of greater injury

The more serious the possible harm to the claimant, the more care the defendant must take.

> *In* Paris v Stepney Borough Council *[1951] AC 367 the claimant was employed by the defendant council. The defendant had not provided the claimant with protective goggles. It was not usual to do so for this type of work, because the risk of this sort of accident occurring was small. However, the defendants knew that the claimant was blind in one eye. In the course of his work a fragment of metal damaged his good eye – with the result that he was blinded. Failure to provide safety goggles had caused the blindness. It was held that the defendant was in breach of duty. The potential injury risked was very serious: the total loss of sight. Therefore, in this case, reasonable care required that goggles should have been provided.*

The magnitude of risk is one half of the equation. The other is to consider the factors which are relevant in deciding how the defendant ought to have responded to that risk. These are examined below.

2.3.2 Cost and practicability of precautions

In deciding whether the defendant has done all that a reasonable person would have done in the circumstances to guard against the risk of injury, the courts will consider what practical measures the defendant could reasonably have taken to reduce the risk of injury and the cost of those measures.

If the risk of injury could have been substantially reduced at a low cost to the defendant, the defendant will have acted unreasonably if he fails to take the necessary precautions. If, on the other hand, the defendant would incur great expense which would produce only a very small reduction in risk, it will be reasonable for the defendant to do nothing. However, great expense will not excuse a defendant where the risk of injury is great. The issues of cost and the practicability of precautions are considered below.

In Latimer v AEC Ltd *[1953] AC 643, the defendants' factory was flooded and the water mixed with an oily liquid leaving the floor very slippery. The defendants spread sawdust over most of the floor but did not have enough to cover it all. They were faced with the decision of either closing the factory until extra sawdust arrived or taking the risk that someone might slip. They decided to keep the factory open. A workman slipped and was injured.*

The court held that the defendant was not in breach of duty. The risk of injury was only slight, while the cost and inconvenience of having to totally eradicate the risk by closing the factory would have been substantial.

In *Latimer v AEC Ltd*, the defendants' decision not to close down the relevant part of the factory was a reasonable one, given the relatively small risk of injury and the potential consequences of a closure. If the risk of injury to the employees had been sufficiently great, a reasonable employer would have closed down.

Example

David lights a garden bonfire quite close to a garden shed belonging to his neighbour Fred. Unfortunately, the fire spreads to the shed and destroys it.

David owed Fred a duty to take care, to avoid damaging his garden shed. David will be in breach of that duty if he fails to take as much care as a reasonable person.

In assessing how much risk was David taking and the precautions he should have taken, the following questions should be considered:

- *How likely was it that the fire would get out of control?*
- *If it did get out of control, how serious was the damage likely to be?*
- *How should David have responded to the risk?*
- *What safety precautions should he have taken?*

On the facts of this example it might appears that David was undertaking a risky activity because it was quite likely that the fire could get out of control, and if it did, serious damage could be caused. It could be argued that he should have responded to the risk by taking the precaution of building the fire well away from his neighbour's shed. Since David actually built the fire close to Fred's garden shed, it could be concluded that David fell below a reasonable standard of care. He was in breach of his duty towards Fred.

The greater the risk of injury, the greater the steps the courts will expect defendants to take in reducing or eliminating the risk. This may require the expenditure of money that the defendant does not have. However, as a general rule, if a defendant's failure to exercise reasonable care is attributable to his lack of resources, the courts will not allow the defendant to use this as an excuse. Impecuniosity is not a defence.

2.3.3 Defendant's purpose

The value to society of the defendant's activities is a factor which the courts consider in determining their reasonableness.

If the defendant's behaviour, therefore, is in the public interest, the defendant is less likely to be held liable in negligence. A claimant is more likely to succeed where injured in the course of a commercial enterprise carried on by the defendant than in the course of a life-saving enterprise.

The degree of risk which a defendant justifiably can take is determined to a large extent by the purpose of the defendant's activity.

In Watt v Hertfordshire County Council [1954] 1 WLR 835, the claimant was a fireman called to an emergency where a woman was trapped under a lorry. Heavy lifting equipment was necessary but the vehicle designed to transport it was not available. Instead, the equipment was transported by an ordinary lorry, with three firemen steadying it. The claimant was injured when the equipment slipped during transport. It was held that the claimant's employers were not in breach of their duty of care. The risk had to be balanced against the end to be achieved and the saving of life justifies the taking of considerable risk.

The case of Watt v Hertfordshire County Council [1954] 1 WLR 835 illustrates the principle that, if human life is at stake, a defendant may be justified in taking abnormal risks. However, the case is not authority for the proposition that the purpose of saving life or limb justifies the defendant taking *any* risk. The emergency services can, therefore, still be liable in negligence by, for example, ignoring a red traffic light and/or failing to use their sirens.

If the defendant's activity has no social utility or is unlawful, the defendant will be required to exercise a very high degree of care to justify even a small risk of harm to others.

2.3.4 Common practice

Defendants sued in negligence may be able to escape liability if they can show that they complied with the accepted practice in their trade or profession.

An example of this is in the case of *Bolam v Friern Hospital Management Committee* (1957), above. Compliance with an accepted trade practice is strong evidence that a defendant has not been negligent, but it is not conclusive. The practice itself may be a negligent one.

It is comparatively rare for courts to condemn a commonly accepted practice as negligence. However, the court did so they in the case of *Re The Herald of Free Enterprise* (1987) Independent, 18 December. This case involved a cross-Channel ferry sinking. The court found that the common practice of ships' masters commanding roll-on roll-off ferries to set sail without checking that the ferry's bow doors were closed was a negligent one.

2.3.5 The current state of knowledge

Since the standard is that of the hypothetical reasonable person, in applying this standard it is necessary to ask what, in the circumstances, the reasonable person would have foreseen. The defendant's activities are judged by the standard of current knowledge.

In Roe v Ministry of Health [1954] 2 QB 66, the claimant entered hospital for minor surgery, but emerged permanently paralysed from the waist down. The anaesthetic had become contaminated by seepage through invisible cracks in the glass in which it was stored. At the time the incident occurred in 1947, the risk of seepage was not known.

It was held that the defendant was not in breach of duty. As the risk of seepage was not known at the time, the defendants could not reasonably be expected to take precautions against it.

2.4 Proving breach of duty

In a claim for negligence, the burden of proving that the defendant has breached the duty of care lies with the claimant. The claimant must prove their case 'on a balance of probabilities'.

In other words, the claimant must establish that it was more likely than not that the defendant was in breach of the duty of care. (This can be contrasted with the stricter standard of proof in criminal cases, ie beyond reasonable doubt.)

So, the most usual way for a claimant to prove a breach of duty is by using witness evidence:

- Witnesses of fact are people who saw what happened in the accident in question. For example, a witness to a road accident might say that the defendant was exceeding the speed limit. This is evidence that the defendant fell below the standard expected of the ordinary reasonable motorist and was in breach of his duty of care.

- Expert witnesses. For example, people who could say what the normal practice or level of precautions would be for a particular activity or operation. A medical expert could give evidence that a doctor failed to carry out the usually expected tests before administering treatment and so was in breach of his duty to take reasonable care.

However, there are sometimes situations in which there are no relevant witnesses to an accident. In the next paragraph we consider a rule which may help the claimant in such circumstances.

2.4.1 *Res ipsa loquitur*

The claimant must show that their loss was caused by a breach of duty on the part of the defendant. If there are no witnesses to describe how the accident happened, the claimant may have no direct evidence to show that the defendant was in breach of their duty of care.

In a very small number of cases, however, the circumstances in which the damage occurred will be such that a court may be prepared to draw an inference of negligence against the defendant without hearing detailed evidence of what the defendant did or did not do.
In such a case the Latin maxim (or phrase) *res ipsa loquitur* will assist the claimant. This translates as 'the thing speaks for itself'. When the maxim may be available to a claimant is considered below.

In the case of Scott v London and St Katherine Docks Co *(1865), the claimant was walking near to a warehouse belonging to the defendant where bags of sugar were being loaded by the defendant's employees using a hoist. A bag of sugar fell from the hoist, injuring the claimant. There were no witnesses to the accident so that the claimant had no direct evidence of any failure to exercise reasonable care on the part of the defendant's employees.*

The court held that the three conditions for the application of the maxim '*res ipsa loquitur*' are:

- The thing causing the damage must be under the control of the defendant or someone for whom the defendant is responsible.
- The accident must be such as would not normally happen without negligence.
- The cause of the accident is unknown to the claimant – so that the claimant has no direct evidence of any failure by the defendant to exercise reasonable care.

It should be noted that the three conditions set out above are only satisfied in a *very* small number of cases. In the vast majority of cases one or all of the conditions are not met and the claimant must prove their case in the normal way.

In practical terms, when the maxim applies it raises a prima facie inference of negligence against the defendant. The defendant then has to provide a reasonable explanation of how the accident could have occurred without negligence.

The defendant can do this in either of two ways. They need to produce evidence to show:

- how the accident actually happened and that this was not due to negligence on their part; or
- if they cannot show how the accident actually happened, that they had at all times used all reasonable care.

2.4.2 The Civil Evidence Act 1968

The effect of s 11 of the Civil Evidence Act 1968 is that a defendant who has been convicted of a criminal offence is presumed, in any subsequent civil proceedings, to have committed that offence.

This statutory provision can help a claimant to prove that a defendant has fallen below a reasonable standard of care where the offence of which the defendant has been convicted involved careless conduct. The claimant can rely upon the conviction as evidence that this careless conduct did take place. The claimant does not need to prove that behaviour again in the civil proceedings.

⭐ *Example*

A car accident occurs and the defendant is convicted of driving without due care and attention. The claimant in a subsequent civil claim can use this conviction as evidence that the defendant failed to take reasonable care when driving. This is because the criminal conviction is relevant to the claim in negligence.

However, this provision will not always be of assistance to the claimant. For example, if a driver is convicted of driving without insurance, this does not provide the claimant with any evidence that the defendant failed to drive carefully. The criminal conviction is not relevant to the claim in negligence.

Summary

- The claimant has the burden of proving that the defendant has breached their duty of care. The claimant needs to prove this on the balance of probabilities.
- The standard of care is that of the reasonable person in the defendant's position. This is an objective standard. For example, if the defendant is a driver, the defendant needs to reach a standard of the reasonable competent driver.
- In deciding whether there has been a breach, the courts analyse the facts of the case and consider the factors considered above, eg magnitude of the risk.
- In *limited* circumstances, the maxim *res ipsa loquitur* may help the claimant.
- In other circumstances, a *relevant* criminal conviction will assist the claimant.

The essential elements of duty and breach in a negligence claim have been considered in **Chapters 1** and **2**. In **Chapter 3**, the other important issues of causation of damage are considered.

Summary flowchart

Figure 2.1 Negligence: breach of duty flowchart

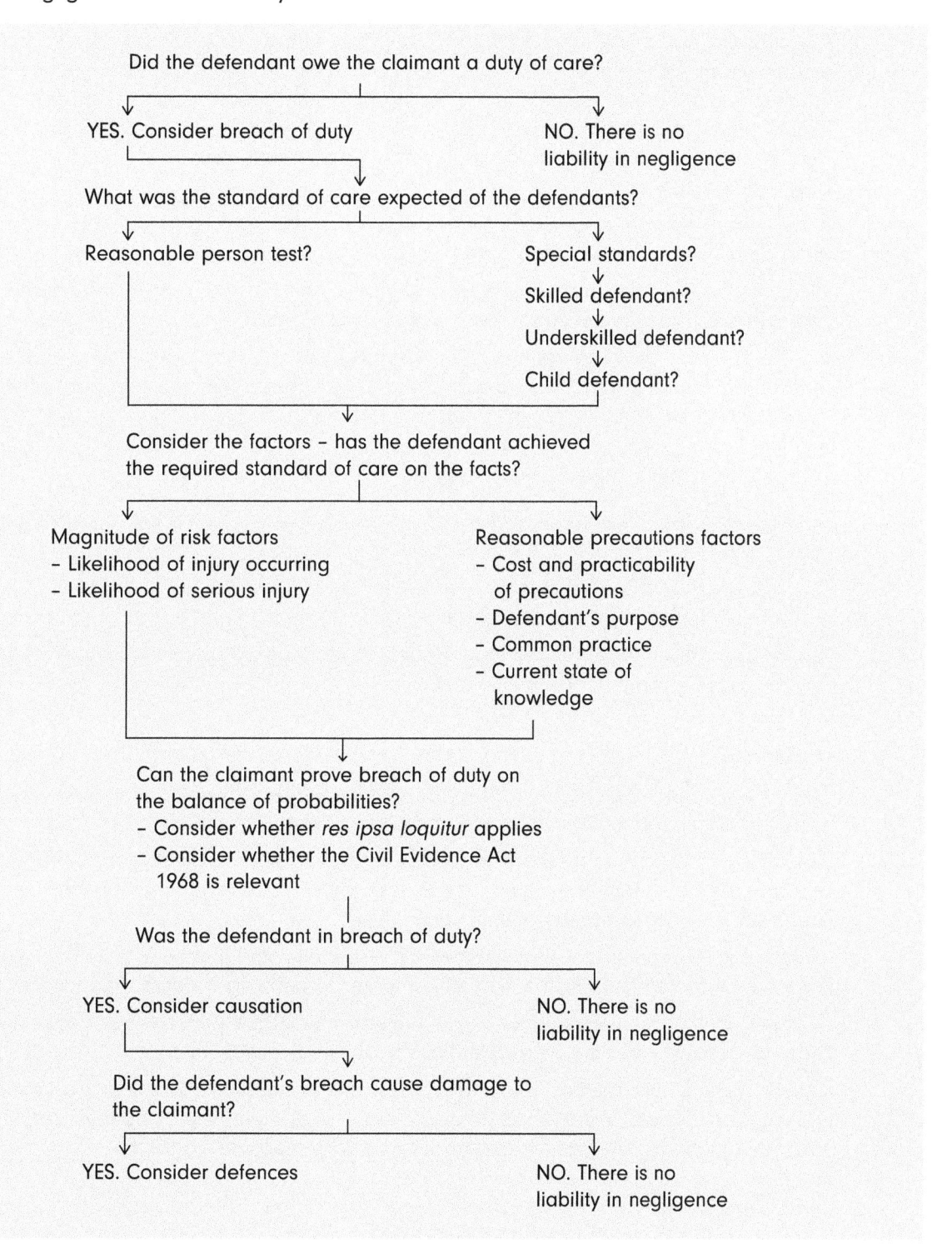

Did the defendant owe the claimant a duty of care?
- YES. Consider breach of duty
- NO. There is no liability in negligence

What was the standard of care expected of the defendants?
- Reasonable person test?
- Special standards?
  - Skilled defendant?
  - Underskilled defendant?
  - Child defendant?

Consider the factors – has the defendant achieved the required standard of care on the facts?

Magnitude of risk factors
- Likelihood of injury occurring
- Likelihood of serious injury

Reasonable precautions factors
- Cost and practicability of precautions
- Defendant's purpose
- Common practice
- Current state of knowledge

Can the claimant prove breach of duty on the balance of probabilities?
- Consider whether *res ipsa loquitur* applies
- Consider whether the Civil Evidence Act 1968 is relevant

Was the defendant in breach of duty?
- YES. Consider causation
- NO. There is no liability in negligence

Did the defendant's breach cause damage to the claimant?
- YES. Consider defences
- NO. There is no liability in negligence

Tort

Sample questions

Question 1

The claimant was injured in a road traffic accident and taken by ambulance to their local hospital. The defendant (a newly qualified casualty doctor) who saw the claimant incorrectly diagnosed the claimant as having merely a sprained ankle and sent her home. In fact, the claimant's ankle was broken in two places, and the failure to diagnose and treat the injury lead to permanent limp, which the claimant would not have if the break had been treated correctly.

Independent medical evidence has been obtained which shows that the breaks showed quite clearly on the x-rays taken at the time.

Which of the following statements best explains whether the defendant breached the duty of care that they owed the claimant in negligence?

A   No, because the defendant is a conscientious and careful doctor who only missed seeing the breaks on the X-rays due to the increased pressure of work and the fact that ward was understaffed at the time.

B   No, because the defendant had only just qualified and was performing as well as any newly qualified doctor in their position.

C   Yes, because the defendant was at fault for not identifying the broken ankle on the X-rays.

D   Yes, because the defendant failed to meet the standard of care expected of the reasonably competent newly qualified casualty doctor.

E   Yes, because the defendant failed to meet the standard of care expected of the reasonably competent casualty doctor.

Answer

Option E is correct – the defendant would be measured against the standard of care expected of the reasonably competent casualty doctor.

Option A is wrong because the standard of care expected is objective and impersonal. The fact that the defendant was doing their best in difficult circumstances will not prevent them from being in breach of their duty of care.

Option B is incorrect because no allowance is made for the inexperience of a junior doctor. They are expected to show the level of competence befitting a doctor holding the same post.

Option C is not the best explanation as, while this may be true, it does not correctly state the legal position whether the defendant has breached their duty of care.

Option D is also not the best explanation as, while the defendant may or may not have met the standard of care expected of the reasonably competent newly qualified casualty doctor, this is not the standard that the defendant would be measured against.

Question 2

A man owns a house near to the boundary of his local cricket club. His garden boundary is only 30 metres (100 feet) away from the cricket ground, and his house is only 18 metres (60 feet) further away. Cricket balls have been hit onto his property 12 times in the last 12 months causing minor damage to his house.

The cricket club has a four-metre (13 feet) fence around the ground but have refused to consider building a higher fence to prevent cricket balls from leaving the ground. The club have stated that they do not have the money to fund the building of a newer fence. The club have also stated that the man should appreciate that the playing of sport is a 'good thing' and that he should simply put up with the risk of his house being hit by cricket balls 'every now and then'.

Which of the following statements best describes whether a court would decide that the cricket club have breached their duty of care in negligence?

A   Yes, because the cricket club could reasonably foresee that the damage to the man's house was likely.

B   Yes, because the cricket club could reasonably foresee that the damage to the man's house was likely and the cost of building a higher fence was reasonable in the circumstances.

C   Yes, because the cricket club could reasonably foresee that the damage to the man's house was likely and the public interest in the playing of sport is not a relevant consideration.

D   No, because, the cricket club could reasonably foresee that the damage to the man's house was likely but the cricket club did not have the resources to prevent the risk.

E   No, because the cricket club could reasonably foresee that the damage to the man's house was likely and the court are bound by the fact that it is the common practice of cricket clubs to have fences that are not higher than four metres.

Answer

Option B is correct – the court would consider the how likely the risk created by the club's activities was and what reasonable precautions should be taken to eliminate the risk.

OptionA is wrong because it fails to appreciate what precautions the club ought to reasonably have taken in response to a foreseeable risk.

Option C is wrong as the public interest in the activities undertaken by the club is a relevant consideration.

Option D is wrong as, if the court were to decide that it was reasonable to build a higher fence, the lack of resources of the club are not generally a relevant consideration.

Option E is wrong as, while the court do consider common practice, it is not conclusive and the court can ignore it if the practice was considered to be negligent.

Question 3

A defendant is being sued for damages arising out of a road traffic incident. The allegation is that the defendant failed to wait at a 'Give way' sign and pulled out into the path of the claimant at a road junction. The claimant was riding a bicycle and suffered a broken collar bone as a result of falling off their bike while, the claimant alleges, swerving to avoid the defendant's car. The defendant denies the allegations and believes that the claimant fell off their bike because they were texting on a mobile phone.

The police attended the incident and the defendant subsequently received a fixed penalty fine for driving a vehicle without road tax. The claimant's solicitor has reported that they have two independent witnesses who will support the claimant's version of events. The defendant's solicitor has not been able to locate any witnesses to support the claimant's version of events.

Tort

Which of the following statements best explains why it is likely that the defendant would be found to have breached their duty of care to the claimant?

A   Because the claimant will be able to rely upon the criminal conviction.

B   Because the defendant will not be able to prove on the balance of probabilities that they did not fall below the standard of the reasonable driver.

C   Because the claimant will be able to rely upon the maxim *res ipsa loquitur* as the defendant was in control of the car and such incidents do not normally happen without a defendant's negligence.

D   Because, on the balance of probabilities, the court is likely to decide that the claimant's evidence has proven that the defendant fell below the standard of the reasonable driver.

E   Because the claimant will be able to rely upon the maxim *res ipsa loquitur* as the defendant was in control of the car, such incidents do not normally happen without a defendant's negligence and the cause of the accident is not known to the claimant.

Answer

Option D is correct as it recognises that the burden of proof is on the claimant to prove breach of duty and that the issue will be decided on the basis of the available evidence.

Option A is wrong as, while a relevant criminal conviction can be relied upon to prove breach of duty (eg dangerous driving), the defendant's conviction for failing to purchase road tax is not relevant as it does not involve careless driving as an element of the offence.

Option B is wrong because the burden of proof is on the claimant to prove their case. The burden of proof only switches to the defendant if they raise any defences, eg contributory negligence.

Option C is wrong because it does not set out all three conditions that are required to be satisfied before the claimant can rely on the maxim *res ipsa loquitur*.

Option E is wrong as, while it sets out the necessary requirements of *res ipsa loquitur*, they are not satisfied on the facts of the question. Such incidents do happen without any defendants being negligent and the cause of the accident is known to the claimant as they have evidence from independent witnesses of the defendant's failure to comply with the 'Give way' sign.

3 Negligence: Causation

3.1	Introduction	30
3.2	Causation in fact	31
3.3	Divisible injury: proportionate damages	34
3.4	Indivisible injury: contribution between tortfeasors	34
3.5	Breaking the chain of causation: intervening acts	35
3.6	Remoteness of damage	37

SQE1 syllabus

This chapter will enable you to achieve the SQE1 Assessment Specification in relation to Functioning Legal Knowledge concerned with the core principles of tort on negligence and causation of damage as the requirement that there must be a causal link between the defendant's breach of duty and the claimant's damage.

Note that for SQE1, candidates are not usually required to recall specific case names or cite statutory or regulatory authorities. Cases are provided for illustrative purposes only.

Learning outcomes

By the end of this chapter you will be able to apply relevant core legal principles and rules appropriately and effectively, at the level of a competent newly qualified solicitor in practice, to realistic client-based and ethical problems and situations in the following areas:

- negligence and the law that determines whether the defendant's breach was a factual cause of the claimant's damage;
- negligence and the limitations on recoverable damage imposed by the rules on intervening acts and remoteness of damage.

3.1 Introduction

In the Example used at **2.3.2** above, David carelessly lit a garden bonfire too close to a garden shed belonging to his neighbour Fred, with the result that the fire spread to the shed and destroyed it.

David owed Fred a duty of care. David breached that duty by failing to reach a reasonable standard of care. It is now necessary to consider causation of damage.

Is it possible to say that the damage to the shed was caused by David's breach of duty? On the simple facts of this case it is clear that it was. It can be said that, but for David's negligence, the damage to Fred's shed would not have occurred. David should therefore pay compensation to Fred for the damage to his shed.

The first issue is one of 'causation in fact', and it is considered more fully in **3.2.1** below.

However, if the facts of the scenario are changed, it can be used to illustrate some of the more complex issues of causation which may arise.

⊛ *Example*

David built the garden bonfire as before but then left it unattended for a few moments. Without David's knowledge another neighbour, John, added several old car tyres to the fire. This made the fire much bigger and caused it to spread to Fred's shed.

*The question of who is responsible for causing the damage to the shed is now more difficult. Had it not been for David's actions in building the fire next to the shed in the first place, the damage could never have happened. However, it might be said that the real cause of the damage is John's intervention. David's actions provide the background, but John's careless intervention is the real cause of the damage to Fred's property. This situation is described as a 'new intervening act' or 'novus actus interveniens'. This is considered further in **3.5** below.*

⊛ *Example*

The facts of the scenario above are changed again. This time David is the only person responsible for the fire. As above, it is clear that he should pay for the damage to the shed itself. However, Fred's garden shed happens to overlook a prestigious racecourse and Fred had agreed to rent out the shed to a photographer for the week of a big race meeting. The rent was £1,000 per week. When the shed is burnt down, Fred loses the rent.

*Clearly, as a matter of fact, David's actions have caused Fred to lose the rent. But for David's negligence in lighting the fire, Fred would not have suffered this loss. However, would it be fair to hold David responsible for all the consequences of his negligent actions? In an example like this, it could be said that Fred's damage of the lost rent was too far removed from David's actions. When a court decides that damage is too far removed so that a defendant should not be responsible for it, the damage is said to be too remote. This is the issue of remoteness of damage, and it is consider it further in **3.6** below.*

To summarise, the concept of causation of damage has been expanded and it covers three questions:

- As a matter of fact, was the defendant's negligence a cause of the claimant's harm?
- Even if the defendant's negligence was a cause of the claimant's harm was there any intervening act?
- Even if the defendant's negligence was a cause of the claimant's harm, was the damage too remote?

3.2 Causation in fact

3.2.1 The 'but for' test

When dealing with causation of damage, the first question that needs to ask is:

'As a matter of fact, was the defendant's negligence a cause of the claimant's damage?' This test is explored further below.

> *In Barnett v Chelsea and Kensington Hospital Management Committee [1969] 1 QB 428, a nightwatchman finished his duty early in the morning and felt unwell. He called at the casualty department of the local hospital and asked to see someone. A doctor in the casualty department told him to leave and see his own doctor. The casualty doctor did not examine him. Later on that same day the nightwatchman died of arsenic poisoning. The medical evidence was that even if he had been seen in hospital that morning, he would have died anyway, as the arsenic poisoning was too far advanced.*
>
> *The court held that, while the hospital had breached its duty of care to the deceased, that breach was not the cause of his death. The hospital did not administer the arsenic to the deceased, neither could it have prevented his death. It is only when the actions of the defendant cause the damage to the claimant that the defendant should be held liable for that damage.*

When factual causation is considered it is necessary to ascertain whether the defendant's breach of duty actually caused the loss about which the claimant is complaining. If it did not then the claimant has no cause of action.

The test applied by the court in *Barnett v Chelsea and Kensington Hospital Management Committee* [1969] to determine this question is known as the 'but for' test. The question that should be asked in each case is:

But for the defendant's breach of duty, would the harm to the claimant have occurred?

If the answer to the question is yes – the harm would still have occurred in any event – then the claimant has failed to establish causation and his claim against the defendant must necessarily fail.

If the answer to the question is no – the harm would not have occurred but for the defendant's negligence – then causation is satisfied and the claimant is able to proceed with his claim.

This requirement that the act or omission of the defendant should be linked to the loss or damage suffered by the claimant is often referred to as the 'chain of causation'. The chain of events and the ways in which the chain might be broken is considered in more detail at **3.5** below.

3.2.2 Proof of factual causation: the 'all or nothing' approach

In a civil case a person alleging a particular fact must prove it. The standard of proof is on a balance of probabilities, ie 'more likely than not'.

In a claim for negligence this means that to establish causation, the claimant must show, on the balance of probabilities, that the harm suffered was caused by the defendant. If the claimant fails to prove that the defendant's breach caused the loss, the claimant's claim will fail.

> *In Hotson v East Berkshire Area Health Authority [1987] 2 All ER 909, the claimant fell from a tree and was injured, but was then treated negligently by the defendant. There was a 75% chance that the claimant's medical condition following the fall would have been the same irrespective of diagnosis and treatment. The claimant had therefore failed to satisfy the causation test, as there was only a 25% chance the defendant's breach had caused his disability and this did not satisfy the balance of probabilities.*

In this kind of case the court is being asked to decide what the cause of the claimant's injury was. Was it the 'innocent' fall from the tree, or was it the defendant's negligent medical treatment?

This question can be much more difficult to answer when there are several possible *alternative* causes of the claimant's injury.

The application of the balance of probabilities test in cases where there is more than one possible cause of harm to the claimant was considered in Wilsher v Essex Area Health Authority *[1988] AC 1074.*

The claimant was born prematurely and was placed in a special baby care unit at a hospital managed by the defendants. The claimant needed oxygen but a catheter was wrongly inserted into an umbilical vein as opposed to an artery and the claimant was supersaturated with oxygen. He developed a condition which resulted in blindness. A likely cause of the condition but not a definite or the only cause was that he had been administered too much oxygen. The evidence was that there could have been five different causes of the baby being blind, only one of which was due to the defendant's breach of duty.

The House of Lords considered the fact that the burden falls on the claimant to prove that the defendant's breach of duty caused the harm on the balance of probabilities. As there were so many possible causes of the harm in the case, the court held that the claimant had not discharged the burden.

In Wilsher *the claimant failed to establish that the defendant's negligence was the cause of his damage because there were several possible alternative causes of his blindness, only one of which was the defendant's negligence. The claimant could not prove that he had been harmed by the defendant rather than by one of the other causes.*

However, it is sometimes possible for a claimant to prove that several causes have *together* contributed to his harm. This is considered below.

3.2.3 Proof of factual causation: the material contribution approach

In Bonnington Castings Ltd v Wardlaw *[1956] AC 613, the claimant was employed by the defendant for eight years in the dressing shop of their foundry, and while employed he contracted pneumoconiosis (a lung disease) by inhaling air which contained minute particles of a noxious dust. However, there were two causes of the noxious dust. The first was 'guilty dust' as it originated from swing grinders, in respect of which the defendant admitted it was in breach of duty because they had not been properly maintained. The second 'innocent dust' was from a pneumatic hammer, in respect of which the defendant was not in breach of its duty of care.*

The House of Lords held that the claimant had succeeded in establishing causation because he could show that the defendant's breach of duty created the 'guilty dust' which materially contributed to the disease from which he suffered.

The case law makes it clear that in a multiple causes case the claimant need not show that the defendant's breach of duty was the only cause of the damage to the claimant, or even the main cause. The claimant simply has to show that it *materially contributed* to the damage.

This approach was not applied by the House of Lords on the facts of *Wilsher* (above) because the claimant was able only to show that there were five different possible risk factors, each of which could have caused his damage. The defendant was responsible for only one of those factors. The defendant had simply added to the list of risks faced by the claimant. The defendant's negligence could not be shown to have made a material contribution to the claimant's harm.

3.2.4 Factual causation: material increase in risk?

In the case of *McGhee v National Coal Board* [1973] 1 WLR 1, it appeared that the House of Lords had extended the material contribution approach even further, to cover creation of a material increase in the *risk* of injury, rather than a material contribution to the injury itself. In *McGhee*, there was again two types of dust but the claimant was not able to prove that the 'guilty dust' connected to the defendant's breach had in fact contributed to his dermatitis. The court found in favour of the claimant on the basis that the defendant's breach had materially increased the risk of dermatitis. However, the case of *Sienkiewicz v Greif (UK) Ltd* [2011] UKSC 10 casts some doubt on any such general extension. The Supreme Court allowed the claimant to rely upon the material increase in risk approach and found the defendant liable. However, the judgments in the case suggest that the principle of material increase in risk is now strictly limited to cases of scientific uncertainty. Moreover, it appears that mesothelioma may be the only case of such scientific uncertainty currently recognised.

The principle of material increase in risk is best viewed as an exception to the usual rules of causation, strictly confined to cases of scientific uncertainty like mesothelioma. In all other cases the claimant must prove causation according to the usual 'but for' test; or, exceptionally, in cases of multiple contributing causes, the material contribution to damage test from *Bonnington*.

3.2.5 Factual causation: what if a claimant is injured more than once?

The problems of causation which arise where a claimant suffers one injury which may have more than one cause were considered above. In *Bonnington*, for example, the two causes ('guilty' dust and 'innocent' dust) were happening at the same time. In *Holtby* (at **3.3** below), the causes (periods of employment with different employers) were happening one after the other but they still contributed to one injury.

It is necessary to briefly consider a different problem: where the claimant suffers more than one injury, one after the other.

Obviously, a claimant might happen to have two completely separate accidental injuries. For example, C might slip on the stairs and suffer a broken wrist. Later, he might be a passenger in a car accident and suffer a broken leg. If the two injuries are unrelated and have no impact on each other, no specific problems of causation are caused.

Difficulties of causation arise, though, where one injury follows another and the two injuries do impact on each other. A simple example of this is provided by the case of *Performance Cars v Abraham*, which deals with two incidents of property damage.

> *In* Performance Cars v Abraham *[1962] 1 QB 33, the defendant negligently collided with a Rolls Royce owned by the claimants. As a result the car would have needed a partial re-spray. However, the same part of the car had already been damaged in an earlier accident. Therefore, it would have needed a re-spray in any event.*
>
> *The Court of Appeal held that the claimant could not claim the cost of the re-spray from the defendant in the second incident because the defendant's breach had not caused the need for the re-spray. Such a need already existed. (Of course, the cost of the re-spray could be claimed from the defendant in the first incident.)*

So, where a claimant (or his property) has already suffered damage, a later defendant who causes a subsequent injury should be liable only to the extent that he makes the claimant's damage worse.

The next issue to consider is: if the defendant has only contributed towards the claimant's injury, should the defendant pay damages which reflect the full extent of the harm suffered? Would it be fairer if the defendant only paid a sum which reflected the extent of their contribution? These questions are examined at **3.3** below.

3.3 Divisible injury: proportionate damages

> *In Holtby v Brigham and Cowan (Hull) Ltd [2000] 3 All ER 421, the claimant developed asbestosis as a result of exposure to asbestos dust during his work. However, the disease had developed over a period of time during which he had worked for several different employers. He brought his claim against one of those employers and was able to prove that this employer's negligence had made a material contribution to his damage. Therefore he was able to succeed in proving causation. The defendant employer argued that it should be responsible only for a proportion of the harm suffered by Mr Holtby. The court agreed. The court apportioned the damages to be paid according to the length of time Mr Holtby had worked for each employer and been exposed to asbestos.*

Where the court has evidence which will enable it to divide up the injury suffered by the claimant, it will apportion the damages accordingly. In *Holtby*, the injury could be divided in this way because the cumulative exposure to asbestos caused a disease which got progressively worse the longer the exposure continued.

This is an issue of great practical importance for both defendants and claimants. It is an important issue for defendants because it determines how much money they must pay to the claimant as damages. It is also an important issue for claimants because if their injury is divided up in this way between several defendants, a claimant will need to sue all of them in order to recover damages in full.

It is important to note that most injuries cannot be divided up in this way.

Example

> *Jack is injured in a road accident caused by the negligence of two separate drivers. He is a passenger in Elise's car who is travelling too fast and it collides with another car driven by Adrianna, who pulls out from a side road without looking. Jack suffers a broken leg.*
>
> *Clearly, both car drivers have made a material contribution to Jack's injury. In this case, however, Jack's broken leg is one single injury which cannot be divided up between the two potential defendants. Both of the drivers are responsible to Jack for his injury.*

In this kind of situation the claimant is entitled to recover his damages in full from either of the defendants. This is much better for the claimant than the situation in *Holtby* above, because the claimant needs to bring proceedings against only one defendant in order to recover his damages in full. (Note, however, that the claimant cannot recover his damages more than once.)

Again, however, it is necessary to consider the position of the defendants. If both are liable to the claimant in full, how should the court deal with damages as between the defendants themselves? This is considered below.

3.4 Indivisible injury: contribution between tortfeasors

Under ss 1(1) and 2(1) of the Civil Liability (Contribution) Act 1978, where two or more people are responsible for the *same* damage, the court has the power to apportion the damage between them. Damages are apportioned according to each person's share of responsibility for the damage.

It should be noted that the apportionment under the Civil Liability (Contribution) Act 1978 applies only as between the defendants themselves. It does not affect the damages recovered by the claimant.

This means that there is an important difference between this situation and the one in *Holtby* above. In a case like *Holtby*, the court can divide up the damage so that each defendant is liable to the claimant only for the particular share of the damage which it caused.

By contrast, where two (or more) defendants are liable to the claimant in respect of the same damage, each defendant is liable to the claimant in full. The claimant will be able to recover full damages from one defendant even if the other is insolvent or untraceable.

The position of the claimant

Where two or more persons are liable to the claimant in respect of the same damage, the claimant is entitled to sue any or all of them and is entitled to recover the full amount of their loss from any or all of them.

Note that this does not mean that the claimant can recover loss several times over.

The position of the defendants

Under the Civil Liability (Contribution) Act 1978, a person (D1) liable for any damage suffered by another person (C) may recover a contribution from any other person (D2) liable for the same damage.

Although the court may apportion blame between the defendants, the apportionment does not affect the claimant as far as the enforcement of any judgment is concerned.

✪ Example

C is awarded damages of £20,000. D1 is found 90% to blame and D2 is found 10% to blame.

- *The total amount of damages C can recover is £20,000.*
- *C may enforce against D1 for the whole £20,000. However, D1 may seek a contribution from D2 for £2,000, ie 10% or*
- *C may enforce against D2 for the whole £20,000. However, D2 may seek a contribution from D1 for £18,000, ie 90%.*

3.5 Breaking the chain of causation: intervening acts

✪ Example

*The example of a bonfire lit by David which destroyed a shed belonging to his neighbour Fred, was considered at **3.1** above. The position when a third party – John – was the real cause of the destruction because he added tyres to the fire, causing it to flare up and spread to the shed was examined.*

If the issue of factual causation is considered, and the 'but for' test is applied, it can be said that David's negligence was a cause of the destruction – but for his building too close to the shed it could not have spread. However, David's negligence was only a background cause. He was not the actual cause of the shed's destruction. The real cause was the intervention by John in adding the tyres.

This can be described by saying that the chain of causation, linking David's negligent act with Fred's damage, has been broken. John's actions have intervened to break the chain of causation. John's actions would be referred to as a new intervening act (the Latin name for this is a 'novus actus interveniens'). The effect of the chain of causation being broken is that Fred's claim against David would fail. (Fred could, of course, bring a separate claim against John.)

The most obvious example of a new intervening act is the action of a third party, such as John in the example above. This is considered below first. However, it is possible for the claimant's own actions to intervene to break the chain of causation. This is considered second.

It can be noted that it is also possible for an event (rather than the actions of a person) to intervene to break the chain of causation. However, the rules for both are similar, so it is possible to concentrate on intervening acts.

3.5.1 Breaking the chain of causation: intervening acts; the actions of a third party

3.5.1.1 The instinctive intervention of a third party

The instinctive interventions of a third party do not break the chain of causation.

> *In the case of* Scott v Shepherd *(1773) 2 Wm Bl 892, the defendant threw a lighted firework into a crowd. X instinctively picked it up and threw it away from himself. Y then did the same. It then landed in front of the claimant and exploded. The court decided that the defendant was still liable to the claimant. The acts of the third parties (X and Y) in throwing the firework about constituted an instinctive reaction in a moment of alarm. They did not break the chain of causation.*

3.5.1.2 The negligent intervention of a third party

The chain of causation is unlikely to be broken by a negligent action of a third party which the defendant ought to have foreseen as a likely consequence of his negligence.

> *In the case of* Knightley v Johns *[1982] 1 WLR 349, the defendant's negligent driving caused his car to block the exit of a busy tunnel. A police inspector took charge and ordered the claimant, a constable, to drive back against the traffic to close the tunnel. The claimant was struck by a vehicle in the tunnel and was injured. The Court of Appeal held that the defendant was not liable. The defendant could not have foreseen the act of the police inspector. This intervening act broke the chain of causation between the claimant and the defendant.*

This can be compared with the case of *Rouse v Squires* [1973] QB 889. The facts of the case were that a lorry driver, A, negligently drove his lorry so that it jack-knifed and blocked two lanes of a motorway. A car then collided with the lorry. Another lorry, driven by Mr Rouse, stopped to provide assistance. However, a further lorry, driven by B, then approached, and its driver negligently failed to notice the accident until it was too late. He collided with the vehicles and Mr Rouse was killed. The Court of Appeal held that both A and B were liable. On the facts, B did not break the chain of causation. A remained liable because it was foreseeable that other drivers might come along too fast and not keep a proper lookout.

(This is a case in which driver A and driver B each made a material contribution to the single injury suffered by Mr Rouse – his death. Both drivers were liable to Mr Rouse in respect of the same wrong, and the court apportioned liability between them under the Civil Liability (Contribution) Act.)

3.5.1.3 The intervening conduct of a third party is reckless or intentional

It is more likely that the conduct of a third party that is reckless or intentional rather than just negligent will be treated as a *novus actus interveniens*.

> *In the case of* Lamb v Camden London Borough Council *[1981] QB 625, the defendants had negligently caused damage to the claimant's house. While the house was being repaired and left unoccupied, squatters entered and caused damage. The court held that the defendants were not liable for the squatter's actions.*

However, the defendant was held liable in *Stansbie v Troman* [1948] 1 All ER 599. Here the defendant was decorating a house. He left it unattended for two hours to fetch wallpaper.

He had been told by the owner of the house to ensure that it was closed when he left. A thief entered and stole a diamond bracelet belonging to the claimant. The Court of Appeal held that the defendant was liable to the claimant. The defendant was negligent, as he had not taken reasonable care to prevent thieves entering. The Court placed importance on the relationship between the parties. The defendant had impliedly agreed to take reasonable care. The theft did not break the chain of causation.

Whether or not the chain of causation has been broken is often a question of fact which depends on the judgment the court makes about the circumstances of the particular case.

However, as a broad rule it can be said that the chain of causation is unlikely to be broken by an action which the defendant ought to have foreseen as a likely consequence of his negligence.

One example of this is the situation where a defendant negligently causes an injury to the claimant, which is then followed by negligent medical treatment. Case law indicates that negligent medical treatment is unlikely to break the chain of causation. This is because a defendant who negligently causes an injury ought to foresee that medical treatment will then be necessary and that this carries some risk that the treatment could be negligent. This is not to say that negligent medical treatment can never break the chain of causation. Medical treatment which was grossly negligent, amounting to a completely inappropriate reaction to the claimant's injury, probably would break the chain.

3.5.2 Breaking the chain of causation: intervening acts; the actions of the claimant

The situation to be considered here is where the claimant does something after the defendant's negligent act which causes the claimant to suffer further harm. When would the claimant's actions break the chain of causation so that the defendant is not liable for the further harm suffered by the claimant?

In the case of McKew v Holland & Hannen & Cubitts (Scotland) Ltd [1969] 3 All ER 1621, the defendant's negligence had weakened the claimant's leg, leaving it with a tendency to give way. When the claimant descended a steep staircase which had no handrail, his leg gave way and he suffered further injuries. The House of Lords held that the claimant had acted unreasonably and had broken the chain of causation.

This can be compared with the case of *Wieland v Cyril Lord Carpets Ltd* [1969] 3 All ER 1006. The claimant injured her neck due to the defendant's negligence. She was fitted with a neck collar which made it difficult to use her spectacles. She further injured herself falling down stairs. The court held that this did not break the chain of causation. The claimant had acted reasonably.

From these cases it can be seen that to amount to a *novus actus interveniens* the claimant's act has to be entirely *unreasonable* in all the circumstances, otherwise the act will simply be a natural event and will not break the chain of causation.

In most cases, if the claimant acts in a careless manner, rather than say that the claimant's act amounts to a *novus actus interveniens* the defendant will raise the defence of contributory negligence (see **Chapter 7**). If that defence is successful it will lead to a reduction in the claimant's damages. This is more favourable to the claimant than a finding that their actions broke the chain of causation because, if the chain of causation is broken, the defendant will not be liable for the claimant's injury.

3.6 Remoteness of damage

3.6.1 Remoteness of damage: the basic rule

There is one further aspect of causation of damage: remoteness of damage.

⭐ Example

The example of a bonfire lit by David which destroyed a shed belonging to his neighbour Fred, was considered at **3.1** above. Fred's garden shed happened to overlook a prestigious racecourse and Fred had agreed to rent out the shed to a photographer for the week of a big race meeting. The rent was £1,000 per week. When the shed is burnt down, Fred loses the rent.

The key point is that the loss of the rent was a kind of damage which was unusual and unexpected. As a matter of fact, David's actions have caused Fred to lose the rent. However, it might not be considered fair to hold David responsible for all the consequences of his negligent actions. Since the lost rent was a kind of damage which was unusual and unexpected, it could be said that it was too far removed from David's actions.

When a court decides that damage is too far removed, so that a defendant should not be responsible for it, the damage is said to be too remote. This is the issue of remoteness of damage.

The case which sets out the test for remoteness of damage is Overseas Tankship (UK) Ltd v Morts Dock and Engineering Co. Ltd, The Wagon Mound (No 1) *[1961] 1 All ER 404. This case is usually simply referred to as 'The Wagon Mound (No 1)'.*

In the Wagon Mound (No 1), *the defendant was operating a ship, the Wagon Mound. Its employees carelessly allowed oil to spill from the ship on to the water of Sydney harbour. The claimant was a ship builder who owned a wharf in the harbour where its employees were using welding equipment. Oil from the Wagon Mound collected around the wharf. The claimant's manager ordered work to stop while he made enquiries. He then concluded that oil floating on water in the open was not likely to ignite. He ordered the welding work to recommence. Unfortunately, the oil did ignite. Hot metal from the claimant's welding set fire to debris in the water which then ignited the oil. The claimant's wharf and a ship under repair were damaged. Could the claimant recover the cost of the damage from the defendant?*

The Wagon Mound (No 1) *held that the test for remoteness of damage is one of* reasonable foreseeability. *The court should ask: Is the damage of such a kind that the reasonable person would have foreseen it? If a reasonable person would not have foreseen the damage then the claimant cannot recover that damage from the defendant. The Privy Council found that the defendant was not liable for the fire damage because it was not reasonably foreseeable.*

⭐ Example

This test can be applied to the example above. A reasonable person would have foreseen that lighting a garden bonfire close to a shed might cause physical damage to or destruction of the shed. Therefore Fred can recover the cost of repairing or replacing the shed. However, a reasonable person probably would not have foreseen Fred's loss of a very profitable rental agreement. Therefore Fred cannot recover the £1,000 lost rent from David.

The *Wagon Mound* rule for remoteness of damage is, 'If a reasonable person would not have foreseen the damage it cannot be recovered'.

However, there are two provisos to this rule, which are referred to as:

- the 'similar in type' rule; and
- the 'egg-shell skull' rule.

These provisos are considered below, beginning with the 'similar in type' rule.

3.6.2 Remoteness of damage: the 'similar in type' rule

If the claimant suffers an injury of a type which was foreseeable, it does not matter that the precise way in which the claimant was injured was not foreseeable.

In Hughes v Lord Advocate *[1963] 1 All ER 705, Post Office employees repairing an underground cable left a manhole with a canvas tent over it and paraffin lamps around the site before going on a tea break. The claimant, a boy aged 8, and another boy aged 10, took one of the lamps, entered the tent and, using ladders, climbed into the manhole. As they climbed back out, the claimant knocked over the lamp which fell into the hole. This caused a huge explosion, with flames climbing over 30 feet high. The claimant fell into the hole and suffered bad burns.*

The court confirmed the rule that an injury must be reasonably foreseeable. As a result of the defendant's employees negligently leaving lit paraffin lamps unattended, an injury by burning was foreseeable. It was not foreseeable that a paraffin lamp would be knocked down the hole and explode. However, since the claimant did suffer an injury of the type *which was foreseeable (injury by burning), it did not matter that the precise way in which he was injured was not foreseeable. The court held that the defendant was liable to the claimant for his burns.*

In *Tremain v Pike* [1969] 3 All ER 1303, the 'similar in type' test was not satisfied. The claimant worked on the defendant's farm. The defendant negligently allowed rats to proliferate on the farm. The claimant came into contact with the rats. He contracted a rare condition, Weil's disease, which is caught by contact with rats' urine.

The court said that this kind of injury was not foreseeable. The type of injury which was foreseeable in those circumstances was injury from rat bites. The injury suffered by the claimant was unusual and unexpected so that it was not foreseeable, even under the 'similar in type' proviso. Therefore, the claimant could not recover damages from the defendant.

It should be noted that in *Tremain v Pike* all of the other elements of a claim in negligence were satisfied. However, the claimant failed on the last aspect of causation of damage: remoteness of damage. The claimant could not prove that his damage was a reasonably foreseeable consequence of the defendant's negligence, so his claim failed.

From this example it is possible to see how the rule of remoteness operates to limit the liability of the defendant.

3.6.3 Remoteness of damage: the 'egg-shell skull' rule

The basic rule for remoteness of damage is that the claimant's injury must be reasonably foreseeable. However, there is a second proviso to the *Wagon Mound* test known as the 'egg-shell skull' rule. This is also described as the rule that 'you take your victim as you find him'.

In Robinson v Post Office *[1974] 1 WLR 1176, the claimant suffered slight injuries to his leg as a result of the defendant's negligence. The claimant saw a doctor who gave him an anti-tetanus injection. Unfortunately the claimant suffered a severe allergic reaction to the injection. The claimant sued the defendant both for the original injury and for the further injury arising out of the allergic reaction.*

The claimant succeeded. The defendant had to take the claimant as he found him. The defendant ought reasonably to have foreseen that as a result of his negligence, the claimant would require medical treatment, so the necessity for the anti-tetanus injection was reasonably foreseeable. The defendant was liable for the consequences of the medical treatment even though he could not reasonably foresee the precise extent of the consequences and could not have foreseen that they would be so severe.

The 'egg-shell skull' rule means that you take your victim as you find them. This means that if the claimant suffers a particular disability or has a particular condition, they can recover in full from the defendant for their losses, even though the defendant could not have foreseen the full extent of the claimant's loss. This rule extends the rule of remoteness as stated in *The Wagon Mound (No 1)*.

✪ Examples

Hareem injures Ola in a car accident due to her negligent driving. Ola is a haemophiliac and bleeds to death. Hareem would be liable for the losses resulting from the death even though a person who did not have that condition would have suffered only minor cuts and bruises.

Joseph is a professional footballer and a high salary-earner. Alex negligently causes an injury which prevents Joseph from playing. Alex must pay for Joseph's loss of wages. The fact that Joseph earns a very high salary, and so has a much larger loss of wages than the average person, is irrelevant as Alex must still pay damages to compensate Joseph for that loss. Alex must take his victim as he finds him.

Summary

Factual causation

- The burden is on the claimant to prove the causal link between the breach and the loss.
- The basic test is the 'but for' test, which takes the following form:
    - But for the defendant's breach, would the harm to the claimant have occurred?
    - If the answer is no – the harm would not have occurred were it not for the defendant's breach – then causation is satisfied.
    - In most cases, this basic test is sufficient to establish causation.
- In some circumstances, where there are multiple simultaneous causes, a modified test is applied, so that causation has been satisfied by showing that the defendant's breach materially contributed to the damage.
- Where the claimant suffers one injury which has more than one cause:
    - if the injury which the claimant suffers is divisible, the court will apportion damages accordingly;
    - if the claimant's injury is not divisible – so that two or more defendants are liable for the same damage – the claimant can recover damages in full from any defendant, but as between defendants the Civil Liability (Contribution) Act 1978 will apply.

Intervening acts

- Actions of a third party may break the chain of causation if not a foreseeable consequence of defendant's negligence, or if the third party acted intentionally or recklessly.
- Actions of the claimant themselves may break the chain of causation if entirely unreasonable in all the circumstances.

Remoteness of damage

- The courts apply the test from *The Wagon Mound (No 1)*: Was the claimant's damage reasonably foreseeable? If the damage was not reasonably foreseeable, the defendant is not liable for it.
- However, there are two provisos to this rule:
    - The 'similar in type' rule: provided the type of damage was reasonably foreseeable, the defendant is liable, even if the precise way in which it occurred was not foreseeable.

- The 'egg-shell skull' rule: provided the type of harm was reasonably foreseeable, the defendant is liable for the full extent of the harm, even if the precise extent of the damage was not foreseeable.

Summary flowchart

Figure 3.1 Negligence: causation flowchart

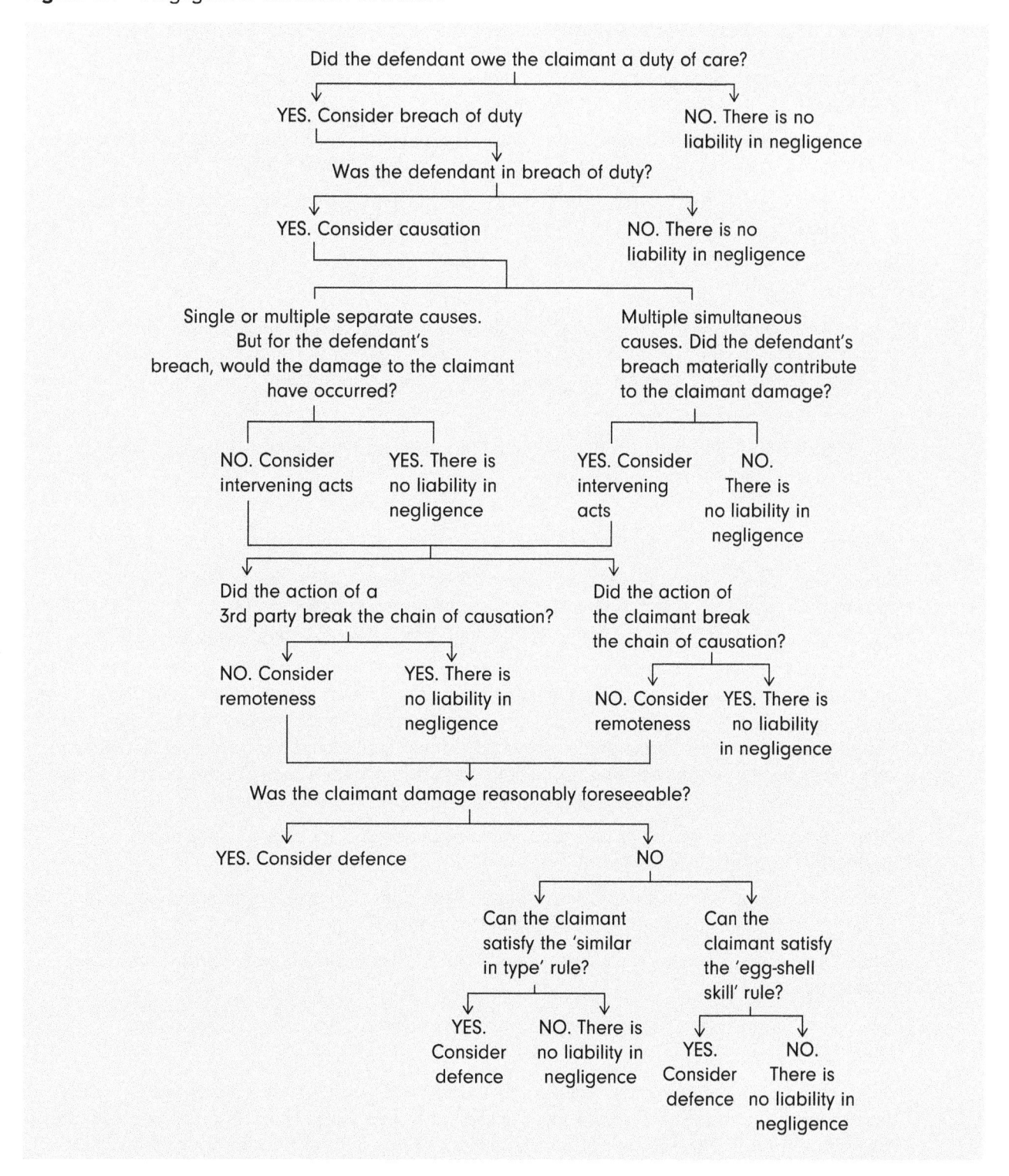

```
                    Did the defendant owe the claimant a duty of care?
                         │                                    │
                    YES. Consider breach of duty      NO. There is no
                         │                            liability in negligence
                    Was the defendant in breach of duty?
                         │                                    │
                    YES. Consider causation            NO. There is no
                         │                             liability in negligence
         ┌───────────────┴───────────────┐
    Single or multiple separate causes.    Multiple simultaneous
    But for the defendant's                causes. Did the defendant's
    breach, would the damage to the        breach materially contribute
    claimant have occurred?                to the claimant damage?
         │                                    │
    ┌────┴────┐                          ┌────┴────┐
  NO.        YES. There is           YES.         NO.
  Consider   no liability in         Consider     There is
  intervening negligence             intervening  no liability in
  acts                               acts         negligence
    │                                    │
  Did the action of a                 Did the action of
  3rd party break the chain of        the claimant break
  causation?                          the chain of causation?
    │                                    │
  ┌─┴─┐                                ┌─┴─┐
  NO. Consider  YES. There is       NO. Consider  YES. There is
  remoteness    no liability in     remoteness    no liability
                negligence                        in negligence
           │
    Was the claimant damage reasonably foreseeable?
           │
      ┌────┴────┐
    YES.        NO
    Consider    │
    defence   ┌─┴──────┐
         Can the claimant    Can the
         satisfy the 'similar  claimant satisfy
         in type' rule?       the 'egg-shell
                              skill' rule?
         ┌──┴──┐              ┌──┴──┐
       YES.   NO. There is   YES.   NO.
       Consider no liability in  Consider There is
       defence  negligence       defence  no liability in
                                          negligence
```

Tort

Sample questions

Question 1

A solicitor acts for a client who was injured while a passenger in a taxi. The client was travelling in the taxi when a motorbike driver pulled out of a side road and drove into the path of the taxi. The client says that no collision in fact occurred between the vehicles but the client was thrown sideways when the taxi driver had to swerve quickly to avoid the motorbike. This caused the client to injure their head as it hit the inside window of the taxi.

The Police Accident Report confirms that the motorbike driver had ignored a 'Give Way' sign and that the taxi driver was travelling at 40 mile per hour on a road where the speed limit was 30 miles per hour. Expert evidence confirms that, if the taxi driver had been driving within the speed limit, then they would not have had to swerve to avoid the motorbike.

Which of the following statements best explains how the client will be able to show that the breach of duty by the taxi driver is a factual cause of their injury?

A   Because but for the breach of duty by the taxi driver, the client would not have been injured.

B   Because but for the breach of duty by the motorbike driver, the client would not have been injured.

C   Because the actions of the motor bike driver should have been reasonably foreseeable by the taxi driver.

D   Because the breach of duty by the taxi driver made a material contribution to the injuries suffered by the client.

E   Because the injury suffered by the client is a reasonably foreseeable consequence of the taxi driver's breach of duty.

Answer

Option D is correct – it states the correct test for factual causation where there are two separate tortious acts, which simultaneously cause damage to the client.

Option A is wrong because this is a case of multiple causes. Here there are two separate tortious acts, which simultaneously cause damage to the client. The client's injury was caused by the breach of duty by the taxi driver but also by the breach of duty by the motorbike driver. Satisfying the 'but for' test in this situation would be problematic because the taxi driver could allege that but for the actions of the motorcycle driver they would not have had to swerve at all. Equally, the motorbike driver could allege that, but for the fact that the taxi driver was speeding, their pulling out of the junction would not have injured the client.

Option B is therefore wrong for the same reason (although it focuses on the breach by the motorbike driver and not the taxi driver).

Option C is wrong because it considers whether the actions of the motorbike driver may have broken the chain of causation and not factual causation.

Option E is wrong because it considers the question of remoteness rather than factual causation.

Question 2

A claimant suffered a badly broken leg while being a passenger on a motorbike driven by the defendant. The defendant pulled out of side road into the path of an oncoming car. The claimant feared that the car would hit the defendant's motorbike. In order to avoid this, they jumped from the motorbike and broke their leg in the fall. In fact, the car driver managed to swerve around the defendant's motorbike and avoided a collision.

Which of the following statements best explains how the claimant will be able to show that the fact that she jumped off the motorbike did not act as an intervening act that broke the chain of causation?

A   Because the claimant's act of jumping off the motorbike was entirely reasonable in the circumstances that she was in at the time.

B   Because the claimant's act of jumping off the bike ought to have been foreseen by the defendant as a likely consequence of their negligence.

C   Because the claimant's act of jumping off the bike caused an injury that was reasonably foreseeable.

D   Because the claimant's act of jumping off the bike caused an injury of a type that was reasonably foreseeable, even if the precise way it happened was not foreseeable.

E   Because the claimant's act of jumping off the bike caused an injury of a type that was reasonably foreseeable, even if the precise extent of the injury was not foreseeable.

Answer

Option A is correct – the test that is applied for when the act of the claimant themselves may be an intervening act and break the chain of causation is whether their act was entirely reasonable in the circumstances that they were in at the time.

Option B is wrong as it is the test that is applied when the negligent act of a third party may break the chain of causation.

Option C is wrong as this is the basic rule for remoteness of damage from *The Wagon Mound*.

Option D is incorrect as this is the 'similar in type' rule for remoteness.

Option E is incorrect as this is the 'egg-shell skull' rule for remoteness.

Question 3

A solicitor is instructed by a client who has suffered a bad head injury due to an accident at work. His employers' have admitted that they breached the duty they owed the client but are disputing liability on the issue of causation. The employers' argument is that, while the client was healthy at the time of the incident, medical evidence shows that concussion injuries from playing rugby resulted in the long-term effects of the head injury due to the accident being much worse than they would have been otherwise. The employers have made an offer to settle based upon the effects of the head injury on a person who did not have any pre-accident concussion injuries.

Which of the following statements best explains whether the solicitor should advise the client to accept the employers' offer?

A   No, because the additional long-term effects of the client's head injury were reasonably foreseeable.

B   No, because the head injury was reasonably foreseeable and the employer is liable for the full extent of the harm, even if the additional long-term effects of the client's head injury were not foreseeable.

C   No, because the head injury was reasonably foreseeable and the employer is liable for the full extent of the harm, even if the precise way the head injury occurred was not foreseeable.

D   Yes, because the additional long-term effects of the client's head injury were not reasonably foreseeable.

E   Yes, because the additional long-term effects of the client's head injury were caused by the client.

Answer

Option B is correct as this explains the 'egg-shell skull' rule and why the offer should be rejected.

Option A is wrong because it is likely that a court would find that the additional long-term effects of the client's head injury were not reasonably foreseeable, ie the client would fail on the basic rule on remoteness as it was not foreseeable that the effects of the injury would be worse because of the client's concussion injuries. However, the 'egg-shell skull' proviso to the basic rule on remoteness would apply. This means that the employers must take the client as they find them, ie with the pre-existing concussion injuries.

Option C is wrong because, while it explains the 'similar in type' proviso to the basic rule on remoteness, this proviso is not relevant on the facts of the question.

Option D is wrong because it neglects to consider the 'egg-shell skull' rule.

Option E is wrong because whether the client was in any way at fault in causing the pre-existing concussion injuries is not relevant to an application of the 'egg-shell skull' rule. (If a claimant's own unreasonable act, if done after the defendant's breach of duty, results in their injuries being more severe, then there may be a break in the chain of causation. However, this does not apply to the facts of the question.)

4 Negligence: Pure Economic Loss

4.1	Introduction	46
4.2	Economic loss caused by acquiring a defective item of property	47
4.3	Economic loss unconnected to personal injury to the claimant or physical damage to the claimant's property	49
4.4	Pure economic loss: breach of duty and causation of damage	55
4.5	Exclusion of liability	56

SQE1 syllabus

This chapter will enable you to achieve the SQE1 Assessment Specification in relation to Functioning Legal Knowledge concerned with the core principles of tort on negligence and the special rules for duty of care which apply in the limited duty situation of pure economic loss.

Note that for SQE1, candidates are not usually required to recall specific case names or cite statutory or regulatory authorities. Cases are provided for illustrative purposes only.

Learning outcomes

By the end of this chapter you will be able to apply relevant core legal principles and rules appropriately and effectively, at the level of a competent newly qualified solicitor in practice, to realistic client-based and ethical problems and situations in the following areas:

- negligence and distinguishing between consequential economic loss and pure economic loss;
- negligence and the special rules for duty of care which apply in the limited duty situation of pure economic loss.

4.1 Introduction

This chapter returns to the issue of when a defendant may owe a claimant a duty of care and considers the 'limited duty situation' which arises where a claimant has suffered pure economic loss. **Chapter 5** considers another limited duty situation which arises where a claimant has suffered pure psychiatric harm.

The test for a duty of care requires a sufficiently proximate relationship between the claimant and the defendant. There is generally a lack of a sufficiently proximate relationship between a claimant who has suffered pure economic loss, and a defendant who may have caused this type of loss. The lack of proximity between claimant and defendant means that the defendant's potential liability could be boundless, to an indeterminate number of claimants. This is the reason why the courts place limits upon the duty of care in cases of pure economic loss and why, as a general rule, a defendant does not owe any duty of care to a claimant not to cause pure economic loss.

⭐ Example

A journalist negligently reports that shares in X plc would be a good investment. Several readers invest in X plc but lose money because X plc was already in financial difficulty when the journalist published the article.

If this example is compared with the situation of a householder who negligently burns down the garden shed belonging to his neighbour, so causing property damage, it is possible to note some important differences between the two examples.

The readers who invest and lose money have not suffered any physical damage to property. It can be seen that the relationship between the readers and the journalist is much less close than that between the householder and his neighbour. There may not, therefore, be a sufficiently proximate relationship for a duty of care to arise between the reader and the journalist.

This example demonstrates that the kind of loss suffered by a claimant can determine that a duty of care may not be owed to them. It is important to remember that, when it is stated that no duty of care is owed, this means that the claimant cannot recover the loss suffered. So, in the example above, the readers cannot recover their loss on the shares from the journalist. The defendants have been negligent and their negligence may have caused the damage suffered by the claimants. The negligence of the journalist has caused their readers to lose money on their investment. Nevertheless, in such cases the journalist does not have to pay for the consequences of their negligence.

There are some limited situations in which damages can be recovered for pure economic loss. This explains why it is a 'limited duty' situation and not a 'no duty' situation. In these limited situations recovery is allowed because it is possible to identify a sufficiently close relationship between the particular claimant and the defendant.

As a general rule, a defendant does not owe any duty of care to a claimant not to cause pure economic loss. In other words, as a general rule, where a claimant suffers damage which is classed as pure economic loss, that loss is not recoverable.

It is necessary, therefore, to look more carefully at what constitutes pure economic loss. To do this, the easiest way to begin is to identify what is not pure economic loss.

⭐ Example

A householder, David, negligently lights a garden bonfire which destroys the shed belonging to his neighbour Fred. Fred has to pay £500 for a replacement shed. Fred also pays £5.00 per week to a local garage to store his lawn mower for three weeks while the old shed is out of use.

The £515 spent by Fred is not pure economic loss. Fred has lost money in repairing the shed and paying for storage, but his loss was caused by the physical damage to his property. The money loss follows on from the physical damage, so it can be called 'consequential economic loss'.

There are no special rules for consequential economic loss. Just as David owes Fred a duty of care not to cause damage to his shed, so he also owes a duty not to cause the consequential economic loss which follows from that damage. Fred will be able to recover the £515 for repairs and lost use from David.

Example

Adam's negligence causes Bill to suffer a broken leg. Bill is unable to go to work for six months and suffers a loss of wages of £10,000. It also costs him £500 for physiotherapy treatment.

The £10,500 for lost wages and medical treatment is not pure economic loss. Bill has lost money in not receiving his wages and in paying for the physiotherapy, but his loss was caused by the physical injury caused to him. The money loss follows on from the physical injury, so we call it 'consequential economic loss'.

As stated above, there are no special rules for consequential economic loss. Just as Adam owes Bill a duty of care not to cause him physical injury, so he also owes a duty not to cause the consequential economic loss which follows from that physical injury. Bill will be able to recover the £10,500 for lost wages and medical treatment from Adam.

The examples above have identified money losses which are not pure economic loss. However, the law is not always as logical when considering the kinds of damage which are classed as pure economic loss. Nevertheless, it is possible to begin with one situation of pure economic loss which is clear. This is considered in the next section below.

4.2 Economic loss caused by acquiring a defective item of property

Examples

Maria buys a compact disc player as a gift for her son James. The player does not work because it is faulty. James has no contract with the retailer. (Assume that the Contract (Rights of Third Parties) Act does not apply.)

Maria buys a hairdryer for herself from a retailer 'Super Cheap Ltd'. Super Cheap Ltd goes out of business. The hairdryer does not work because it is faulty. Maria discovers that the hairdryer was manufactured by Electrics Co. Maria has no contract with Electrics Co.

James could not sue the retailer in negligence for the cost of replacing the faulty CD player. Maria could not sue Electrics Co in negligence for the cost of replacing the faulty hairdryer. The proper remedy would be for the person who purchased the goods (Maria in each case) to sue the person with whom she had a contract (the retailer in each case).

James and Maria would be seeking to sue in negligence because they cannot have a remedy in contract. James wants to sue in negligence because he never had a contract to purchase the player. Maria wants to sue the manufacturer of the hairdryer in negligence because the retailer has gone out of business.

There would have been a close relationship between the parties to the relevant contracts. By contrast, there is no sufficiently close relationship between James and the retailer, or

Maria and the manufacturer. Another way that this could be looked at is to say that, if claimants like James and Maria were allowed to sue in negligence in cases like this, the law of tort would interfere with and undermine the law of contract. So, James and Maria cannot sue for these losses in negligence.

The situations above can be summarised as:

- the damage they have suffered is economic loss caused by acquiring a defective item of property;
- this damage is classed as pure economic loss;
- no duty of care is owed in respect of pure economic loss.

Thus, once James and Maria's damage is identified as pure economic loss, it is possible to know that it cannot be recovered in negligence.

It is relatively easy to identify why the damage in the above examples is classed as pure economic loss. A more complex example of pure economic loss caused by acquiring a defective item of property is considered below.

In Murphy v Brentwood DC [1990] 2 All ER 908, the claimant bought a newly constructed house. Eleven years later the claimant discovered that the foundations were dangerous. The foundations were subsiding, causing serious cracking in the walls of the house. The claimant eventually sold the house for £35,000 less than its market value would have been if it had been in a sound condition. The plans for the foundations had been approved by Brentwood District Council. The claimant sued Brentwood District Council for negligently approving the foundation plans.

The House of Lords held that the loss suffered by the claimant was pure economic loss – so not recoverable.

The key point in *Murphy* was that the defects in the house had become apparent before they caused any physical damage to any person or other property. The only thing suffering damage from the cracking and subsiding was the house itself. A claimant in that situation would incur the cost of repairs, or suffer a reduction in value of the property – and the court held that this amounted to pure economic loss. Essentially, the claimant had simply acquired something which was less valuable than the price he paid for it.

Example

Kate decides to have a new swimming pool built in her garden. She contracts with EZ Build Co for them to build the pool. During construction the pool is inspected by the local authority to check that the pool walls are strong enough to meet safety regulations. When the pool is completed Kate pays EZ Build. However, later, Kate finds that the walls of the pool are collapsing because they were not constructed properly. No one has been hurt, but the pool will cost a lot to repair. When Kate tries to contact EZ Build she finds that they have gone out of business. Kate obtains evidence which proves that the local authority was negligent when it inspected the walls of the pool. Could Kate sue the local authority in tort for the cost of repairing the pool?

Applying Murphy it is clear that Kate cannot sue the local authority for the cost of repairs to the pool. Even though Kate may be able to prove that the local authority was negligent and that this caused her loss, she still cannot recover damages from the local authority. The damage which Kate has suffered is economic loss caused by acquiring a defective item of property (the pool). This is classed as pure economic loss. No duty of care is owed in respect of pure economic loss, therefore the loss is not recoverable.

However, where a claimant has suffered personal injury or damage to property that is caused by acquiring a defective item of property, the law is much more ready to accept that there is a sufficiently close relationship between claimant and defendant for a duty of care to arise.

⊛ *Example*

Suppose that, in the example above, the hairdryer bought by Maria caught fire and burned her hand. In this case Maria has suffered personal injury. The special rules on pure economic loss would not apply. However, the cost of replacing the hairdryer is pure economic loss and is, therefore, not recoverable in negligence.

Suppose that, in the example above, the compact disc player given to James overheated and burned a hole in his bag. In this case James has suffered physical damage to his bag. The cost of replacing the bag is consequent on that physical damage. James has not suffered pure economic loss and the special rules would not apply. However, the cost of replacing the compact disc player is pure economic loss and is, therefore, not recoverable in negligence.

Another kind of loss which is also classified as pure economic loss is considered below. It might be thought that the next kind of loss does not bear much logical relation to 'defective products' loss. It may help to remember the reason why certain kinds of loss are classified as 'pure economic loss'. In each case it is because they do not involve the defendant in a sufficiently close relationship with the claimant.

4.3 Economic loss unconnected to personal injury to the claimant or physical damage to the claimant's property

⊛ *Examples*

A journalist negligently advises that shares in X plc would be a good investment. Several readers of his paper suffer losses when they invest in X plc.

The lost investment is classed as pure economic loss because there is no physical damage to person or property.

Tony agrees to lend Dale his new suit to wear for a smart wedding. The day before the wedding Tony's suit is destroyed in a fire caused by the negligence of Sam. Dale cannot wear Tony's suit to the wedding so he has to hire a replacement costing £100 instead.

In this example there is physical damage to property – Tony's suit. However, Dale would be the claimant for his lost £100. In this case there is no physical damage to property belonging to the claimant (Dale). There is only physical damage to property belonging to someone else (Tony). Dale's loss is classed as pure economic loss and Dale cannot recover his £100 from Sam. (Tony's loss of his suit is simply ordinary physical damage. Tony can recover that loss from Sam in the usual way.)

From these examples it is possible to see that this kind of pure economic loss can be sub-divided into two categories. Economic loss unconnected to physical damage to the claimant's person or property can be either:

- economic loss caused by damage to the property of a third party; or
- economic loss caused where there is no physical damage.

These are considered in turn.

4.3.1 Economic loss caused by damage to the property of a third party

Examples

Dale's extra hire costs when Tony's suit is destroyed.

Alison is on her way to the station to catch a train. She is stuck in a large traffic jam caused by a serious road accident. She misses the train and has to purchase another ticket for a later one. This costs Alison more money. Alison finds out that the road accident was caused by the negligence of Conrad, who crashed into a lorry owned by Morris.

In this example there is no damage to any property owned by Alison. The extra cost of her train ticket is classed as pure economic loss. Alison knows that Conrad was negligent. She could also show that his negligence caused her loss. Nevertheless, she cannot recover that loss from Conrad. Conrad does not have to pay for this consequence of his negligent actions.

A more complex example of this kind of pure economic loss is considered below.

In Spartan Steel & Alloys Ltd v Martin & Co (Contractors) Ltd *[1973] QB 27, the claimants manufactured metal in a factory which was directly supplied with electricity by a cable from a power station. The factory worked 24 hours a day. The defendant's employees damaged the electricity cable while drilling a nearby road. The result was a power cut to the factory caused by the defendant's negligence. The damaged electricity cable belonged to the electricity supplier. It did not belong to the claimants.*

The power cut caused the following losses:

- *products (known as 'melts') in a furnace which solidified;*
- *loss of profit on those products;*
- *loss of profits on four further melts which could have been processed during the time the electricity was unavailable.*

In Spartan Steel *the claimant could not recover for the four future melts. This was pure economic loss because it was caused by damage to property belonging to a third party – the cable which belonged to the supplier – so no duty of care was owed. However, the claimant was owed a duty of care for damage to property which it did own, and financial loss consequent on that damage. So, this covered the products in the furnace which solidified and the loss of profit on those products.*

The result in *Spartan Steel* would have been different if the claimant had been the owners of the damaged electricity cable. The lost profit during the time that the electricity was cut off would have been recoverable. This is because it would have been consequential economic loss, following on from damage to property belonging to the claimant (the cable). (If Spartan Steel owned the cable they would also have had a further claim – for the cost of repairs to the cable itself.)

In conclusion:

- If a defendant negligently damages the claimant's property and causes the claimant loss, there is a sufficiently close relationship between the claimant and the defendant. The defendant owes the claimant a duty of care and the claimant can recover their loss from the defendant. This is *not* a situation of pure economic loss.

- If the defendant negligently damages property belonging to a third party and causes the claimant loss, there is not a sufficiently close relationship between the claimant and the defendant. The defendant does not owe the claimant a duty of care and the claimant cannot recover their loss from the defendant. This *is* a situation of pure economic loss.

The next section considers a further instance of pure economic loss caused without physical damage to the claimant.

4.3.2 Economic loss caused where there is no personal injury to the claimant or physical damage to the claimant's property

The section above considered the situation where there is some physical damage, but it is not suffered by the claimant. This section considers cases in which there is no physical damage at all.

The example of the lost investment suffered by the readers as a result of the journalist's negligent financial advice differs from all of the other examples of pure economic loss considered so far. This is because the journalist caused loss by the negligent statement that they made. In all of the other examples so far, the economic loss was caused by negligent actions.

Economic loss caused by acquiring a defective item of property is caused by negligent actions (eg the actions of the inspector in *Murphy*). Economic loss caused by damage to the property of a third party is caused by negligent actions (eg the actions of the workmen who damaged the cable in *Spartan Steel*).

However, economic loss which is caused without any physical damage raises a new possibility. Loss might be caused by negligent statements, as well as by negligent actions. It is therefore possible to sub-divide this kind of loss as follows.

Economic loss caused where there is no physical damage can be either:

- caused by negligent actions; or
- caused by negligent statements.

4.3.2.1 Economic loss caused where there is no physical damage: actions

Economic loss caused by negligent actions where there is no physical damage falls within the general rule that there is no duty of care for pure economic loss.

> *In* Weller & Co v Foot and Mouth Disease Research Institute *[1966] 1 QB 569, the defendants occupied premises where they carried out experiments concerning foot and mouth disease. It was assumed that the defendants had imported a virus onto their premises which had escaped and caused the outbreak of disease. Cattle in the vicinity became infected and two cattle markets in the area had to be closed. The claimants, auctioneers, claimed damages for loss of business against the defendants in negligence for allowing the foot and mouth virus to escape. It was held that the claimant could not recover its loss from the defendant because the loss was not caused by physical damage. It was caused by the forced closure of the cattle market. It was therefore classified as pure economic loss and no duty of care was owed.*

4.3.2.2 Economic loss caused where there is no physical damage: statements

This section considers cases where loss is caused without any physical damage, and by a negligent statement rather than a negligent action.

In this kind of case there is very great potential for unlimited liability. For instance, in the example of the negligent journalist giving bad investment advice, the journalist does not know whether his statement will be read and relied on by 100 readers or 10,000.

As with all other kinds of pure economic loss, the general rule remains, therefore, that no duty of care is owed. There is no duty not to cause pure economic loss, and damages cannot be recovered.

However, this is one instance in which it is recognised that there is an exception to the general rule. The exception is explained in the remainder of this section.

Negligent statements: special relationships

The reason for the general rule for no duty of care for pure economic loss is that there is not a sufficiently close relationship between the claimant and the defendant.

The exception to the general rule arises in cases where the court is able to find that there is, in fact, an especially close relationship between the claimant and the defendant. These cases may be described broadly as situations in which the defendant has assumed a responsibility towards the claimant.

⭐ Example

In the case of the journalist who gave negligent financial advice, one particular reader of the newspaper telephones the journalist and says that he would like some more specific advice. The journalist advises him how many shares to buy. The journalist assures the reader that his advice can be relied on.

It could now be said that the journalist probably does owe a duty of care to this particular reader. This is because the actions of the journalist have created a special relationship between him and the reader. The journalist has undertaken a responsibility towards the reader.

Until 1964 the rule relating to pure economic loss caused by negligent statements was the same as for any other pure economic loss: the claimant could not recover. This position altered dramatically with the case of *Hedley Byrne & Co Ltd v Heller & Partners Ltd*.

In Hedley Byrne v Heller & Partners Ltd *[1964] AC 465, the claimants were supplying services to a company X. The defendant was X's banker who had supplied the claimants with a favourable credit reference for X. The claimant relied on the favourable reference, extended credit to X, and lost a large amount of money when X went into liquidation.*

The question for the court was – even if the bank was negligent – did it owe any duty of care to the claimant? The House of Lords held that there could be liability for a negligent statement, even though the loss was pure economic loss – provided there was an especially close relationship between claimant and defendant. (The House of Lords found that, while a duty of care was owed, the defendant had used an effective disclaimer of liability which meant it escaped liability to the claimant. Such disclaimers that aim to exclude liability are now subject to statutory control – this is considered at **4.5** *below.)*

Hedley Byrne established that a duty is owed if there is a special relationship between the defendant and the claimant. The two elements to a special relationship under *Hedley Byrne* are:

(a) an assumption of responsibility by the defendant;

(b) reasonable reliance by the claimant.

In 1990 the law in this area was considered again by the House of Lords in the case of *Caparo Industries plc v Dickman* [1990] 1 All ER 568. (This case was considered in **Chapter 1** as *Caparo* set the broad general test for novel duty situations.) *Caparo* considered the case of pure economic loss caused by negligent statements and expanded upon the 'special relationship' test in *Hedley Byrne*. *Caparo* expands upon and restates the criteria necessary to establish a special relationship giving rise to a duty of care.

In Caparo Industries v Dickman and others *[1990] 1 All ER 568, the defendants were a firm of auditors, who had prepared the accounts for a company called Fidelity. In the accounts the defendants had stated that Fidelity had made a profit. The claimant was a company which owned some shares in Fidelity. The claimant relied on the defendants' statement by buying additional shares in Fidelity to make a successful takeover bid. The defendants were alleged to have been negligent because the statement in the accounts was incorrect. In fact Fidelity had not made a profit; it had made a loss. The claimant suffered a loss because it had paid an excessive price for the additional shares in Fidelity.*

The House of Lords found that no duty of care was owed by the defendants to the claimant in its capacity as an investor purchasing shares in Fidelity. The necessary special relationship was not established.

The case of *Caparo* laid down the four criteria to be satisfied for a defendant to have assumed a responsibility towards a claimant:

- The defendant knew the purpose for which the advice was required.
- The defendant knew that the advice would be communicated to the claimant (either specifically or as a member of an ascertainable class).
- The defendant knew that the claimant was likely to act on the advice without independent inquiry.
- The advice was acted on by the claimant to its detriment.

Cases which followed *Caparo* have applied this test to determine liability.

In James McNaughton Papers Group Ltd v Hicks Anderson & Co (a firm) [1991] 1 All ER 134, the Court of Appeal decided that a company accountant owed no duty of care to a prospective takeover bidder who relied on the accountant's hurriedly prepared draft accounts. This decision was made on the basis that there was insufficient proximity of relationship between the accountant and the bidder. The accountant did not know his statement, the accounts, would be communicated to the bidder for that particular transaction.

In Morgan Crucible Co plc v Hill Samuel Bank Ltd [1991] 1 All ER 148, the Court of Appeal decided that in a contested takeover battle, if, after an identified bidder has emerged, the directors and financial advisers of a target company make express representations with a view to influencing the bidder's conduct, they may owe a duty not to mislead him negligently. In this case the identity of the bidder is known and the nature of the transaction is known, so proximity of relationship can be established.

The general rule is that, usually, no duty of care will be owed in respect of advice given in a social situation because there is no assumption of responsibility. This is confirmed in the case of *Chaudhry v Prabhakar* [1989] 1 WLR 29. While *Chaudhry* predates *Caparo*, it nevertheless illustrates the issues to be considered in applying the *Caparo* test.

In Chaudhry v Prabhakar [1989] 1 WLR 29, the court stated that, generally, a duty of care will not be owed in respect of advice given in a social situation, but then found that on the particular facts of that case a duty was owed. On the facts, the claimant and defendant were friends. The defendant gave advice to the claimant about the purchase of a motor car. The claimant relied on the advice but the car turned out to be unroadworthy and worthless, so the claimant suffered a loss.

It was held that the defendant did owe the claimant a duty of care, despite the fact that they were friends. This was because the defendant had more experience and knowledge about cars than the claimant, and the claimant had made it clear that she would be relying on his skill and judgment. In those circumstances this was not simply advice given on a social occasion. The defendant had gone beyond this and had assumed a responsibility to the claimant – so that a duty was owed.

Although *Caparo* did not alter the law drastically in the case of negligent statements, the re-stating of the criteria necessary to determine whether there is sufficient proximity of relationship does have the effect of making it more difficult for the claimant to prove the case.

In terms of the relationship between the test established in *Hedley Byrne* and that in *Caparo*, the four-stage test established in *Caparo* is used to determine whether the defendant has assumed a responsibility to the claimant – so as to give rise to a special relationship.

A checklist of the overall test derived from both *Hedley Byrne* and *Caparo* is as follows:

Is there a special relationship between the defendant and the claimant?

- Did the defendant assume a responsibility towards the claimant?
    - Did the defendant know the purpose for which the advice was required?
    - Did the defendant know that the advice would be communicated to the claimant (either specifically or as a member of an ascertainable class)?
    - Did the defendant know that the claimant was likely to act on the advice without independent inquiry?
    - Was the advice acted on by the claimant to its detriment?
- Was it reasonable for the claimant to rely on the defendant for advice?

When the test is applied there is likely to be some overlap between the different parts of it. For example, if the defendant knows that the claimant has sought its advice for a particular purpose and intends to rely on it, this could tend to show that it was reasonable for the claimant to rely on the advice.

In the next section you will see that the duty of care established in *Hedley Byrne* and *Caparo* has been extended to some new situations. In these new situations it is not always easy to see how the test set out above is satisfied in full. You may not always be able to identify reliance by the claimant. However, you will see that the cases can still be explained as ones in which there is an assumption of responsibility by the defendant.

Economic loss caused where there is no physical damage: extension of the special relationship

The *Hedley Byrne* principle has been extended to cover a wider class of cases of pure economic loss – essentially, cases where the defendant has assumed a responsibility towards the claimant.

In Spring v Guardian Assurance plc *[1994] 3 WLR 354, the claimant's former employer provided a reference to his prospective new employers. The reference had been prepared negligently. As a result it was incorrect and was very unfavourable towards the claimant. This resulted in the claimant not being employed by the prospective new employers.*

The claimant claimed damages for the pure economic loss which he suffered as a result of the negligent statements in the reference. It was held that a duty of care was owed to him by his former employer.

Spring is different to the cases considered above because the negligent statement was not made to the claimant. It was made to a third party (the prospective employer), who relied on it to the detriment of the claimant. *Spring* extends the *Hedley Byrne* principle to this wider class of cases. It can be explained on the basis that the employer had assumed a responsibility to the claimant to take care in providing the reference.

In White v Jones *[1995] 1 All ER 691, a client instructed a solicitor to draft a new will for him. The solicitor negligently delayed in drafting the will. Unfortunately the testator died before the new will was drawn up. This meant that the testator's old will took effect.*

The claimant in this case would have been a beneficiary under the new will. He was not a beneficiary under the old will. The solicitor's negligence had therefore caused him to lose his prospective inheritance under the new will.

The court held that a duty was owed to the claimant. Although it could not be said that the beneficiary had relied on the solicitor, it was still possible to find a sufficiently close relationship between them. This was because the solicitor could clearly foresee that if the will were not drafted before the testator died, the potential beneficiaries would not be able to claim their inheritances. Again, the case can be explained on the basis that the solicitor undertook a responsibility towards the potential beneficiaries (as well as to the testator).

There is one further key feature of the facts in *White* which make it different from the cases considered above. In this case the solicitor did not make a negligent statement. He provided services in a negligent way. Thus, in *White v Jones* it is possible to see the extension of the *Hedley Byrne* principle from negligent statements to pure economic loss caused in the negligent provision of professional *services*, where there has been an assumption of responsibility.

Henderson v Merrett Syndicates Ltd [1994] 3 All ER 506 is a more complex example of the extension of the *Hedley Byrne* principle to the negligent provision of professional services. Some of the claimants *in Henderson* had a contract with the defendant for the provision of professional services. Nevertheless, they were still allowed to bring a claim in tort against the defendant. It was very important that the duty in tort (to take reasonable care) was consistent with the duty owed under the contract (also a duty to take reasonable care).

Henderson established that a claimant can rely on a claim in tort even though they also have a contract with the defendant for the professional services. However, this is possible only if the duty in tort is consistent with the duties owed under the contract.

4.4 Pure economic loss: breach of duty and causation of damage

The discussion above has been wholly concerned with the first element of a claim in negligence, whether a duty of care is owed. In those situations where a duty of care *is* owed not to cause pure economic loss, it is necessary to go on to consider the other elements of a claim in negligence: breach of duty and causation of damage. It is also necessary to consider possible defences.

⭐ Example

Hannah has a claim for negligent financial advice by an accountant, Kate. In considering breach of duty, Hannah would need to prove that Kate has failed to meet the standard of care expected of a reasonable member of that profession. The case of Bolam *would be relevant here.*

Hannah must then establish causation of damage. Hannah would need to show that but for Kate's negligent advice, she would not have suffered loss. Usually this will be clear in negligent advice cases because, as discussed above, part of the test for a duty of care to arise in the first place is that the claimant suffered a loss by relying on the advice.

If all elements – duty of care, breach of duty and causation of damage – are satisfied, we must then turn to consider any relevant defences. The defence which is most relevant in the case of negligent statements and services is the exclusion of liability. This is considered in the section below.

4.5 Exclusion of liability

There are two important requirements which any defendant needs to satisfy before they will be able to rely on an exclusion notice. These are:

- Reasonable steps must have been taken to bring the exclusion notice to the claimant's attention before the tort was committed.
- The wording of the notice must cover the loss suffered by the claimant.

The ability of a defendant to exclude liability is further limited by the Unfair Contract Terms Act 1977 and the Consumer Rights Act 2015.

In *Hedley Byrne* the defendant was able to escape liability by relying on a defence. It excluded its liability by using a disclaimer: the information was said to have been supplied 'without responsibility'. However, since then the situation has been changed, firstly by the Unfair Contract Terms Act 1977 (UCTA 1977) and more recently by the Consumer Rights Act 2015 (CRA 2015). These Acts can restrict the ability of a defendant to exclude liability under a disclaimer.

UCTA 1977 applies to claims in negligence. This is because under s 1(1) (b), the Act is said to apply to 'any common law duty to take reasonable care or exercise reasonable skill'. Section 2 of the Act is relevant to the defendant's ability to exclude liability for negligent acts or omissions. Section 2 does not apply to 'consumer contracts' or 'consumer notices'.

For UCTA 1977 to be applicable, the defendant must be acting in the course of business. For CRA 2015 to be applicable, the defendant must be acting as a trader (ie for purposes relating to that person's trade, business, craft or profession) and the claimant must be acting as a consumer (ie for purposes that are wholly or mainly outside the individual's trade, business, craft or profession). Note that where the claimant is not acting as a consumer, UCTA 1977 may still apply.

The defendant cannot exclude liability for death or personal injury resulting from negligence. This is under s 2(1) of UCTA 1977 and s 65(1) of CRA 2015. With regard to any other type of loss or damage, the defendant can exclude or restrict his liability only if the exclusion satisfies the requirements of reasonableness under s 2(2) of UCTA 1977 or fairness under s 62 of CRA 2015.

'Reasonableness' is defined in s 11 of UCTA 1977. Section 11(3) is the relevant provision as far as negligence is concerned. This deals with the effect of a non-contractual exclusion notice. It states that the requirement of reasonableness means that it should be fair and reasonable to allow reliance on the exclusion notice, having regard to all the circumstances. The circumstances are to be looked at as they were at the time when liability would have arisen. 'Fairness' under s 62 of CRA 2015 involves similar considerations but also includes the requirement of good faith, focusing on any significant imbalance in the parties' rights and obligations to the detriment of the consumer.

Where UCTA 1977 or CRA 2015 apply:

- it is not possible for the defendant to exclude liability for death or personal injury;
- it is possible for the defendant to disclaim liability for negligent acts causing other damage, provided the disclaimer is reasonable under the 1977 Act or fair under the 2015 Act.

Although s 11 of UCTA 1977 defines 'reasonable' and s 62 of CRA 2015 defines 'fair', neither Act provides any examples of when a disclaimer might be considered reasonable or fair. The requirement of reasonableness was considered in the case below.

> *In* Smith v Eric S Bush; Harris v Wyre Forest District Council *[1989] 2 All ER 514, the House of Lords found that a duty of care was owed by the defendant valuers/surveyors to the house purchasers. The valuations were given in the course of business. The House of Lords decided that UCTA 1977 governed the use of exclusion notices in these cases. In* Smith

v Eric S Bush, *the exclusion notice said that neither the building society nor the surveyor warranted that the report and valuation would be accurate, and that the report was being supplied without any assumption of responsibility. In* Harris, *the exclusion notice said that no responsibility whatsoever was implied or accepted for the value or condition of the property. The House of Lords did not find that the exclusions satisfied the requirement of reasonableness.*

The House of Lords listed a number of factors which should be taken into account in deciding the question of reasonableness:

- Were the parties of equal bargaining power?
- In the case of advice, would it have been reasonably practicable to obtain the advice from an alternative source taking into account considerations of cost and time?
- How difficult is the task being undertaken for which liability is being excluded?
- What are the practical consequences, taking into account the sums of money at stake and the ability of the parties to bear the loss involved, particularly in the light of insurance?

In conclusion, whether a disclaimer is reasonable or not depends on all the circumstances of the case. It is impossible to produce an exhaustive list of factors which would be considered in deciding whether a disclaimer is reasonable or not. A similar conclusion may be reached when looking at fairness under CRA 2015.

Summary

- There are no special rules on whether a duty of care is owed for *consequential* economic loss.
- If the defendant owes a duty of care not to cause the claimant physical injury or property damage, then the defendant also owes a duty not to cause the consequential economic loss which follows from that injury or damage.
- As a *general rule*, a defendant does *not* owe any duty of care to a claimant not to cause *pure* economic loss. The types of loss that are classified as pure economic loss and are not recoverable are:
    - economic loss caused by acquiring a defective item of property
    - economic loss unconnected to personal injury to the claimant or physical damage to the claimant's property
    - economic loss caused by damage to the property of a third party
    - economic loss where there is no physical damage: actions
    - economic loss where there is no physical damage: statements
- In the case of negligent statements, an *exception* to the general rule arises in cases where the court is able to find that there is, in fact, a *special relationship* between the defendant and the claimant. This special relationship may be found using the following criteria:
    - Did the defendant assume a responsibility towards the claimant?
    - Did the defendant know the purpose for which the advice was required?
    - Did the defendant know that the advice would be communicated to the claimant, (either specifically or as a member of an ascertainable class)?
    - Did the defendant know that the claimant was likely to act on the advice without independent inquiry?
    - Was the advice acted on by the claimant to its detriment?
    - Was it reasonable for the claimant to rely on the defendant for advice?

Tort

Summary flowchart

Figure 4.1 Negligence: pure economic loss flowchart

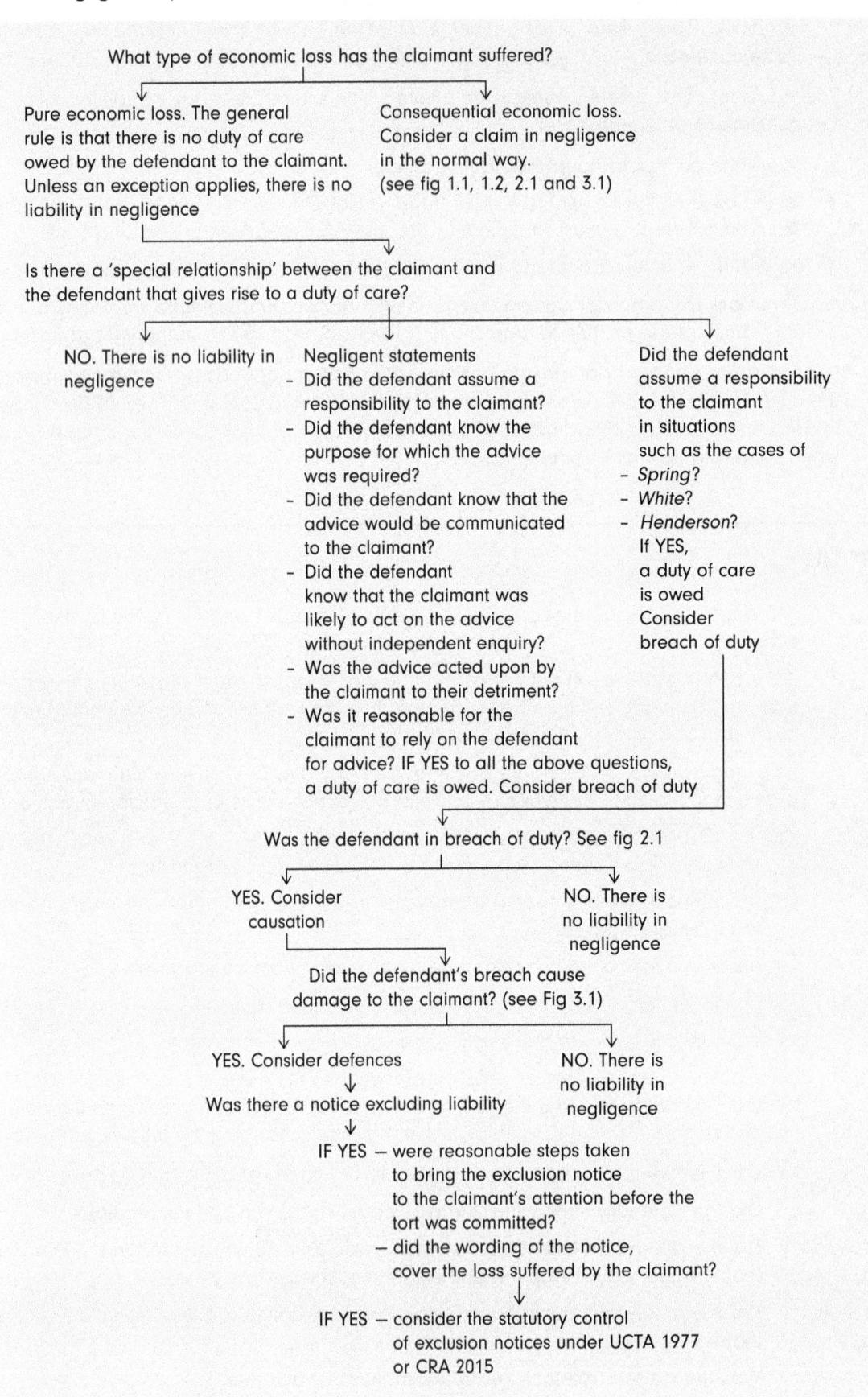

What type of economic loss has the claimant suffered?

Pure economic loss. The general rule is that there is no duty of care owed by the defendant to the claimant. Unless an exception applies, there is no liability in negligence

Consequential economic loss. Consider a claim in negligence in the normal way. (see fig 1.1, 1.2, 2.1 and 3.1)

Is there a 'special relationship' between the claimant and the defendant that gives rise to a duty of care?

NO. There is no liability in negligence

Negligent statements
- Did the defendant assume a responsibility to the claimant?
- Did the defendant know the purpose for which the advice was required?
- Did the defendant know that the advice would be communicated to the claimant?
- Did the defendant know that the claimant was likely to act on the advice without independent enquiry?
- Was the advice acted upon by the claimant to their detriment?
- Was it reasonable for the claimant to rely on the defendant for advice? IF YES to all the above questions, a duty of care is owed. Consider breach of duty

Did the defendant assume a responsibility to the claimant in situations such as the cases of
- *Spring*?
- *White*?
- *Henderson*?
If YES, a duty of care is owed Consider breach of duty

Was the defendant in breach of duty? See fig 2.1

YES. Consider causation

NO. There is no liability in negligence

Did the defendant's breach cause damage to the claimant? (see Fig 3.1)

YES. Consider defences
↓
Was there a notice excluding liability
↓
IF YES — were reasonable steps taken to bring the exclusion notice to the claimant's attention before the tort was committed?
— did the wording of the notice, cover the loss suffered by the claimant?
↓
IF YES — consider the statutory control of exclusion notices under UCTA 1977 or CRA 2015

NO. There is no liability in negligence

Sample questions

Question 1

A solicitor has been instructed by a mother and daughter for advice on potential claims that they may have against a cosmetic surgeon. The mother received cosmetic filler treatment to her face in preparation for the daughter's wedding. This went wrong and caused substantial swelling and pain to her face. As a result of the treatment the mother was unable to work for three months. The mother is a presenter on an online shopping channel and has lost a significant amount of income. The daughter felt that she had no choice but to cancel the wedding because her mother would have been unable to attend. The daughter has lost a substantial amount of money as a consequence of this.

Which of the following statements best explains whether the clients would be compensated for their financial losses if the cosmetic surgeon's negligence was proven to have caused their loss?

A Neither the mother nor the daughter would receive compensation for their financial losses because they have suffered pure economic loss.

B Both the mother and the daughter would receive compensation for their financial losses because there is an established duty of care between doctors and patients.

C Only the mother would receive compensation for her financial losses because they are owed a duty of care for their pure economic loss. The daughter would not be owed a duty of care for her pure economic loss because there was not a 'special relationship' between her and the surgeon.

D Only the mother would receive compensation for her financial losses because there is an established duty of care between doctors and patients. The daughter's loss is too remote.

E Only the mother would receive compensation for her financial losses because there is an established duty of care between doctors and patients. The daughter would not be owed a duty of care for her pure economic loss because there was not a 'special relationship' between her and the surgeon.

Answer

Option E is correct.

Option A is wrong because the mother would be compensated for her financial loss as her lost income is consequential on her personal injury, ie it is not pure economic loss. It is correct, however, that the daughter has suffered pure economic loss (PEL) and that they would not be compensated for this (see further below).

Option B is wrong because, while there is an established duty of care between doctors and their patients, this would not assist the daughter as they are not a patient of the surgeon. It is also wrong because the daughter has suffered PEL. The established duty of care is only relevant for personal injury or property damage and not for PEL.

Option C is wrong as the mother has not suffered PEL. It is correct, however, that the daughter would not be owed a duty of care for their pure economic loss because there was not a 'special relationship' between her and the surgeon. She would not satisfy the test for a 'special relationship' from *Hedley Byrne v Heller* (as expanded upon in *Caparo v Dickman*).

Option D is wrong because the daughter would not be owed a duty of care for their PEL. Their claim would therefore fail at the duty of care stage and the question of remoteness is, therefore, irrelevant.

Tort

Question 2

A client has consulted a solicitor about problems they are having with a new computerised record system. The client provides employers with security checks on prospective new employees. It does this using the computerised record system to search for information about credit records, county court judgments, and criminal convictions.

The record system was purchased from a retail company specialising in the supply of computer systems comprising both hardware and software. The client has encountered a fault in the computer hardware. The client did initially complain to the retail company. However, they have received no reply and it seems that this company may have ceased trading.

The hardware was manufactured by another large and reputable company. This company has accepted that there is a fault in the hardware. It has offered to supply the replacement parts at a discount.

The client has asked for advice on whether they should accept this offer, or whether, in fact, they could sue the manufacturer for the full cost of a new system.

Which of the following statements best explains whether the client should accept the offer by the manufacturer rather than suing the manufacturer for the full cost of a new system?

A   Yes, because, while the manufacturer has admitted liability, the client should avoid incurring unnecessary legal costs.

B   Yes, because the client has suffered pure economic loss and the manufacturer does not owe them a duty of care. If they sue the manufacturer their claim is bound to fail.

C   No, because the manufacturer owes the client an established duty of care and it has admitted that it is in breach of that duty.

D   No, because the client can sue the manufacturer in contract for the full cost of a replacement system.

E   No, because a duty of care is owed as there is a 'special relationship' between the client and the manufacturer, and the manufacturer has admitted that it is in breach of that duty.

Answer

Option B is correct – this is an example of economic loss caused by acquiring a defective item of property. The client's loss is categorised as pure economic loss and is caught by the general rule that there is no duty of care owed for this type of loss. As there is no exception that would apply, the client should accept the offer that has been made by the manufacturer.

Option A is wrong because, while it is generally correct that any unnecessary legal costs should be avoided, this is not the reason why the offer should be accepted as the client's claim is bound to fail in any event. The manufacturer *may* have admitted that it was at fault, but it will not be liable because a duty of care is not owed to the client.

Option C is wrong because the manufacturer's duty of care only encompasses physical damage, personal injury and any *consequential* economic loss. It does not apply to pure economic loss.

Option D is wrong because the client's contract is with the retail company and not the manufacturer. The client does not, therefore, have a claim against the manufacturer in contract.

Option E is wrong because there is nothing on the facts to suggest that a special relationship involving an assumption of responsibility by the manufacturer to the client would apply.

Question 3

A solicitor is instructed by a client who wishes to bring a claim in negligence for substantial losses arising from an investment they have made in buy-to-let properties. The client had asked a friend, who is an estate agent, to advise on suitable purchases. The client had no knowledge of the risks involved in buying properties for letting and had made it clear that they would be relying on their friend's skill and judgment. The client's friend recommended buying two houses near to a university with the stated aim that the houses would convert into separate lettings for multiple occupation by students. The client bought the houses on the basis of the friend's recommendation. The client later discovered that the houses were unsuitable for multiple occupation and has suffered a substantial loss of income from the houses as a result. The client now wishes to recoup these losses from their friend.

Which of the following statements best explains whether the client is owed a duty of care by their former friend?

A No, because there can never be a duty of care in respect of negligent advice given in a social situation.

B No, because the client has suffered pure economic loss.

C Yes, because the former friend had assumed a responsibility to the client and it was reasonable for the client to rely on the former friend for advice.

D Yes, because the former friend had assumed a responsibility to the client and the former friend did not exclude their liability by way of a disclaimer.

E Yes, because it was reasonable for the client to rely on the former friend for advice and the former friend did not exclude their liability by way of a disclaimer.

Answer

Option C is correct as it correctly states the two parts of the test for a duty of care to be owed for negligent statements.

Option A is wrong because, while it is generally true that there is no duty of care in respect of advice given in a social situation, there are exceptions (as per *Chaudhry v Prabhakar* [1989] 1 WLR 29).

Option B is wrong because, while it is true that there is generally no duty of care for pure economic loss, there are exceptions – in particular for negligent statements (as per *Hedley Byrne v Heller & Partners Ltd* [1964] AC 465).

Option D is wrong as, while an assumption of responsibility is one element of when a 'special relationship' may give rise to a duty of care for negligent statements, it must also be reasonable for the claimant to rely on the defendant for advice. Also, the fact that there may or may not have been a disclaimer of liability is not relevant to whether a duty of care was owed.

Option E is wrong for similar reasons to option D, the difference being that there must also be an assumption of responsibility by the defendant to the claimant.

5 Negligence: Pure Psychiatric Harm

5.1	Introduction	64
5.2	Pure psychiatric harm: limiting factors for duty of care	65
5.3	Pure psychiatric harm: different types of victim	66
5.4	Primary victims	67
5.5	Secondary victims	68
5.6	Rescuers	71
5.7	Pure psychiatric harm: breach of duty and causation of damage	72

SQE1 syllabus

This chapter will enable you to achieve the SQE1 Assessment Specification in relation to Functioning Legal Knowledge concerned with the core principles of tort on negligence and the special rules for duty of care which apply in the limited duty situation of pure psychiatric harm.

Note that for SQE1, candidates are not usually required to recall specific case names or cite statutory or regulatory authorities. Cases are provided for illustrative purposes only.

Learning outcomes

By the end of this chapter you will be able to apply relevant core legal principles and rules appropriately and effectively, at the level of a competent newly qualified solicitor in practice, to realistic client-based and ethical problems and situations in the following areas:

- negligence and distinguishing between consequential psychiatric harm and pure psychiatric harm;
- negligence and the special rules for duty of care which apply in the limited duty situation of pure psychiatric harm.

5.1 Introduction

This chapter returns again to the issue of when a defendant may owe a claimant a duty of care and considers another 'limited duty situation'. The situation under consideration here is where a claimant has suffered pure psychiatric harm. While the law determining when a duty of care may be owed for pure psychiatric harm is different to that governing pure economic loss, nevertheless, the themes discussed in relation to pure economic loss in **Chapter 4** are equally relevant in relation to this type of harm.

A prerequisite for a duty of care is a sufficiently proximate relationship between the claimant and the defendant. As with pure economic loss, there is generally a lack of a sufficiently proximate relationship between a claimant who has suffered pure psychiatric harm, and a defendant who may have caused this type of loss. This helps to explains why, as a general rule, a defendant does not owe any duty of care to a claimant not to cause pure psychiatric harm.

⭐ Example

A train company negligently causes a major rail crash. Several hundred bystanders suffer shock and psychiatric illness as a result of witnessing the events.

If this example is compared with the situation of a motorist who negligently knocks down a pedestrian and causes personal injury, it is possible to note some important differences.

The witnesses who suffer psychiatric harm have not suffered any physical injury. The defendant train company has caused harm without having any physical contact with the claimant witnesses. The relationship between the witnesses and the train company is much less close than that between the driver and the injured pedestrian. The lack of proximity between claimants and defendants means that the defendant's potential liability could be boundless, to an indeterminate number of claimants. This is the reason why the courts place limits upon the duty of care in cases of pure psychiatric harm and why, as a general rule, a defendant does not owe any duty of care to a claimant not to cause pure psychiatric harm.

As with pure economic loss, there are some limited situations in which damages can be recovered for pure psychiatric harm. The courts have laid down rules to establish when a defendant does owe the claimant a duty of care not to cause them pure psychiatric harm. The aim of the rules is to define when a claimant has been closely enough affected by the defendant's negligence. If a claimant has been closely enough affected by the defendant's negligence then a duty of care is owed to them.

If the claimant falls outside the class of closely affected victims then no duty of care is owed to them. Such a claimant will not receive compensation for his pure psychiatric harm, even if he can show that the defendant was negligent and that this negligence was the cause of their psychiatric harm. In the example above, the negligence of the train company has caused the witnesses to suffer psychiatric harm. Nevertheless, the train company does not have to pay for the consequences of their negligence.

As a general rule, a defendant does not owe any duty of care to a claimant not to cause pure psychiatric harm. In other words, as a general rule, where a claimant suffers damage which is classed as pure psychiatric harm, that loss is not recoverable.

It is necessary, therefore, to define what constitutes pure psychiatric harm. To do this, the easiest way to begin is to identify what is not pure psychiatric harm.

⭐ Example

A motorist negligently knocks down a pedestrian, Jim, and causes him personal injury. Jim suffers a broken leg. He also suffers from the following further effects of the accident:

- *he feels anxious and has nightmares about the accident;*
- *he has a medically diagnosed phobia of cars.*

The nightmares and phobia may have been caused by the shock of the accident. However, this is not *pure psychiatric harm. The nightmares and phobia follow on from the physical injury which Jim suffered, so they are* consequential *psychiatric harm. There are no special rules for consequential psychiatric harm.*

The consequential psychiatric harm which Jim has suffered simply forms part of his physical injury. A claimant like Jim who suffers physical injury will be compensated for all of his pain and suffering. This will include any consequential distress and mental anguish.

The defining feature of pure psychiatric harm is that it is caused without any physical impact or injury to the claimant.

Note that Jim suffers a medically diagnosed phobia, but he also suffers from simple anxiety and nightmares. All of these effects can be recovered as part of the consequences of his physical injury. By contrast, when pure psychiatric harm is considered, the type of harm that the claimant may receive compensation for is far more restrictive.

The types of psychiatric harm which might be caused without physical impact can include a very wide range of illnesses and conditions. The list might include psychiatric illnesses such as post-traumatic stress disorder, lesser conditions such as worry and anxiety, physical illnesses which might be caused by a sudden shock, such as a heart attack or a miscarriage. The list might also include the gradually developing depression caused by caring for an injured relative. This illustrates the point we made above – that a defendant's potential liability could be indefinite.

In order to address this problem the courts have developed some more specific rules which define more narrowly the kinds of pure psychiatric harm for which a duty of care can be owed. These are considered below.

5.2 Pure psychiatric harm: limiting factors for duty of care

The definition of pure psychiatric harm is psychiatric harm suffered without physical impact. However, only certain kinds of pure psychiatric harm will give rise to a duty of care. This is because the courts have developed rules to define more narrowly the kinds of pure psychiatric harm for which a remedy can be obtained. A summary of these rules is set out below.

Where a claimant has suffered pure psychiatric harm – ie without physical impact – the injury *must* be either:

- a medically recognised psychiatric illness; or
- a shock-induced physical condition (such as a miscarriage or heart attack).

(However, in **Chapter 6** on employers' liability, it will be noted that claims for stress caused within the employment relationship have their own rules, which are different from those considered in this chapter.)

The requirement for a medically recognised psychiatric illness means that there is no duty of care in relation to effects which do not amount to a defined and diagnosed illness. This would rule out, for example, cases of simple worry and anxiety. So, for example, a claimant who has no physical injury and suffers only from worry and anxiety will not be compensated, even if they can show that the defendant was negligent and that this negligence caused the claimant's damage.

A summary of the rules considered above is:

- pure psychiatric harm is psychiatric harm suffered without physical impact;
- it must be a medically recognised psychiatric illness, or a shock-induced physical condition.

However, there are further limitations. The courts have not allowed recovery for pure psychiatric harm unless the claimant has been closely enough affected by the defendant's negligence. This involves considering how far the claimant was involved in the events caused by the defendant's negligence. This is examined in the next section.

5.3 Pure psychiatric harm: different types of victim

The rules for duty of care in relation to pure psychiatric harm are different depending on how far the claimant was involved in the events caused by the defendant's negligence.

Example

Sarah is setting off for work on her motor bike. As Sarah rides carefully down the road, a car driven by Peter comes round the corner too fast and knocks Sarah off the bike. Sarah is unhurt but suffers psychiatric harm. A pedestrian, Jane, witnesses the event from a safe distance. She finds the event very shocking and she also suffers psychiatric harm.

Sarah and Jane are in the same position in that they have both suffered pure psychiatric harm – they have both suffered a psychiatric injury without any physical impact. However, Sarah and Jane are different in that Sarah was actually involved in the incident. Sarah was in the actual area of danger. Jane was never in any danger – she merely witnessed the events.

The above illustration can be described using the terminology from case law. It would be said that:

- *Sarah is a* primary victim *of Peter's negligence.*
- *Jane is a* secondary victim *of Peter's negligence.*

The following sections describe the different tests which apply to determine whether or not a duty of care is owed to a primary and to a secondary victim in relation to pure psychiatric harm. Secondary victims, like Jane, must meet a more stringent set of requirements before a duty can be owed to them.

5.4 Primary victims

Pure psychiatric harm has been defined as that which is suffered without physical impact. If a duty of care is to be owed, the harm must be a medically recognised psychiatric illness, or a shock-induced physical condition. It should be noted that this requirement is the same for *both* primary and secondary victims. Once this requirement is satisfied, however, the further rules for primary and secondary victims are different.

In Page v Smith *[1995] 2 All ER 736, the claimant was involved in a car crash caused by the defendant's negligence. He did not suffer any physical injury. However, the shock of the accident caused a medically recognised psychiatric illness.*

The House of Lords reviewed the law on pure psychiatric harm and held that, since physical injury to the claimant was foreseeable, a duty of care was also owed in respect of the pure psychiatric harm which he actually suffered.

The House of Lords in *Page v Smith* stated that the tests for primary and secondary victims are as follows:

Primary victims

A primary victim is someone who was actually involved in the incident. So, a primary victim:

- was in the actual area of danger; or
- reasonably believed that he was in danger.

The requirements for a duty of care to be owed to a primary victim are:

- primary victims are owed a duty of care in relation to their pure psychiatric harm, provided the risk of physical injury was foreseeable;
- for primary victims it is *not* necessary for the risk of psychiatric harm to be foreseeable.

Secondary victims

A secondary victim is someone who is *not* involved in the incident in the same way. So a secondary victim:

- witnesses injury to someone else; or
- fears for the safety of another person.

The case of Dulieu v White & Sons *[1901] 2 KB 669 provides a good example of the application of the test for duty of care in the case of a primary victim. The claimant was a pregnant barmaid working in a public house. The defendants negligently drove a horse-drawn van so that it crashed into the public house. The claimant suffered severe shock leading to miscarriage. It was held that the defendants did owe a duty of care to her.*

The claimant suffered a shock without any physical impact on her. Thus, she suffered pure psychiatric harm. She suffered a shock-induced physical condition, the miscarriage.

She was a primary victim because she reasonably feared for her own physical safety. The defendants' negligence had created a foreseeable risk of physical harm to the claimant. Therefore they owed her a duty of care, even though the actual harm which she in fact suffered was pure psychiatric harm rather than a physical injury.

A defendant owes a primary victim a duty of care not to cause pure psychiatric harm, provided that the risk of *physical* injury was foreseeable (although it did not in fact occur).

The test for duty in relation to secondary victims is much more stringent, and this is considered below.

5.5 Secondary victims

A secondary victim is someone less closely involved in the incident caused by the defendant's negligence.

⭐ Example

A train company negligently causes a major rail crash. Several hundred bystanders suffer shock and psychiatric illness as a result of witnessing the events.

Everyone who witnesses the event and suffers psychiatric harm as a result, can be described as a secondary victim. However, not all secondary victims are owed a duty of care. Some individuals may suffer psychiatric harm as a result of the defendant's negligence but the defendant will not be required to compensate them. In relation to those victims, the defendant will escape the consequences of his negligence. This is because the courts narrow down the number of secondary victims to whom a duty of care is owed.

The first limitation on whether a secondary victim will be owed a duty of care is considered above. In order to be owed a duty of care, the secondary victim must have suffered a medically recognised psychiatric illness, or shock-induced physical condition. This will rule out, for example, those who have suffered only distress or anxiety, etc. This requirement is the same for both primary and secondary victims.

There are additional requirements which narrow still further the number of secondary victims to whom a duty is owed. These requirements were handed down in the case of *Alcock v Chief Constable of South Yorkshire Police*. This case is the key authority on the rules relating to secondary victims.

Alcock v Chief Constable of South Yorkshire Police [1991] 4 All ER 907. This case arose from the Hillsborough football stadium disaster. This was a tragic event in which a large number of Liverpool Football Club supporters were killed or injured. The incident was caused by the negligence of police officers in allowing the stadium to become overcrowded. As a result of the overcrowding, spectators in one part of the ground were crushed. Claims were brought by relatives of the victims who had witnessed the events and claimed in respect of pure psychiatric harm suffered as a result. The defendants admitted negligence but denied that a duty of care was owed to these particular victims.

The claimants were not allowed to recover damages for the psychiatric harm they suffered. The court held that, in the circumstances, no duty of care was owed to them.

The House of Lords set down the current test to determine whether a duty of care is owed for pure psychiatric harm suffered by a secondary victim.

All of the following requirements must be satisfied:

- Foreseeability of psychiatric harm.

It must be reasonably foreseeable that a person of normal fortitude in the claimant's position would suffer a psychiatric illness.

- Proximity of relationship.

The claimant must have a close relationship of love and affection with the person who is endangered by the defendant's negligence.

- Proximity in time and space.

The claimant must be present at the accident or its immediate aftermath.

- Proximity of perception.

The claimant must see or hear the accident, or its immediate aftermath, with their own senses.

These requirements are often referred to as the '*Alcock* control mechanisms'. The effect of the test in *Alcock* is to impose requirements which will narrow down the number of secondary victims to whom a duty of care is owed. Each of these requirements is considered in more detail below.

5.5.1 Secondary victims: foreseeability of psychiatric harm

It helps to understand the requirement for foreseeability of psychiatric harm for secondary victims by comparing the position for primary victims.

Primary victims are closely involved in the accident caused by the defendant's negligence. Therefore a duty of care is owed to them in relation to pure psychiatric harm, provided only that some *physical* injury to them was foreseeable (even though it does not in fact occur).

The courts have held that in relation to primary victims it is not necessary for the risk of pure psychiatric harm to be foreseeable. In essence, the courts have taken the view that no distinction should be made between physical injury to a primary victim and psychiatric injury to a primary victim.

By contrast, if the claimant is a secondary victim, they are not as closely involved in the accident. They have not been placed in any danger themselves. Their position is clearly different from that of someone who has been exposed to the risk of physical harm.

The courts recognise this difference by requiring a secondary victim to demonstrate that *psychiatric* injury was a foreseeable consequence of the defendant's negligence. In essence, the court should ask: 'If an ordinary person in the claimant's position witnessed these events, is it foreseeable that he would suffer a psychiatric injury?'

⭐ Example

A mother is watching her child at play when he is struck by a car negligently driven by the defendant. The mother suffers psychiatric harm. The court will ask: 'Would any normal person have suffered psychiatric harm in those circumstances?' Clearly, the answer here is likely to be yes. Thus, the mother, as claimant, would satisfy the first requirement of the Alcock *test.*

The first element of the test for duty of care to a secondary victim is:

- Was it reasonably foreseeable that a person of normal fortitude in the claimant's position would suffer a psychiatric illness?

5.5.2 Secondary victims: proximity of relationship

The second requirement under *Alcock* is that the claimant must have a close relationship of love and affection with the person who is endangered by the defendant's negligence (the 'immediate victim'). The House of Lords stated that:

- Where a relationship of parent/child, husband/wife and fiancé/fiancée exists, there is a presumption of a relationship of close ties of love and affection.

- If the defendant knows that, although the claimant falls into a category where love and affection can be presumed, the claimant was not in fact very close to the victim, the defendant can adduce evidence to the court to rebut the presumption of love and affection.
- If the claimant falls outside the categories where close ties of love and affection can be presumed, the claimant must prove that a close relationship of love and affection existed.

5.5.3 Secondary victims: proximity in time and space and proximity of perception

The requirements under *Alcock* are that:

- the claimant must be present at the accident or its immediate aftermath; *and*
- the claimant must see or hear the accident, or its immediate aftermath, with their own senses.

It is convenient to examine these two tests together since there is overlap between them. (It is difficult to envisage how a claimant could see or hear an event with their own senses without being present.)

Proximity in time and space

In McLoughlin v O'Brian [1982] 2 All ER 298, one of the claimant's children was killed and her husband and other two children were severely injured in a road accident. The incident was reported to the claimant while she was at her home, some two miles from the scene. The claimant arrived at the hospital about an hour after the accident. At the hospital the claimant saw the extent of the injuries to her family as they were still in the same condition they had been at the scene of the accident, ie covered in oil and mud. As a result, she suffered severe and persisting psychiatric harm, for which she claimed damages. The House of Lords held that the claimant could recover for her pure psychiatric harm.

The decision in *McLoughlin* can be compared with the position of one of the claimants in the case of *Alcock*. Mr Alcock identified his brother-in-law in the mortuary eight hours after the incident. Mr Alcock did not satisfy the test laid down in *McLoughlin* because the identification could not be described as part of the 'immediate aftermath'.

To satisfy the test of proximity in time and space, the claimant need not actually be present at the time of the incident. However, they must at least come upon the immediate aftermath.

Proximity of perception

McLoughlin considered the question of how the event must be perceived by the claimant. It was decided that:

- the claimant must have personally perceived the event 'through sight or hearing of the event or of its immediate aftermath';
- a claimant cannot be compensated if the event is communicated by a third party.

In *Alcock*, some of the claimants were not physically at the football game but went on to suffer psychiatric harm as a result of what they saw during the live television broadcasts of the tragic events. These claimants did not succeed in showing that a duty of care was owed to them. This meant that their claim for damages failed.

The House of Lords held it was important that, although the claimants had watched live TV pictures of events at the stadium, they were not able to see pictures showing the suffering of identifiable individuals. The court decided that what the claimants did see was not equivalent to seeing and hearing the event or its immediate aftermath.

This aspect of the *Alcock* case therefore illustrates the final part of the test for duty of care:

- The claimant must see or hear the accident, or its immediate aftermath, with their own senses.

If broadcasters were to break their own code of ethics and transmit images of recognisable individuals' suffering, this might amount to a new intervening act (*novus actus interveniens*). Thus, this could break the chain of causation between the defendant's negligent act and the claimant's loss.

In *Alcock*, it was also noted that a live television broadcast might be sufficient to render the tortfeasor liable to claimants in shock if the 'impact of the simultaneous television pictures would be as great, if not greater, than the actual sight of the accident'. The example given in *Alcock* was of 'a special event of children travelling in a balloon, in which there was media interest, particularly amongst the parents, [showing] the balloon suddenly bursting into flames'.

5.6 Rescuers

The House of Lords in White v Chief Constable of the South Yorkshire Police *[1999] 1 All ER 1 arose out of the Hillsborough disaster. The claimants in this case were police officers. In each instance the police officers claiming damages in* White *had suffered pure psychiatric harm. However, the police officers had not gone into the actual area of danger during the incident at the football ground. Although they were involved in rescue activities, they were never at risk of physical injury.*

The claimants pure psychiatric harm came from being exposed to shocking events and scenes during the course of their employment as police officers and while they were acting as rescuers. The claimants' argument was that they should enjoy a special status. A duty of care should be owed to them in respect of pure psychiatric harm either because they were acting as rescuers, and/or because they were in the course of their employment.

The claimants' cases failed. The House of Lords did not accept that being an employee conferred a special status and that a duty of care should be owed to the officers in respect of pure psychiatric harm simply because that harm was suffered during the course of their employment. The House of Lords also did not accept that being a rescuer conferred a special status and that a duty of care should be owed to the officers in respect of pure psychiatric harm simply because that harm was suffered during the course of acting as a rescuer.

The House of Lords' decision means that rescuers (and those acting in the course of their employment) should be treated in the same way as any other victim who suffers only pure psychiatric harm. Therefore:

- If a rescuer has been in the actual area of danger, they are a primary victim. A duty of care is owed to a primary victim, provided there is a foreseeable risk of physical injury (even though the injury he in fact suffers is pure psychiatric harm).

- If a rescuer has not been in the actual area of danger so that they have not been exposed to any risk of physical injury, they will be classed as a secondary victim. They will be owed a duty of care only if they meet all of the tests laid down in *Alcock*.

The tests in *Alcock* are designed to reduce the number of secondary victims to whom a duty of care is owed. A professional rescuer might well be able to meet the first test: that it was reasonably foreseeable that a person of normal fortitude in the claimant's position would suffer psychiatric harm. (There is no special rule which says that professional rescuers are expected to be more than usually resistant to shocking events. Police officers, ambulance staff and fire fighters are not expected to display more than normal fortitude.)

It is also likely that a rescue situation would mean that the two tests of proximity in time and space and proximity of perception are met. However, it is unlikely that the professional rescuer will have any ties of love and affection with the immediate victims whom they are assisting. Thus, the requirement for proximity of relationship is unlikely to be met.

A case which is a very good illustration of a successful claim by a rescuer for pure psychiatric harm is *Chadwick v British Railways Board* [1967] 2 All ER 945. In this case two trains had crashed, resulting in 90 people dying. Mr Chadwick lived near to the disaster and went to help. As he was of small stature, he was asked to crawl into the debris and give injections to the wounded. He was involved in the rescue for many hours. He did not suffer physical injury, but as a result of his experiences he suffered pure psychiatric harm. It was held that a duty of care was owed to him. From the facts it is clear that Mr Chadwick was involved in the incident as a primary victim. He was clearly in the area of danger and at risk of physical injury.

5.7 Pure psychiatric harm: breach of duty and causation of damage

The discussion above considers whether a duty of care is owed in relation to pure psychiatric harm – in relation to primary and secondary victims and rescuers. It is important to remember that in every claim for negligence the claimant needs to demonstrate not only that a duty of care was owed to them, but also that the duty was breached and that the breach caused the damage from which the claimant has suffered.

Often, a defendant in a case of pure psychiatric harm does in fact admit that they fell below a reasonable standard of care and so was in breach of duty. Instead the argument centres on whether or not a duty was owed.

Also, sometimes causation of damage is assumed for the sake of argument, so that the court is free to concentrate on the question of whether or not a duty is owed. In this kind of case, if the court was satisfied on duty, the claimant would then have to go on to actually prove the damage.

In relation to damage, there is one particular issue which needs to be considered in more detail. This relates to remoteness of damage. For damage to be recoverable in the tort of negligence it must not be too remote. Damage is too remote if it is not a reasonably foreseeable consequence of the defendant's negligence. However, a proviso to this requirement is the 'egg-shell skull' rule.

The egg-shell skull rule basically means that the defendant must take his victim as he finds him. It is relevant, for example, where a claimant suffers from some pre-existing characteristic which makes him more vulnerable, so that the damage he suffers is greater than could reasonably have been expected.

Under the 'egg-shell skull' rule, the claimant only needs to show that some damage of the kind they suffered was reasonably foreseeable. Provided this is satisfied, they can recover damages for the full extent of the loss which they actually suffer – it does not matter that the full extent of his loss could not reasonably have been foreseen.

This issue is relevant to the *Alcock* test for secondary victims above and whether it is reasonably foreseeable that a person of normal fortitude in the claimant's position would suffer a psychiatric illness. What if the claimant is not a person of normal fortitude? What if they have an 'egg-shell' personality, in that they are particularly vulnerable to psychiatric harm?

In relation to secondary victims the rules on duty of care and remoteness of damage work together as follows. In order to show that a duty is owed to them, the claimant must still get over the first hurdle of foreseeability. So, they must show that it was reasonably foreseeable that a person of normal fortitude in the claimant's position would suffer a psychiatric illness. (They must then establish breach of duty.)

However, once the claimant has done this they can rely on the 'egg-shell skull' rule in relation to causation of damage. So, they can recover damages for all psychiatric injury they suffer. This is so even if it is greater in extent than could reasonably have been foreseen (and so greater than would have been expected in a person of normal fortitude). In other words, defendants must take their victims as they find them, even in cases of psychiatric injury.

The 'egg-shell skull' rule also applies in the normal way to primary victims. In *Page v Smith* (see **5.4**), the claimant was particularly vulnerable because they suffered from a pre-existing condition. This condition was exacerbated by the accident. The extent of the pure psychiatric harm which the claimant suffered from a simple road accident was more than anyone could reasonably have foreseen. Nevertheless, the claimant recovered damages for the full extent of his psychiatric injury.

Summary

It is important to remember that a claim for psychiatric injury is, ultimately, just another negligence claim. The first element of a negligence claim is duty of care.

There are special rules for duty of care where the claimant has suffered pure psychiatric harm. That is, a psychiatric injury caused without any physical impact.

In all cases of pure psychiatric harm the duty of care is limited, in that the claimant must show that he has suffered either a medically recognised psychiatric illness, or a shock-induced physical condition.

A primary victim is someone who was actually involved in the incident, ie in the actual area of danger; or they reasonably believed that they were in danger. Primary victims are owed a duty of care in relation to their pure psychiatric harm, provided the risk of physical injury was foreseeable.

A secondary victim is someone who is not involved in the incident in the same way, ie they witness injury to someone else or fear for the safety of another person. Secondary victims will be owed a duty of care if they satisfy all of the following requirements:

- Foreseeability of psychiatric harm. It must be reasonably foreseeable that a person of normal fortitude in the claimant's position would suffer a psychiatric illness.

- Proximity of relationship. The claimant must have a close relationship of love and affection with the person who is endangered by the defendant's negligence. Close ties of love and affection are presumed where a relationship of parent/child, husband/wife and fiancé/fiancée exists. If the claimant falls outside the categories where close ties of love and affection can be presumed, the claimant must prove that a close relationship of love and affection existed.

- Proximity in time and space. The claimant must be present at the accident or its immediate aftermath.

- Proximity of perception. The claimant must see or hear the accident, or its immediate aftermath, with their own senses.

Finally, if it has been established that a duty of care is owed, the claimant will need to prove breach of duty and causation of damage. The defendant may wish to rely on any relevant defences.

Summary flowchart

Figure 5.1 Negligence: pure psychiatric harm flowchart

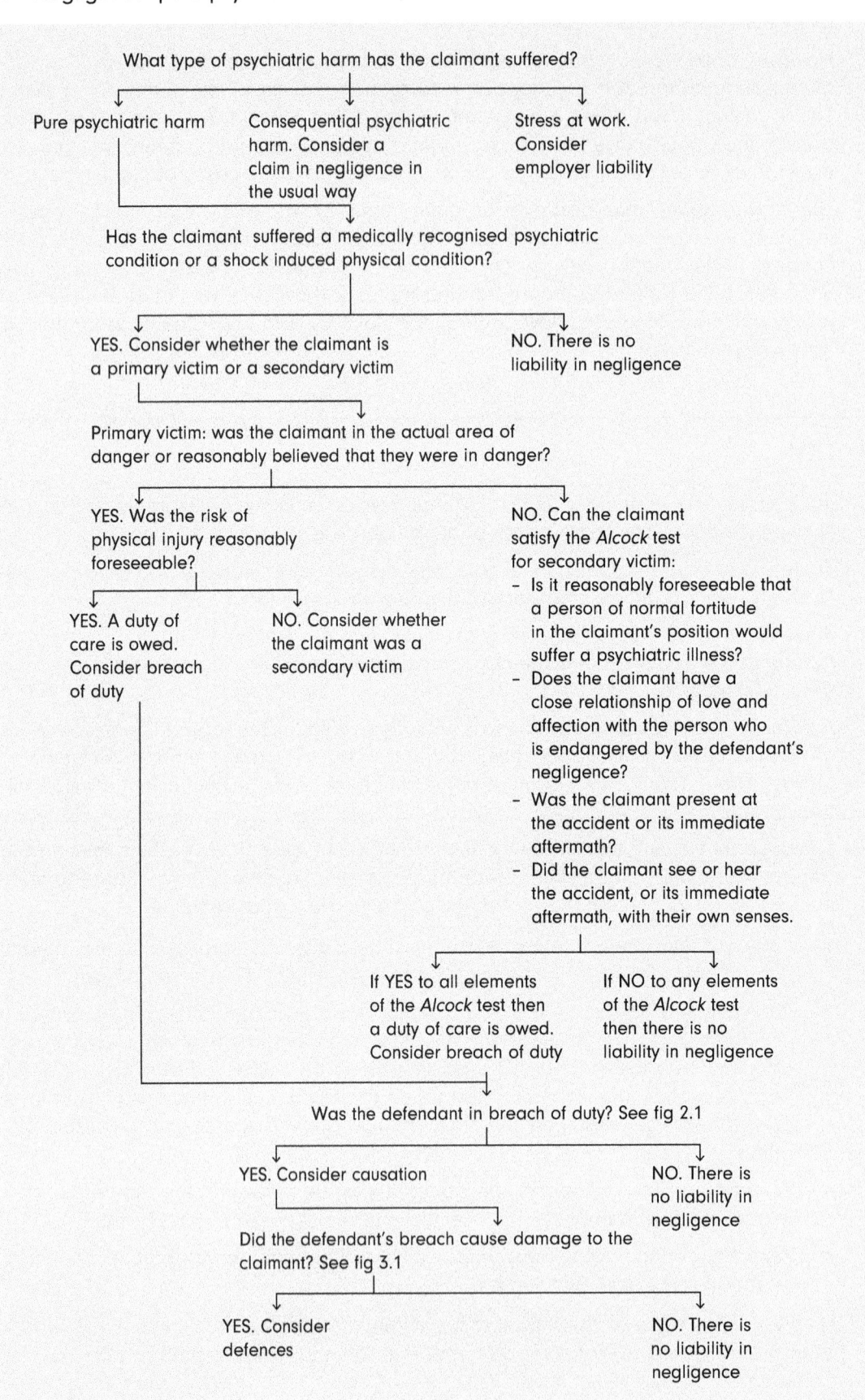

```
What type of psychiatric harm has the claimant suffered?
├── Pure psychiatric harm
├── Consequential psychiatric harm. Consider a claim in negligence in the usual way
└── Stress at work. Consider employer liability
```

Has the claimant suffered a medically recognised psychiatric condition or a shock induced physical condition?

- **YES.** Consider whether the claimant is a primary victim or a secondary victim
- **NO.** There is no liability in negligence

Primary victim: was the claimant in the actual area of danger or reasonably believed that they were in danger?

- **YES.** Was the risk of physical injury reasonably foreseeable?
  - **YES.** A duty of care is owed. Consider breach of duty
  - **NO.** Consider whether the claimant was a secondary victim
- **NO.** Can the claimant satisfy the *Alcock* test for secondary victim:
  - Is it reasonably foreseeable that a person of normal fortitude in the claimant's position would suffer a psychiatric illness?
  - Does the claimant have a close relationship of love and affection with the person who is endangered by the defendant's negligence?
  - Was the claimant present at the accident or its immediate aftermath?
  - Did the claimant see or hear the accident, or its immediate aftermath, with their own senses.

- If **YES** to all elements of the *Alcock* test then a duty of care is owed. Consider breach of duty
- If **NO** to any elements of the *Alcock* test then there is no liability in negligence

Was the defendant in breach of duty? See fig 2.1

- **YES.** Consider causation
- **NO.** There is no liability in negligence

Did the defendant's breach cause damage to the claimant? See fig 3.1

- **YES.** Consider defences
- **NO.** There is no liability in negligence

Negligence: Pure Psychiatric Harm

Sample questions

Question 1

A solicitor has been instructed by two trade union members: an older man and a younger woman. They were both attending their annual conference when a car driver lost control of their vehicle and crashed into the queue of people waiting to get into the conference. The older man was in the queue. He suffered a minor injury to his leg but has also been diagnosed with post-traumatic stress disorder (PTSD). The younger woman was on the other side of the road at the time and saw the accident take place. She has also been diagnosed with PTSD.

Which of the following statements best explains whether the clients would be compensated for their PTSD if the car driver's negligence was proven to have caused their loss?

A   Neither the older man nor the younger woman would receive compensation for their PTSD because they have suffered pure psychological harm.

B   Both the older man and the younger woman would receive compensation for their PTSD because there is an established duty of care between road users and pedestrians.

C   Only the older man would receive compensation for their PTSD because he is owed a duty of care for his pure psychological harm as he is a primary victim. The younger woman would not be owed a duty of care for her pure psychological harm as she is neither a primary victim nor a secondary victim.

D   Only the older man would receive compensation for their PTSD because there is an established duty of care between road users and pedestrians. However, the younger woman's PTSD is too remote.

E   Only the older man would receive compensation for their PTSD because there is an established duty of care between road users and pedestrians. However, the younger woman would not be owed a duty of care for their pure psychological harm as she is neither a primary victim nor a secondary victim.

Answer

Option E is correct.

Option A is wrong because the older man has not suffered pure psychological harm (PPH) as his PTSD has been caused by a physical impact. His PTSD would be compensated for as part of the pain and suffering for the physical injury. It is correct, however, the younger woman has suffered PPH and that she would not be compensated for this (see further below).

Option B is wrong because, while there is an established duty of care between road users and pedestrians, this would not assist the younger woman as she has suffered PPH. The established duty is only relevant for personal injury or property damage and not for PPH.

Option C is wrong because the older man has not suffered PPH. He is owed a duty of care because he has suffered a physical injury and the established duty of care between road users and pedestrians applies. His PTSD would be covered under this established duty and the older man would not have to rely on the special rules that apply for PPH. (The test for a primary victim (PV) only applies for PPH, ie psychological harm without physical impact.) It is correct, however, that the younger woman would not be owed a duty of care for her PPH as she is neither a PV nor a secondary victim (SV). She was not a PV as she was not in the 'danger zone' when the car crashed. There is also nothing on the facts to suggest that she had a close relationship of love and affection with any person who was physically

75

endangered by the car driver. She would not, therefore, be classed as a SV as she would not satisfy all the *Alcock* control mechanisms.

Option D is wrong because the younger woman would not be owed a duty of care for her PTSD. The claim would therefore fail at the duty of care stage and the question of remoteness is, therefore, irrelevant.

Question 2

A client has been diagnosed as suffering from post-traumatic stress disorder. This was caused when the client was in a local park recently. They saw a lorry swerve out of control and crash from a nearby road through the park railings and onto the area of grass where children were playing together. The lorry hit one of the children who subsequently died. The client was sitting on a park bench some distance away from the accident but they witnessed the whole horrific event. They also went to the scene immediately afterwards to try and help.

The insurers of the lorry have admitted liability for the death of the child.

Which of the following statements best explains whether the client would be owed a duty of care for their post-traumatic stress disorder?

A Yes, because the insurance company has admitted liability for the death of the child.

B Yes, because while the client was not in any physical danger, the lorry driver owed a duty of care to all foreseeable rescuers.

C Yes, because the client suffered a foreseeable psychiatric injury due to what they saw and heard.

D No, because the client did not have a close tie of love and affection with the dead child.

E No, because the client was not in any physical danger.

Answer

Option D is correct – while the client will be able to satisfy all the other elements of the *Alcock* test, there is nothing to suggest that they had a close tie of love and affection with the dead child (or indeed any of the children that were playing in the park).

Option A is wrong because the fact that the insurance company has admitted liability for the death of the child does not, in itself, mean that it admits that the client was owed a duty of care for their pure psychiatric harm. (The admission will, however, prove breach of duty.)

Option B is wrong because the established duty of care between a defendant and foreseeable rescuers only applies to cases where the rescuer has suffered physical injuries or property damage. (If this duty did apply, a rescuer can also claim for their *consequential* psychiatric harm.)

Option C is wrong as, while this is one element of the *Alcock* test for secondary victims, there are others, eg a necessary close tie of love and affection with the person who was physically injured.

Option E is wrong because secondary victims do not have to be in physical danger. They do, however, have to satisfy all elements of the *Alcock* test.

Question 3

A client is a firefighter and has been diagnosed as suffering from depression. This was caused when the client attended an accident on a motorway. Two cars had collided and crashed into the central reservation. The fire engine arrived on the scene within five minutes of the accident. The client crawled into the wreckage to free a passenger in one of the cars. Petrol was leaking from the car during this event but it did not, fortunately, ignite.

Which of the following statements best explains whether the client would be owed a duty of care for their depression?

A   Yes, because the client has suffered a foreseeable psychiatric injury due to what they saw and heard.

B   Yes, because the client was in danger of suffering a physical injury during the rescue.

C   No, because the risk of physical injury was low as the fuel did not actually ignite.

D   No, because the client did not have a close tie of love and affection with the passenger in the car.

E   No, because the client is a professional rescuer and they should be used to seeing horrific scenes as part of their job.

Answer

Option B is correct – the client is owed a duty of care as they have suffered a medically recognised psychiatric condition as a result of a sudden shock and they are a primary victim. There was a foreseeable risk of physical injury (burns) due to the fact that petrol was leaking from the car.

Option A is wrong because, while the client may have suffered a foreseeable psychiatric injury due to what they saw and heard, they would not be owed a duty of care as a secondary victim. This is because they would not have a close tie of love and affection with the passenger in the car. In any event, the client is a primary victim and it is not necessary that psychiatric injury is reasonably foreseeable.

Option C is wrong because there was a foreseeable risk of physical injury – the fact that it did not occur is irrelevant.

Option D is wrong as, while the client did not have a close tie of love and affection with the passenger in the car, this is irrelevant as the client is a primary rather than a secondary victim.

Option E is wrong as the foreseeability of psychiatric injury is not relevant to primary victims. In any event, there is no special rule that requires professional rescuers who are secondary victims to be more than usually resistant to shocking events. Professional rescuers are not expected to display more than normal fortitude.

6 Negligence: Employers' Liability

6.1	Introduction	80
6.2	Employer's common law duty	80
6.3	Breach of duty	84
6.4	Causation	85
6.5	Defences	86

SQE1 syllabus

This chapter will enable you to achieve the SQE1 Assessment Specification in relation to Functioning Legal Knowledge concerned with the core principles of tort on negligence and how the duty of care operates in relation to employers, including how the duty of care has evolved to protect those who suffer stress through pressures of work.

Note that for SQE1, candidates are not usually required to recall specific case names or cite statutory or regulatory authorities. Cases are provided for illustrative purposes only.

Learning outcomes

By the end of this chapter you will be able to apply relevant core legal principles and rules appropriately and effectively, at the level of a competent newly qualified solicitor in practice, to realistic client-based and ethical problems and situations in the following areas:

- the elements which an employee needs to prove in order to establish a claim in negligence against their employer;
- the scope of the employer's duty in negligence in so far as it relates to stress at work.

Tort

6.1 Introduction

Claims by employees injured at work are some of those most commonly brought before the courts. The majority of employers are required by statute (Employers' Liability (Compulsory Insurance) Act 1969) to take out insurance against such claims. An employee will know, therefore, that embarking on litigation will not be a worthless exercise. The employer should have the means to pay any damages it is ordered to pay.

There are two potential areas of liability in tort for the employer. This chapter considers an employers' primary liability in negligence for breach of the personal duty an employer owes to every employee. **Chapter 9** considers the secondary liability of employers under the principle of vicarious liability for the torts of employees committed in the course of their employment.

6.2 Employer's common law duty

The general nature of the duty owed by the employer to his employees is a duty to take reasonable care for its employees' safety while at work. Case law has further defined the employer's duty in more specific terms.

The House of Lords in *Wilsons & Clyde Coal Co Ltd v English* [1937] 3 All ER 628 defined the employer's common law duty as comprising three separate duties.

The duties are to take reasonable steps to provide:

- competent staff;
- adequate material (ie plant, equipment and machinery); and
- a proper system of work and supervision.

In *Latimer v AEC Ltd* [1953] 2 All ER 449, the House of Lords added a fourth duty to the list, ie the duty to take reasonable steps to provide:

- a safe place of work.

A feature that is common to all four duties is that the duty owed by employer to employee is 'personal to the employer'. This means that an employer cannot escape liability for the negligent performance of its duty by saying that it delegated its performance to someone else (eg an independent contractor or one of its own employees) whom it reasonably believed to be competent to perform it. It is a non-delegable duty. The practical implications of this are considered further below.

Personal nature of the employer's duty

> ⭐ *Examples*
>
> *Fiona, a factory worker, is badly injured when a machine she was operating exploded. The machine was recently serviced by a local contractor who negligently failed to spot an obvious electrical fault.*
>
> *The factory will be liable to Fiona. It owes Fiona a duty to provide adequate plant and equipment. Although it has delegated the servicing of the machine to a local contractor, its duty is non-delegable and so the negligent failure of the contractor to rectify the wiring problem will place the factory in breach of this duty. (Although the factory will be liable to Fiona, it will have a claim in contract against the contractor whereby it could recoup any compensation it has to pay out.)*
>
> *This can be compared with the example of Robert, who is also employed by the factory, and who is knocked over outside the factory by a lorry being driven negligently by Simon, who is delivering goods from a supplier.*

*The factory has not delegated the performance of any of its duties to Simon. As Robert is injured outside the factory by someone not employed by the factory, this incident falls outside the scope of the factory's duties as Robert's employer. Robert's claim would therefore lie in negligence against Simon (or, if Simon is an employee of the supplier for whom he was delivering, against the supplier under the principle of vicarious liability which is considered in **Chapter 9**).*

The reason why the duty of care owed by an employer to their employees is non-delegable is because the relationship is a close personal relationship, based on mutual trust and confidence. The employee does not have to identify exactly who was to blame for an accident. The employee can simply allege that a given event or given state of affairs proves that the employer has breached its personal common law duty.

Each of the duties are considered below.

6.2.1 Competent staff

An employer owes an employee a duty to provide the employee with competent fellow workers.

In Hudson v Ridge Manufacturing Co Ltd [1957] 2 QB 348, the claimant was injured while at work through a prank practised on him by a fellow workman. The claimant claimed damages for personal injuries against his employers, the defendants. The claim was based on a breach by the defendants of their duty at common law to take care for the safety of their workmen. Over a space of four years the fellow workman in question had been in the habit of tripping people up, or otherwise engaging in horseplay. During this period, he had been reprimanded over and over again by his foreman and told that if he did not stop his horseplay somebody would be likely to be hurt. The claimant succeeded. The judge made it clear that the important factor in the case was that the employer knew about the risk that the workman was posing to fellow staff. Had this been the first occasion that the workman had played a prank then the duty of care would not have arisen.

The duty to provide competent staff will not therefore arise merely from the fact that a worker is incompetent. Rather, it arises where an employer knows, or ought to know, about the risk a particular worker is posing to fellow workers. This was confirmed by the House of Lords in *Waters v Commissioner of Police for the Metropolis* [2002] 1 WLR 1607. The House of Lords also confirmed, in this case, that the risk being posed by the worker could be of psychological as well as physical harm. This duty is therefore important in respect of bullying in the workplace.

(In the circumstances covered by this duty, an injured employee may often also be able to bring a claim against his employer through vicarious liability, which is considered in **Chapter 9**.)

The duty to provide competent staff means that an employer will need to carefully consider many practical issues, including:

- selection of staff;
- provision of training to ensure staff are equipped to do their job;
- provision of supervision as necessary;
- dismissal of employees who despite adequate training, etc, continue to pose a risk to fellow staff.

If an employer does not, for example, adequately train or supervise their workers then they may well have on their staff workers who are not competent. The employer would either know about this incompetence, or ought reasonably to know about it. Such knowledge gives rise to the duty of care to other employees.

The second duty from *Wilsons & Clyde Coal* was a duty to provide adequate material. This has been interpreted widely by the courts and is usually now referred to as the duty to provide adequate plant and equipment. This is considered below.

6.2.2 Adequate plant and equipment

An employer owes an employee a duty to provide the employee with adequate plant and equipment.

This duty is relevant in two situations:

- Where an employer does provide plant and/or equipment to his employees but it is inadequate in some way. For these purposes 'equipment' covers anything provided by an employer for the purposes of its business.
- Where an employer does *not* in fact supply all the plant and equipment needed for the job. This aspect of the duty overlaps with the duty to provide a safe system of work, and this is considered at **6.2.3** below.

⭐ Example

Lucas owns a factory in which there are several machines, some of which are inherently dangerous. The various ways in which the machinery could be or become inadequate for an employee to use include:

- *problems caused by wear and tear or the age of the machines;*
- *problems caused by lack of servicing and inspection;*
- *lack of safety devices (such as hand guards) on the machines;*
- *inherent defects in the machines themselves (such as a design fault or manufacturing defect).*

The employer's duty to provide adequate plant and equipment is therefore a demanding one. An employer must provide all necessary equipment and maintain it to a safe standard. However, one reason equipment may be inadequate is because of inherent defects. This is considered below.

Employer's Liability (Defective Equipment) Act 1969

The purpose of the above Act is to save an employee from experiencing the potential difficulty of identifying and suing the manufacturer of defective equipment supplied to their employer. The employee can simply sue the employer for breach of its duty to provide adequate plant and equipment instead as, under s 1(1), 'the injury shall be deemed to be also attributable to negligence on the part of the employer'.

The injured employee needs to establish two things:

- fault on the part of the third party (most commonly the manufacturer of the equipment, but a supplier would also come within the statutory provision);
- causation (ie that the fault of the third party caused the employee's injury).

The third duty from *Wilsons & Clyde Coal Co Ltd* involves the provision of a safe system of work. This is considered below.

6.2.3 Safe system of work

An employer owes an employee a duty to provide the employee with a safe system of work.

This is the widest and therefore most frequently invoked branch of the employer's duty. The duty to provide a safe system of work includes, amongst other things, the physical lay-out of the job, the sequence in which the work is carried out, and, where necessary, the provision of training, warnings, notices, safety equipment and the issue of special instructions. It also covers cases where, through lack of a safe system of work, an employee has suffered stress (as opposed to some physical injury). The courts have, however, devised some special rules to apply in this context, which are considered at **6.2.5** below.

It is not enough for an employer simply to devise a safe system; this duty also requires an employer to take reasonable steps to ensure that it is complied with. The steps which a reasonable employer would take to ensure the safe system is being implemented include:

- providing adequate training to employees in the operation of the new system;
- ensuring the employees are supervised, at least at the outset;
- monitoring the operation of the system to ensure it is being fully complied with; and
- taking disciplinary action against any employee who fails to comply with the system.

Complying with the duty to provide a safe system of work therefore requires an employer to continuously assess the risks inherent in its particular working environment. It is a wide-ranging and potentially onerous obligation as evidenced by the number of cases in which the 'safe system of work' duty has been in issue.

6.2.4 Safe workplace

An employer owes an employee a duty to provide the employee with a safe place of work.

In *Latimer v AEC Ltd* [1953] 2 All ER 449, the House of Lords confirmed that, in addition to the duties set out in *Wilsons & Clyde Coal*, an employer owes a duty to an employee to take reasonable steps to provide a safe place of work.

There is an overlap between this common law duty in negligence and the statutory duty provided by the Occupiers' Liability Act 1957 (which is considered in detail in **Chapter 10**). Under this Act, where there are dangers due to the state of the premises, an occupier owes a duty to visitors to take reasonable care for their safety. An employer would qualify as an occupier in respect of work premises and an employee as a visitor.

Although there is an overlap, the employer's common law duty to employees is more onerous than the duty under the 1957 Act in two respects:

- Under the 1957 Act, an employer can comply with its duty by delegating work to an independent contractor (s 2(4)(b)). The employer's common law duty is, in contrast, non-delegable.
- The 1957 Act duty only applies to premises of which the employer is 'occupier'. In *General Cleaning Contractors v Christmas* [1953] AC 180 the House of Lords confirmed that the common law duty to provide a safe system of work (considered at **6.2.3** above) applies regardless of where the employees are at work. This means an employer has to assess premises to which his employees are sent for dangers and then, if such dangers are found, devise and implement a system of work so as to eradicate or minimise those dangers.

6.2.5 Stress at work

In the case of *Walker v Northumberland County Council* [1995] 1 All ER 737, the Court of Appeal confirmed that the duty to provide a safe system of work can extend to an employee who has suffered stress as a result of his work. Although this stems from the 'safe system of work' duty, later cases have refined the law applicable in this context.

In *Hatton v Sutherland* [2002] 2 All ER 1, the Court of Appeal laid down guidelines as to how courts should deal with such claims. These have since been approved by the House of Lords in *Barber v Somerset County Council* [2004] 2 All ER 385.

Stress at work: the Hatton Guidelines on when a duty of care may be owed

The Court of Appeal said that the *'threshold question'* to determine whether a duty would arise was whether injury to health through stress at work was reasonably foreseeable.

The Court went on to say that in deciding this threshold question the court should consider:

- the nature and extent of the work done by the employee (eg was the workload obviously too demanding in terms of type or amount; was there a high degree of absenteeism or sickness in the relevant department, etc); and
- signs from the employee themselves. The Court stated that an employer is generally entitled to assume an employee was up to the normal pressures of the job and was entitled to take what an employee told it at face value.

⭐ Examples

Alison is a teacher who has been taking on extra work in the hope of securing a promotion. She has recently seen her GP and is complaining that her workload is causing her to be depressed. She does not want to jeopardise her job prospects so has not told anyone at school of her problems.

Alison's employer is unlikely to know of the problems that Alison is facing. A duty of care is therefore not likely to arise unless the amount of Alison's extra work is so excessive that it alone makes future problems foreseeable.

Clement works in the prison service. He is going through a difficult divorce, which is making him depressed. He discusses matters with his employer and asks to take two weeks' immediate holiday. His employer is sympathetic but is unable to grant his request. Clement is then signed off work with a stress-related illness.

Clement's stress problems are not caused by his work but by personal problems and therefore fall outside the ambit of a duty.

Bilal is a social worker. He suffers a nervous breakdown as he is not able to cope with his workload. He is absent from work recovering for two months. On his return his employer promises to give him some extra assistance but nothing further happens. Bilal has now suffered a second nervous breakdown.

The fact that Bilal was previously off work for stress caused by his work makes it foreseeable that this could occur again unless steps are taken by the employer. This foreseeability gives rise to the duty to take such steps. (Note that this example is based on the facts of the Walker *case referred to above.)*

In *Hatton*, the Court of Appeal confirmed that the control mechanisms which apply to other claims for psychiatric harm (considered above in **Chapter 5**) have no role to play in claims for stress at work.

The four duties considered above together make up the employer's duty in negligence to take reasonable care for an employee's safety. The issue of breach of the employer's duty is considered below.

6.3 Breach of duty

Each of the duties owed by an employer requires the employer to take such steps as are *reasonable*. An employer will be in breach of its duty if it fails to meet the standard of care to be expected of a reasonable employer in its position.

Negligence: Employers' Liability

The approach to breach of duty is the same in this area of negligence as in relation to general negligence. The court will assess the standard of care to be expected by looking at all the circumstances of the case, including the magnitude of the foreseeable risk and also the cost and practicality of precautions.

An employer's duty is a personal one deriving from the close relationship of mutual trust between employer and employee. As well as making the employer's duty non-delegable, this also means that the duty is owed to each individual employee. This is considered below.

*In the case of Paris v Stepney Borough Council [1951] 1 All ER 42 (considered in **Chapter 2**), the defendant was required to take extra precautions for the claimant's safety because it knew he had only one sound eye and, therefore, risked total blindness if that eye was damaged. His colleagues, on the other hand, risked blindness in only one eye.*

To be in breach of duty, the risk must be known to the defendant. Accordingly, if the defendant had (reasonably) been ignorant of the claimant's special circumstances, it would not have been liable, unless the risk of injury was so great that fully-sighted garage hands should have been provided with goggles.

Health and Safety at Work etc Act 1974 (HSWA 1974)

It should be noted that regulations governing health and safety in the workplace are made under HSWA 1974. These regulations cover a vast range of issues arising in the workplace, such as the obligations to carry out risk assessments and the provision of information and training for employees. Breach of regulations made under the HSWA 1974 is a criminal offence. Section 47 of the HSWA 1974 provides that breach of regulations made under the HSWA 1974 are not actionable in a civil claim (unless the particular regulations in question provide otherwise). This means that an employee injured at work will not be able to bring a claim for breach of statutory duty based on regulations made under the HSWA 1974.

Although such regulations cannot be relied upon as the basis for a claim for breach of statutory duty, the provisions remain relevant where an injured employee brings a claim in the tort of negligence. The employers' duty is to take reasonable care for the safety of employees. The content of statutory health and safety regulations will be relevant in assessing breach of duty. A court assessing breach of duty in negligence will ask two basic questions:

- What risks ought the employer to have foreseen?
- What precautions ought the employer to have taken in response to those risks?

Where a particular risk is covered by statutory health and safety regulations, the content of those regulations will be highly relevant in answering both of the above questions. In other words, precautions which are required by statutory health and safety regulations are likely to be regarded as a guide to the standard which a reasonable employer ought to meet. Therefore, it will continue to be important for practitioners to have a good understanding of statutory health and safety regulations.

6.4 Causation

Once an employee has established a breach of the employer's duty of care, the issues of causation, *novus actus interveniens* and remoteness must be considered, applying the usual tests (see **Chapter 3**). Many of the leading cases on causation arise from claims against employers.

6.5 Defences

The main defences raised by an employer are likely to be consent (voluntary assumption of risk) and contributory negligence. These are considered in **Chapter 7**.

Summary

- This chapter establishes how the law of negligence impacts on the employer/employee relationship. An employer owes some well-established duties to an employee, including an obligation to provide a safe system of work. This duty has been interpreted widely by the courts, and extends to cover an employee who has suffered stress at work.

- This chapter also considers how the other elements of a claim in negligence against an employer are the same as studied in **Chapters 2** and **3**.

Summary flowchart

Figure 6.1 Negligence: employers' liability flowchart

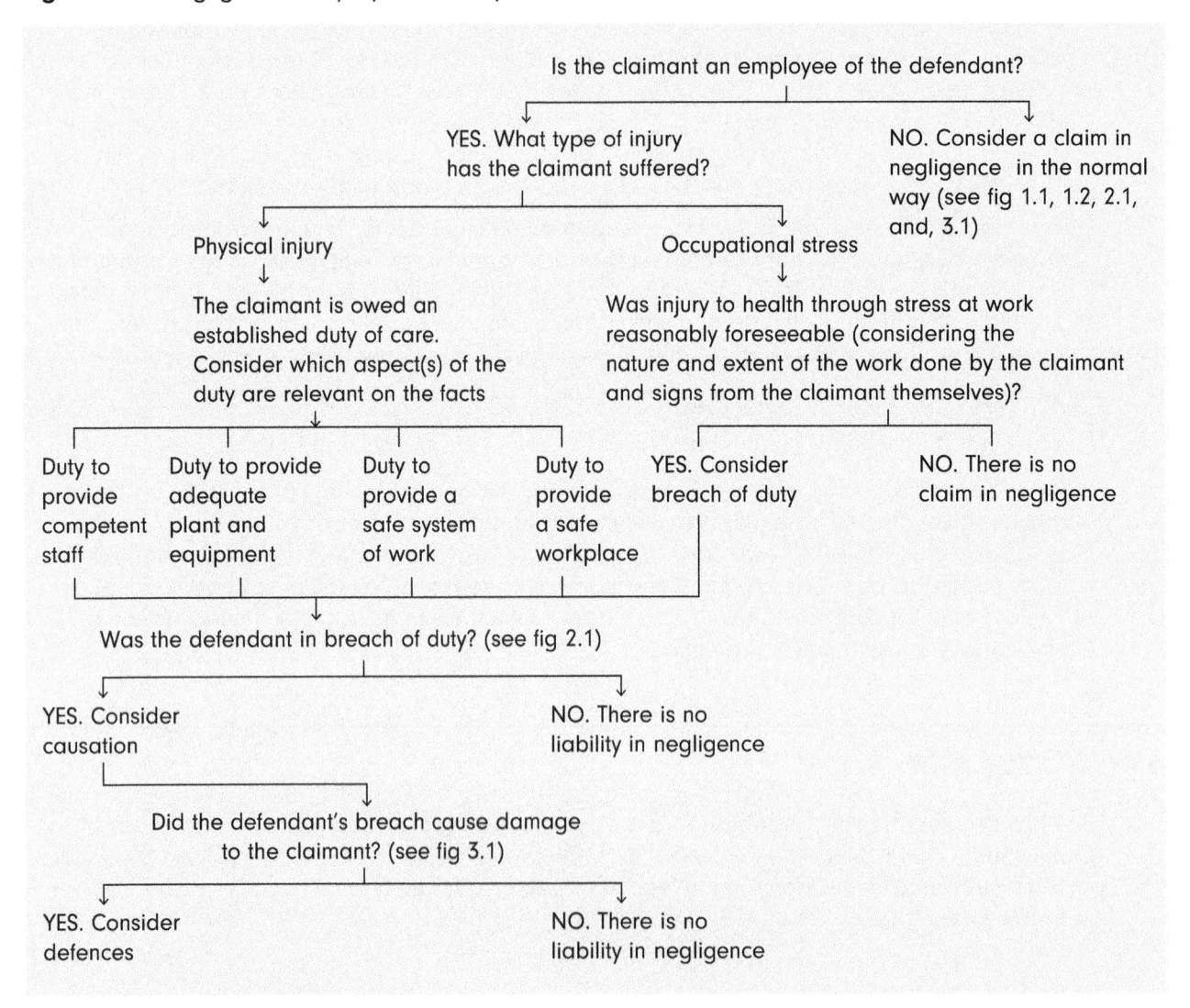

```
                    Is the claimant an employee of the defendant?
                    ├─────────────────────────────┬─────────────────────────────┐
          YES. What type of injury                         NO. Consider a claim in
          has the claimant suffered?                       negligence in the normal
                    │                                      way (see fig 1.1, 1.2, 2.1,
          ┌─────────┴─────────┐                            and, 3.1)
    Physical injury      Occupational stress
          │                    │
The claimant is owed an    Was injury to health through stress at work
established duty of care.  reasonably foreseeable (considering the
Consider which aspect(s) of the  nature and extent of the work done by the claimant
duty are relevant on the facts   and signs from the claimant themselves)?
                                           ┌───────────┴───────────┐
                                    YES. Consider        NO. There is no
                                    breach of duty       claim in negligence
```

Duty to provide competent staff | Duty to provide adequate plant and equipment | Duty to provide a safe system of work | Duty to provide a safe workplace

Was the defendant in breach of duty? (see fig 2.1)

YES. Consider causation — NO. There is no liability in negligence

Did the defendant's breach cause damage to the claimant? (see fig 3.1)

YES. Consider defences — NO. There is no liability in negligence

Sample questions

Question 1

A solicitor's client is an employee of a plastics company and works in its factory as an operator of a machine that makes plastic cups. The plastics company has contracted with a maintenance company for the maintenance of its plant and equipment.

The maintenance company had installed a fence to guard the dangerous moving parts on the plastic cup machine. When the client first began to use the machine, they discovered that, although there was a safety guard over the dangerous moving parts on the plastic cup machine, the safety guard could easily be moved to one side. The client found that this made their work on the machine much quicker. Due to this, the client developed the habit of moving the safety guard to one side when they were working on the machine.

One day the client caught their hand in the machine and suffered severe injury, necessitating the amputation of their hand.

Which of the following statements best explains whether the plastics company has breached the duty of care that it owes to your client?

A   No, because the plastics company has supplied safe plant and equipment as there was a safety guard around the dangerous parts of the machine.

B   No, because the plastics company took all reasonable care in selecting the maintenance company to carry out the maintenance of its plant and equipment.

C   No, because the client was at fault in moving the safety guard to one side.

D   Yes, because the duty to provide a safe system of work is relevant as the client should not have been able to move the safety guard and continue working on the machine.

E   Yes, because the plastics company will automatically be found to be liable in negligence as there is a regulation under the Health and Safety at Work etc Act 1974 that covers safety guards.

Answer

Option D is correct because the duty to provide a safe system of work is relevant and the client should not have been able to move the safety guard and continue working on the machine (the usual safeguard is that such machines should automatically switch off if a safety guard is moved).

Option A is wrong because, the fact that the plastics company may (arguably) have supplied safe plant and equipment will not, in itself, mean that it will not be found to have breached other elements of the duty of care that it owes its employees.

Option B is wrong because the duty of care the plastics company owes its employees is personal and non-delegable. While the task of maintaining the plant and equipment has been contracted out to the maintenance company, this is irrelevant as it cannot contract out of the duty of care it owes its employees.

Option C is wrong because while this may be relevant to the issue of the defence of contributory negligence (see **Chapter 7**), it is not relevant to whether the employer has breached its duty of care. Defences are only considered after the liability under the elements of the relevant tort (here duty, breach and causation) has been established.

Option E is wrong because a breach of any regulation under the Health and Safety at Work etc Act 1974 does not automatically lead to a finding that there has been a breach of a duty of care in negligence. The breach of the regulation is, however, relevant to the breach of duty question in negligence.

Tort

Question 2

A solicitor is instructed by a supermarket in relation to a claim that a female employee is bringing against it in negligence.

A male employee was employed to collect up shopping trolleys from the supermarket car park. This man often decided to gather all the available shopping trolleys at once so as to make his job quicker. This was in direct contravention of an instruction from the supermarket that he should only gather and move five trolleys at a time. As the man was pushing a long row of trolleys he lost control of them. They crashed into the female employee, causing a nasty injury to her ankle.

The team leader in charge of the man's work had previously noticed his practice of collecting more than five trolleys at a time. The team leader told the man on three occasions that he must collect only five trolleys at a time. However, the man ignored these instructions. The team leader eventually gave up ordering the man not to collect more than five trolleys at a time and did nothing more about it.

Which of the following statements best explains whether the supermarket would be found to have breached the duty of care that it owes to the female employee?

A   Yes, because the male employee is clearly incompetent.

B   Yes, because the team leader is clearly incompetent.

C   Yes if the female employee can show that the supermarket either knew that the team leader was not properly supervising the male employee, or that it ought to have known.

D   No, because the supermarket had put in place a safe system of work which was implemented by employing a team leader to supervise its employees.

E   No, because the team leader was responsible for the relevant aspect of the safe system of work.

Answer

Option C is correct – the supermarket will have breached its duty to provide competent staff if it either knew that the team leader was not properly supervising the male employee, or that it ought to have known (as per *Hudson v Ridge Manufacturing Co Ltd* [1957] 2 QB 348).

Options A and B are incorrect as, while the male employee and team leader are clearly incompetent, their employer must either know or ought to know this fact before it will be found to be in breach of its duty of care.

Option D is wrong because, while it may not have breached the duty to provide a safe system of work, it may still be found to have breached the duty to provide competent staff.

Option E is incorrect because, while the task of implementing a safe system of work may have been allocated to a supervisor, the responsibility for the duty of care is the employer's and cannot be delegated to their employees.

Question 3

A company has been notified of a claim for damages for occupational stress by a former employee. The former employee was the company's human resources (HR) manager. Prior to their resignation, the former employee dealt with redundancy dismissals of several staff. The former employee has been diagnosed with depression and alleges that this was caused by the actions of the company.

Negligence: Employers' Liability

The company has instructed its solicitor to defend the claim. The company's instructions are that they were aware that dealing with the redundancies was a very stressful task and that a director therefore offered to help the former employee on a number of occasions. However, the former employee told the director that they were happy to deal with redundancies on their own.

Which of the following statements best explains whether the company would be successful in arguing that it did not owe a duty of care to the former employee for occupational stress?

A   Yes, because there is an established duty of care between employers and their employees.

B   Yes, because there is an established duty of care between employers and their employees. The relevant aspect of the duty is a safe system of work.

C   Yes, injury to health through stress at work was reasonably foreseeable because the former employee was carrying out a particularly stressful task.

D   No, because the former employee was neither at risk of foreseeable physical injury nor the witness to a shocking event involving someone they were in a close tie of love and affection with.

E   No, because injury to health through stress at work was not reasonably foreseeable because the former employee was a HR manager and the former employee told the director that they were happy to deal with redundancies on their own.

Answer

Option E is correct. Employers are (under the Hatton Guidelines) entitled to take what an employee tells them at face value. The facts indicate that there was nothing to suggest that injury to health through stress at work was reasonably foreseeable.

Option A is wrong because the established duty of care between employers and their employees only covers physical injuries and not occupational stress, ie pure psychological harm.

Option B is wrong for the same reason as A. (It is correct, however, that the duty to provide a safe system of work *can* extend to an employee who has suffered stress as a result of their work.)

Option C correctly states the 'threshold question' from *Hatton* determines whether an employee would be owed a duty of care for occupational stress. However, option C is incorrect because (under the Hatton Guidelines) an employer is generally entitled to assume an employee was up to the normal pressures of the job. Dealing with redundancies is (unfortunately) a normal part of a HR manager's job.

Option D is wrong because it seeks to apply the primary and secondary victim tests for the duty of care in cases of pure psychological harm (considered in **Chapter 5**). These tests do not apply to claims for occupational stress.

7 Defences

7.1	Introduction	92
7.2	Consent (voluntary assumption of risk)	92
7.3	Contributory negligence	94
7.4	Illegality (*ex turpi causa non oritur actio*)	98
7.5	Excluding liability	99

SQE1 syllabus

This chapter will enable you to achieve the SQE1 Assessment Specification in relation to Functioning Legal Knowledge concerned with the core principles of tort on negligence and the defences that a defendant may rely upon where the claimant has established liability.

Note that for SQE1, candidates are not usually required to recall specific case names or cite statutory or regulatory authorities. Cases are provided for illustrative purposes only.

Learning outcomes

By the end of this chapter you will be able to apply relevant core legal principles and rules appropriately and effectively, at the level of a competent newly qualified solicitor in practice, to realistic client-based and ethical problems and situations in the following areas:

- the defence of consent (voluntary assumption of risk);
- the defence of illegality;
- the defence of contributory negligence.

7.1 Introduction

In a negligence claim, even if a claimant can prove all the elements of negligence – duty of care, breach of duty and causation of damage – the claim may still fail if a defendant can successfully raise a defence. This chapter considers the defences which a defendant might raise in a negligence claim that may either eliminate or reduce the liability a defendant may otherwise have to compensate a claimant for their losses. These defences are known as general defences in that they may also apply to torts other than negligence. The applicability of these defences to other torts is considered later in this book.

Other torts discussed in this book may be subject to defences other than the general defences considered in this chapter. These are considered in the following chapters in relationships to those torts:

- Chapter 10 – Occupiers' liability
- Chapter 11 – Product liability
- Chapter 12 – Nuisance

7.2 Consent (voluntary assumption of risk)

The defence of consent (also referred to as voluntary assumption of risk or *volenti non fit injuria*) operates as a complete defence for the defendant, preventing the claimant recovering at all for the defendant's breach of duty.

For the defence of consent to succeed, a defendant must establish:

- that the claimant had full knowledge of the nature and extent of the risk; and
- that the claimant willingly consented to accept the risk of being injured due to the defendant's negligence.

Each of these key elements is examined in turn.

7.2.1 Claimant's knowledge of the risk

For the defence to succeed, the claimant must have had *full* knowledge of both the nature and the extent of the risk which the claimant is alleged to have assumed. It is not sufficient for the claimant simply to know that the risk exists.

7.2.2 Claimant's consent

For the defence of voluntary assumption of risk to succeed, it is not enough for a defendant to prove that the claimant knew of the risk. The defendant must also prove that the claimant freely consented to run the risk of injury. The courts have frequently pointed out that knowledge is not consent ('*sciens* is not *volens*').

The two cases below consider this element of the defence.

In Dann v Hamilton [1939] 1 KB 509, the claimant, knowing that the driver of a motor car was under the influence of drink nevertheless chose to travel by the car. She was injured in an accident caused by the drunkenness of the driver, in which the driver was killed. In an action against the personal representative of the driver, the defendant raised the defence of volenti non fit injuria.

The court held that, while the claimant knew that the driver had been drinking so that there was a risk that he might drive carelessly, it could not be said that knowledge of the risk was sufficient to imply consent to the risk.

> *In Morris v Murray [1990] 3 All ER 801, the claimant had been drinking for some hours with the deceased when they decided to go for a ride in the deceased's light aircraft. The claimant assisted in preparing the aircraft, which took off, piloted by the deceased in conditions in which flying at the aerodrome had been suspended. The plane crashed, and the claimant brought an action for negligence against the deceased's estate.*
>
> *The Court of Appeal held that the claimant's claim was barred by the defence of* volenti non fit injuria. *The claimant must have realised how drunk the pilot was and thereby implicitly waived his right to damages. The drunkenness of the pilot was so extreme and glaring that the claimant could be said to have accepted the risk of his negligence.*

Note that there is now a statutory provision which deals with the defence of consent in the case of motor vehicles. Section 149 of the Road Traffic Act 1988 applies to any motor vehicle where insurance for passengers is compulsory. Its effect is that any acceptance of risk by the passenger is invalid. The defence of consent or *volenti* cannot be relied on.

Section 149 applies only in the specific case of motor vehicles. In any other case the defence of consent can still be raised. *Dann* is still relevant here because it illustrates how difficult it will be for a defendant to establish the defence of consent. The conclusion to be drawn from *Dann* is that in practice very few cases are likely to satisfy the stringent requirements for the defence of consent to succeed.

Two further situations which illustrate just how difficult it is in practice to establish the defence of consent: employees and rescuers.

The claimant's consent must be given freely and voluntarily and not be obtained as a result of fear or duress. The claimant therefore must have been in a position to choose freely. If, therefore, the relationship between the parties is such that there is doubt as to whether the claimant can truly decide voluntarily whether or not to assume the risk of danger, consent cannot apply. An example of one such relationship is considered below.

7.2.3 Consent and employees

The defence of consent rarely succeeds in claims by employees against their employers. An employee acts under a duty and therefore has no real freedom of choice when carrying out a dangerous task requested by the employer.

If an employee refuses to carry out the task, they run the risk of losing their job. Policy considerations may also be relevant. Employees will usually be under economic and/or other pressures, which will make it unjust for an employer to say that the worker ran the risk of injury freely and willingly.

Smith v Baker [1891] AC 325 is an example of a case where the defence did not succeed against an employee. The claimant was injured when a heavy crane lifting stones overhead dropped its load on him. The court held that, just because the claimant had continued to work, knowing the risks involved, it did not mean he had consented in law to the risk.

7.2.4 Consent and rescuers

Another instance in which a claimant does not necessarily act voluntarily is where they are acting as a rescuer. The courts take the view that rescuers often act under moral compulsion. (This is true whether the rescuer acts immediately and instinctively, or first takes time to reflect before encountering the risk.)

Rescuers will not be considered to have consented to the risk of injury if:

- they were acting to rescue persons or property endangered by the defendant's negligence; and
- they were acting under a compelling legal, social or moral duty; and
- their conduct in all the circumstances was reasonable and a natural and probable consequence of the defendant's negligence.

> *In* Haynes v Harwood *[1935] 1 KB 146, the claimant, a police constable, was on duty inside a police station in a street in which there were a large number of people, including children. Seeing the defendants' runaway horses with a van attached coming down the street he rushed out and eventually stopped them, sustaining injuries in consequence, in respect of which he claimed damages. The defendant pleaded the defence of* volenti. *However, the court held that, as the claimant was injured while rescuing people from a situation of imminent danger, he acted under compulsion and did not willingly accept the risk of injury.*

Haynes demonstrates that the rules on rescuers apply equally to professional rescuers and to lay rescuers.

In considering the requirements of the defence of consent and how the courts have applied them, it is possible to understand that the defence rarely succeeds. One of the reasons for this is that the courts have the power to reduce the damages awarded to a careless claimant under the principle of contributory negligence, and this is regarded as being fairer than denying a claimant any remedy whatsoever against a negligent defendant. The defence of contributory negligence is considered below.

7.3 Contributory negligence

A defendant who is unable to escape liability by relying on any of the complete defences may, nevertheless, be able to raise the partial defence of contributory negligence.

Example

Fred is driving his car along a road and carelessly fails to give way at a junction. He pulls out into the path of a car driven by Gavin. Gavin is injured and his car is damaged. However, Gavin was exceeding the speed limit. If he had been driving more slowly, he would have been able to avoid the collision.

Fred owes Gavin a duty of care – as a road user. From the facts it can be seen that Fred has breached his duty. He has fallen below the standard to be expected of a reasonably competent driver. It is clear that Fred's negligence has caused Gavin's injury.

However, on these facts Fred would be able to rely on the partial defence of contributory negligence.

Contributory negligence comprises the following two elements:

- carelessness on the claimant's part; and
- that carelessness has contributed to the claimant's damage.

In a negligence claim, therefore, it will not always be the defendant alone who is to blame for the claimant's loss. Sometimes the claimant, too, will be at fault. If such fault contributed to the claimant's loss then the defendant will argue contributory negligence against the claimant.

7.3.1 The effect of a finding of contributory negligence

The law relating to the effects of contributory negligence is contained in the Law Reform (Contributory Negligence) Act 1945.

> *Section 1(1) of the 1945 Act provides that:*
>
> *Where any person suffers damage as the result partly of his own fault and partly of the fault of any other person or persons:*
>
> *(a) a claim in respect of that damage shall not be defeated by reason of the fault of the person suffering the damage,*

(b) but the damages recoverable in respect thereof shall be reduced to such extent as the court thinks just and equitable having regard to the claimant's share in the responsibility for the damage.

Where there is a finding of contributory negligence, the claimant's damages are to be reduced. The court will first calculate the full amount of damages which would have been payable had it not been for the claimant's contributory negligence. Then it will make an appropriate reduction to take the contributory negligence into account.

For example, in the case of *Reeves v Metropolitan Police Commissioner* [1999] 3 All ER 897, the deceased hanged himself while in police custody. He was found 50% to blame and so only 50% of the damages were recoverable.

Where a finding of contributory negligence is made by the court, damages should be reduced:

- to such extent as the court thinks just and equitable;
- having regard to the claimant's share in the responsibility for the damage.

    Case law demonstrates that in making this assessment the court will take into account:

- culpability, ie the relative blameworthiness of the parties;
- causation, ie the extent to which the claimant's carelessness has caused or contributed to the loss suffered.

In considering the issue of causation, the claimant needs to have contributed to the loss which they have suffered. The claimant does not need to have contributed to the accident itself. The relevant issue is not who caused the accident, but who caused *the damage*. So, the partial defence of contributory negligence could still apply even where a defendant is solely responsible for the accident in which the claimant was injured.

The simplest example of this is the case of a road accident in which the claimant is injured because they are not wearing a seatbelt. The claimant may have been driving perfectly carefully and have done nothing to cause the accident to happen, so that the accident is caused entirely by the negligence of the defendant. Nevertheless, if the claimant's failure to wear a seatbelt contributes to their injuries, their damages will be reduced.

The section below considers seatbelts as an example of how the courts reduce damages for contributory negligence.

7.3.2 Examples of contributory negligence

7.3.2.1 Seatbelts

Even before it became compulsory to wear a seatbelt, the courts took the view that a passenger in a car who failed to wear a seatbelt could be found contributorily negligent if this failure contributed to the passenger's injuries. The leading case on this issue is *Froom v Butcher*.

In the case of Froom v Butcher *[1975] 3 All ER 520, the Court of Appeal handed down the following scale of reductions to be made when a claimant fails to wear a seatbelt:*

Result of claimant's failure to wear a seatbelt	Likely % reduction
1. Claimant suffered injuries which would have been avoided had a seatbelt been worn.	25%
2. Claimant suffered injuries which would have been less severe had a seatbelt been worn.	15%
3. The wearing of a seatbelt would have made no difference to the extent of the claimant's injuries.	0%

The case of *Froom v Butcher* demonstrates that a defendant must establish *a causal link* between the claimant's failure to wear a seatbelt and the loss the claimant has suffered, ie the claimant's failure to wear a seatbelt must have caused or contributed to the injuries.

7.3.2.2 Crash helmets

Motorcyclists who suffer head injuries due to a failure to wear a crash helmet will have their damages reduced for contributory negligence. In the case of *Capps v Miller* [1989] 2 All ER 333, the Court of Appeal adopted the same tariff for failure to wear crash helmets as that laid down for seatbelts in *Froom v Butcher*. As for seatbelts, the defendant will need to establish the causal link between the lack of any crash helmet and the claimant's injuries.

7.3.2.3 Drunken drivers

Passengers who accept lifts from a driver whom they know to be drunk, can expect to have their damages reduced if they are injured in an accident caused by the driver's intoxicated state.

This principle applies even if the passengers were too drunk to appreciate the driver's intoxication but knew that, by going out drinking together, they would later be driven home by the driver when the driver would be drunk. In other words, self-induced intoxication cannot be used as an excuse by claimants for failing to take reasonable care of themselves (*Owens v Brimmell* [1997] QB 859).

7.3.3 The kind of behaviour that may amount to contributory negligence

A claimant's damages can be reduced if they are guilty of negligence which contributes towards the injury which they suffer. It is therefore necessary to consider what kind of behaviour amounts to contributory negligence.

The test for contributory negligence is whether the claimant has failed to take reasonable care for their own safety.

When assessing the standard of care required of a defendant in the tort of negligence, the defendant's behaviour is measured against that of the reasonable person. The same is true for a claimant when contributory negligence is assessed. The court must decide whether or not the claimant has failed to take reasonable care for their own safety, and their behaviour should be measured against that of an ordinary reasonable person in the circumstances.

The application of this test for contributory negligence to certain classes of claimant is considered below.

7.3.3.1 Children

It is usually said that there is no age below which, as a matter of law, a child cannot be contributorily negligent. However, the older the child, the more likely a court is to make a finding of contributory negligence.

> *In the case of* Gough v Thorne *[1966] 3 All ER 398, a lorry driver stopped, put out a hand to stop other traffic on his right, and waved the claimant, a girl aged 13½, across in front of him. The defendant drove past the lorry on the right as the claimant emerged without looking out and injured her. In an action by the claimant against the defendant for damages for negligence, the defendant pleaded contributory negligence by the claimant.*
>
> *The Court of Appeal held that: '(a) judge should only find a child guilty of contributory negligence if he or she is of such an age as reasonably to be expected to take precautions for his or her own safety.' The child must also be 'blameworthy'. On the facts, this was not the case. The claimant had come up to the standard of any ordinary child of 13½ in the circumstances and was not, therefore, contributory negligent.*

It can be noted that, had the claimant been an adult, it is very likely that there would have been a finding of contributory negligence. A reasonable adult pedestrian, with a fully developed road sense, would have leant forward to see whether there was anything overtaking the lorry before stepping out.

The test which the court will apply in deciding whether a child has been contributorily negligent, is whether an ordinary child of the claimant's age would have taken more care for his safety than the claimant did.

The age of the child is a crucial factor, just as it is when judging a child defendant's conduct. Thus, in the case of a very young child, it is most unlikely that a finding of contributory negligence would be made.

Note that in some situations an injury to a child may be due partly to the defendant's negligence but also partly to the negligence of the child's parents. In this situation the child is *not* 'identified' with the negligence of his parent. In other words, the child's damages cannot be reduced on account of the negligence of his parents.

(If the parent is partly to blame for the injury to the child, the defendant could seek to show that the parent was liable to the child for the same damage as the defendant, and could seek a contribution under the Civil Liability (Contribution) Act 1978. This is considered in **Chapter 3**.)

7.3.3.2 Rescuers

If the defendant's negligence creates a situation of peril, and a brave person rushes in to the rescue and is injured during the attempt, the defence of consent is unlikely to succeed against the rescuer. A defendant may allege that the rescuer has, nevertheless, been contributory negligent. The leading case on whether this may be successful is considered below.

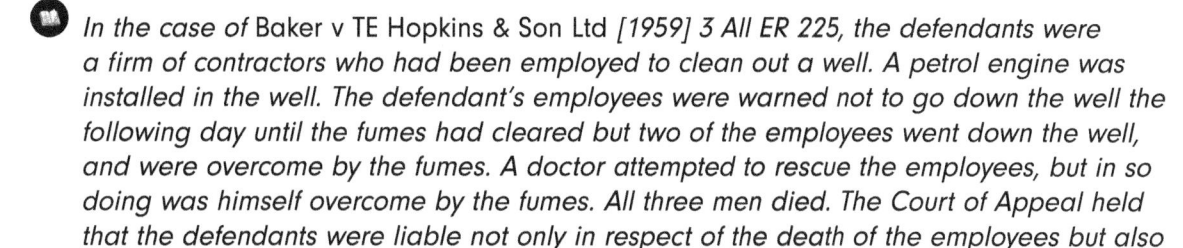

In the case of Baker v TE Hopkins & Son Ltd *[1959] 3 All ER 225, the defendants were a firm of contractors who had been employed to clean out a well. A petrol engine was installed in the well. The defendant's employees were warned not to go down the well the following day until the fumes had cleared but two of the employees went down the well, and were overcome by the fumes. A doctor attempted to rescue the employees, but in so doing was himself overcome by the fumes. All three men died. The Court of Appeal held that the defendants were liable not only in respect of the death of the employees but also in respect of the death of the doctor with no finding of contributory negligence against the doctor.*

The relevant principle from *Baker v TE Hopkins & Son Ltd* is that:

- For the purposes of contributory negligence, a rescuer will be judged against the standard of the reasonable rescuer. Allowance will be made for the emergency situation in which many rescuers will find themselves.

- Only if a rescuer has shown a 'wholly unreasonable disregard for his or her own safety' is there likely to be a finding of contributory negligence. Such cases are likely to be rare in practice as the courts will always be reluctant to accept criticism of a rescuer's conduct.

7.3.3.3 Employees

A claimant might be injured at work partly because of his employer's fault but also as a result of their own carelessness.

In deciding whether a careless employee's actions are sufficient to amount to contributory negligence, the court will take into account all of the relevant circumstances. For example, it will be relevant that the work might be noisy, repetitive or dull, and these factors could lead a claimant to take less care for his own safety.

In *Caswell v Powell Duffryn Associated Collieries Ltd* [1940] AC 152 Lord Atkin said:

> I am of opinion that the care to be expected of the plaintiff in the circumstances will vary with the circumstances; and that a different degree of care may well be expected from a workman in a factory or a mine from that which might be taken by an ordinary man not exposed continually to the noise, strain, and manifold risks of factory or mine.

Courts will therefore be slower to make a finding of contributory negligence against such an employee than against other employees (eg office workers).

7.3.3.4 Dilemma cases

The defendant's negligence may sometimes put the claimant in a situation of imminent danger, compelling the claimant to take some action to try to save themselves. The issue is whether, in these circumstances, the defendant would be successful in arguing contributory negligence against a claimant who is injured while trying to save themselves.

> In the case of *Jones v Boyce* [1814-23] All ER Rep 570, the defendant, a coach owner, negligently drove the coach. This caused the claimant to have to jump off the coach and break his leg.
>
> The court held that the method used by the claimant to try to save himself 'in the agony of the moment' was found to be a reasonable one, given the perilous situation in which he was placed. For this reason, there was no finding of contributory negligence, even though, with hindsight, he would have been safer had he opted for the alternative course of action.

A claimant who acts in the 'agony of the moment' due to the defendant's negligence will not be contributory negligent if the court is satisfied that the claimant's actions were a reasonable response to the danger.

The claimant in *Jones v Boyce* faced a dangerous situation, and in the light of that danger his actions were found to be reasonable. An example in which the claimant did not act reasonably is the case of *Sayers v Harlow UDC*.

> In *Sayers v Harlow UDC* [1958] 1 WLR 623, as a result of the defendant's negligence, the claimant became trapped in a public lavatory owned by the defendant. After unsuccessfully calling for assistance, the claimant thought that she could get out by climbing over the door. She stood with her right foot on the seat of the lavatory and her left foot on the toilet roll and its attachment. Having got into this position, she then realised she could not in fact get over the door. In trying to get down, she slipped, fell and sustained injury. The court reduced her damages by one quarter for contributory negligence.

7.4 Illegality (*ex turpi causa non oritur actio*)

The fact that the claimant was involved in an illegal enterprise at the time they were injured may sometimes provide the defendant with a defence. The maxim '*ex turpi causa non oritur actio*' translates as 'no action arises from a disgraceful cause'. It is commonly referred to as the defence of illegality. Illegality operates as a complete defence for the defendant, preventing the claimant recovering at all for the defendant's breach of duty.

⭐ Example

> Karl and Ben find a safe in the house they are burgling. Karl negligently blows the lock off the safe, injuring Ben. Karl would be able successfully to raise the defence of illegality if Ben sued him for his injuries.

Another example of illegality working as a defence is the case of Ashton v Turner *[1981] QB 137. There, the claimant and the defendant were escaping from a burglary they had just carried out. The defendant's negligent driving caused a crash in which the claimant was injured. The court held that the defence of illegality applied.*

The leading authority on the defence of illegality is the case of *Pitts v Hunt*.

In Pitts v Hunt *[1990] 3 All ER 344, the claimant was a pillion passenger on a motorcycle which was involved in a collision with a car. The rider of the motorcycle was killed and the claimant was injured. Both the claimant and the rider had been drinking prior to the accident. The claimant knew that the rider had no licence and was uninsured, and the claimant had encouraged him to drive in a reckless manner. The claimant sued the car driver and the motorcycle rider's personal representatives for damages for his injuries.*

The claimant's case failed as the action by the claimant arose directly ex turpi causa, *in that the reckless driving, which was the cause of the claimant's injuries, was an inherent part of their joint criminal enterprise.*

For the defence of illegality to succeed there must be a very close connection between the illegal activity of the claimant and the injury which they suffer, so that the damage arises directly out of the illegal activity in such a way that it would be contrary to public policy to allow the claimant a remedy.

Example

Adriana leaves her car parked in a restricted zone so that she is guilty of a traffic offence. Later, Janet, driving carelessly, crashes into the car and damages it. In this case the defendant could not succeed in the defence of illegality. The above requirements would not be satisfied.

7.5 Excluding liability

A person may try to exclude or limit his liability to another in tort. For example, by way of a notice which states: 'No liability is accepted for any loss or damage ...'

The extent to which an attempt to exclude liability may be successful is considered in **Chapter 4** on pure economic loss and in **Chapter 10** on the Occupiers' Liability Acts, as it is particularly relevant to these areas.

Summary

- If all the elements of negligence – duty of care, breach of duty, and causation of damage – are made out, the last argument open to a lawyer acting for a defendant is to seek to establish that a defence applies.

- The defences of consent and illegality are complete defences – this means that if the defendant succeeds in establishing them, then they will avoid paying any amount in compensation to the claimant.

- For the defence of consent to succeed, a defendant must establish: that the claimant had full knowledge of the nature and extent of the risk; and that the claimant willingly consented to accept the risk of being injured due to the defendant's negligence.

- For the defence of illegality to succeed, a defendant must establish: that there is a very close connection between the illegal activity of the claimant and the injury which they

suffer, so that the damage arises directly out of the illegal activity in such a way that it would be contrary to public policy to allow the claimant a remedy.
- The defence of contributory negligence is a partial defence. This means that where is a finding of contributory negligence, the claimant's damages are reduced. The court will first calculate the full amount of damages which would have been payable had it not been for the claimant's contributory negligence. Then it will make an appropriate reduction to take the contributory negligence into account.
- For the defence of contributory negligence to succeed, the defendant must establish: carelessness on the claimant's part; and that carelessness has contributed to the claimant's damage.
- There is contributory negligence where the claimant's injuries have been caused partly by the negligence of the defendant and partly by the claimant's own carelessness. It is necessary to consider whether the claimant failed to take reasonable care for their own safety and whether this contributed to the damage the claimant suffered. It is important to remember that only the claimant can be contributorily negligent.

Summary flowchart

Figure 7.1 Negligence: defences

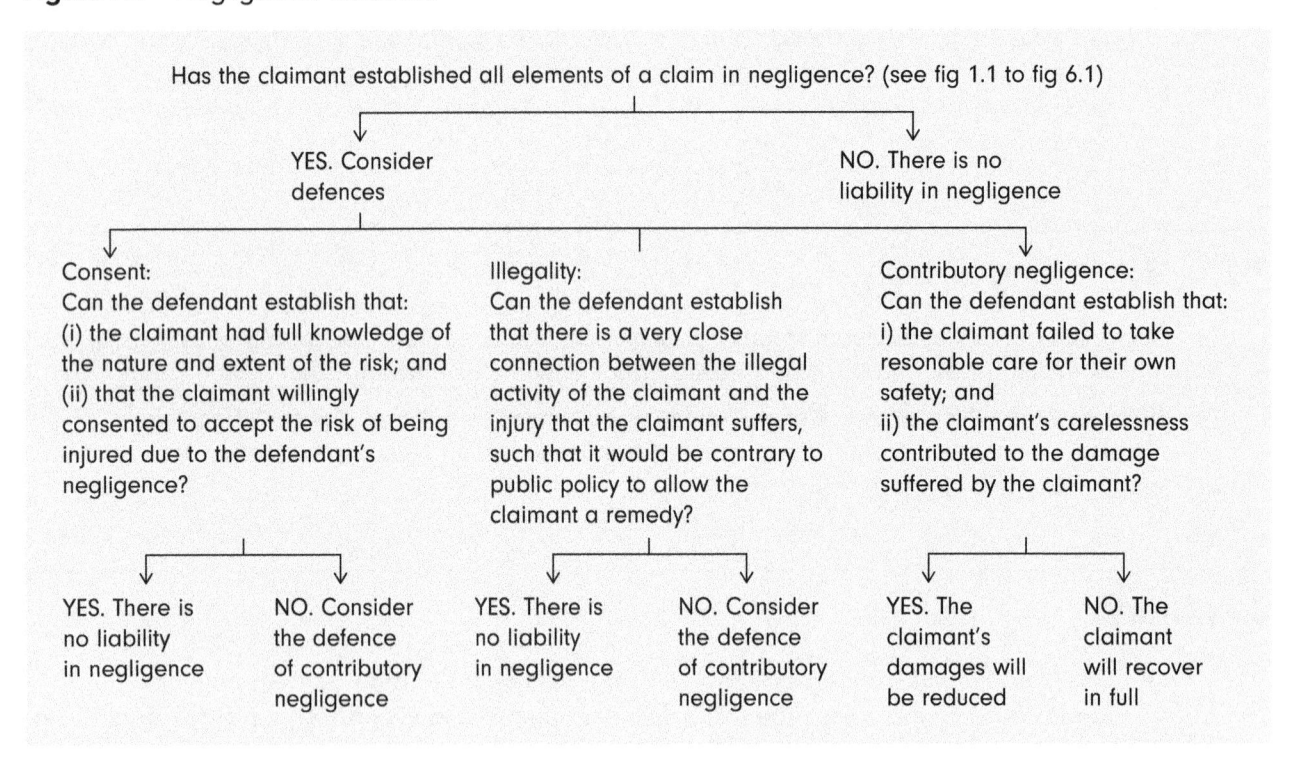

```
Has the claimant established all elements of a claim in negligence? (see fig 1.1 to fig 6.1)
                                    │
            ┌───────────────────────┴───────────────────────┐
            ▼                                               ▼
      YES. Consider                                   NO. There is no
        defences                                    liability in negligence
            │
   ┌────────┼────────┐
   ▼        ▼        ▼
Consent:         Illegality:                    Contributory negligence:
Can the defendant establish that:   Can the defendant establish   Can the defendant establish that:
(i) the claimant had full knowledge of   that there is a very close   i) the claimant failed to take
the nature and extent of the risk; and   connection between the illegal   resonable care for their own
(ii) that the claimant willingly   activity of the claimant and the   safety; and
consented to accept the risk of being   injury that the claimant suffers,   ii) the claimant's carelessness
injured due to the defendant's   such that it would be contrary to   contributed to the damage
negligence?              public policy to allow the           suffered by the claimant?
                         claimant a remedy?

   ┌────┴────┐           ┌────┴────┐              ┌────┴────┐
   ▼         ▼           ▼         ▼              ▼         ▼
YES. There is  NO. Consider  YES. There is  NO. Consider  YES. The      NO. The
no liability   the defence   no liability   the defence   claimant's    claimant
in negligence  of contributory in negligence of contributory damages will will recover
               negligence                   negligence      be reduced    in full
```

Sample questions

Question 1

A solicitor acts for a client who is being sued in negligence. The solicitor's instructions are that the client was giving the claimant (the 8-year-old son of the client's friend) a lift in the client's car when they had to carry out an emergency stop. The claimant was thrown forward and hit the back of the driver's seat. The claimant suffered a broken collar bone as a result. The client confirms that they did not ensure that the claimant was wearing a seatbelt. They had presumed that either the claimant's father had secured the claimant's seatbelt when they had sat the claimant in the car or that the claimant themselves had fastened the seatbelt.

The solicitor has advised the client that it is likely that they will be held to have breached the duty of care they owed to the claimant and that the breach caused the claimant's injury. The solicitor is considering the applicability of any available defence(s).

Which of the following statements best explains whether the client will be able to successfully rely on an applicable defence?

A Yes, because the claimant's father was clearly contributorily negligent and this can be argued to reduce the level of compensation the client will have to pay the claimant.

B Yes, because the claimant was clearly contributorily negligent.

C Yes, because the claimant's father consented to the risk of their son's injury when they sat the claimant in the client's car without ensuring that the seatbelt was fastened.

D No, because the claimant's age makes it highly improbable that the claimant would be found to have been contributorily negligent.

E No, because, as the claimant's father did not know of the risk of the client carrying out an emergency stop, they could not be said to have consented to the risk.

Answer

Option D is correct. While there is no age below which a child cannot be contributorily negligent, the claimant's age makes it highly improbable that the claimant would be found to have been contributorily negligent. The ordinary 8 year old would not be expected to have fastened their own seatbelt.

Option A is wrong because the defence of contributory negligence is used as against a claimant ie the child in this case and not their father. The claimant's father may have been negligent but the child is not 'identified' with the negligence of their parent. If the claimant's father has been negligent, then the client can seek a contribution under the Civil Liability (Contribution) Act 1978. However, this does not prevent the claimant from recovering all of their compensation from the client.

Option B is wrong because it cannot be said that the claimant was clearly contributory negligent (see above).

Option C is wrong because the defence of consent only applies as against the claimant. Any apparent consent by the claimant's father is irrelevant.

Option E is wrong for the same reason as option C.

Question 2

A claimant suffered a badly broken leg while being a passenger on a motorbike driven by the defendant. The defendant pulled out of a side road into the path of an oncoming car. The claimant feared that the car would hit the defendant's motorbike. In order to avoid this, they jumped from the motorbike and broke their leg in the fall. In fact, the car driver managed to swerve around the defendant's motorbike and avoided a collision. The claimant was not wearing a crash helmet. The Police Accident Report confirms that the defendant was required to undertake a breath test after the accident. This indicated that the defendant's blood alcohol level was in excess of the legal limit.

Tort

Which of the following statements best explains why the defendant may be able to successfully rely on an applicable defence?

A Because the defendant will be able to rely upon the defence of illegality as the claimant was not wearing a crash helmet.

B Because the defence of contributory negligence could be relied upon by the defendant if it can be proven that the claimant must have known that the defendant was intoxicated.

C Because the claimant was clearly contributory negligent by jumping off the motorbike.

D Because the claimant was clearly contributory negligent by not wearing a crash helmet.

E Because the claimant clearly consented to the risk of injury by travelling as the defendant's passenger when it would have been obvious that the defendant was intoxicated.

Answer

Option B is correct – the defence of contributory negligence could be relied upon by the defendant if it can be proven that the claimant must have known that the defendant was intoxicated.

Option A is wrong because, while it is a criminal offence not to wear a crash helmet while travelling on a motorbike, it is not a sufficiently serious offence and there is not a very close connection between the illegal activity of the claimant and the injury which they suffered. It would not be contrary to public policy to allow the claimant a remedy in this case.

Option C is wrong because the claimant acted in the 'agony of the moment' due to the defendant's negligence. The claimant's actions were a reasonable response to the danger created by the defendant.

Option D is wrong because, while the failure to wear a crash helmet is treated as an unreasonable failure to take care of one's own safety, there must be a causal connection between the carelessness and the claimant's injury. Here, the claimant suffered a broken leg rather than a head injury, ie their carelessness did not contribute to their injury.

Option E is wrong because, in accordance with s 149 Road Traffic Act 1988, it is not possible for the driver of a motor vehicle to use the defence of consent against a claimant who was a passenger in their vehicle.

8 Principles of Remedies for Personal Injury and Death Claims

8.1	Introduction	104
8.2	Compensatory damages: general principles	105
8.3	Damages for personal injury	106
8.4	Damages on death	115

SQE1 syllabus

This chapter will enable you to achieve the SQE1 Assessment Specification in relation to Functioning Legal Knowledge concerned with the core principles of the remedy of damages for personal injury and the awards of damages which are available when the victim of a tort has died.

Note that for SQE1, candidates are not usually required to recall specific case names or cite statutory or regulatory authorities. Cases are provided for illustrative purposes only.

Learning outcomes

By the end of this chapter you will be able to apply relevant core legal principles and rules appropriately and effectively, at the level of a competent newly qualified solicitor in practice, to realistic client-based and ethical problems and situations in the following areas:

- the principles by which damages are assessed;
- the pecuniary and non-pecuniary elements of an award of damages for personal injury;
- the awards of damages which are relevant when the victim has died.

8.1 Introduction

So far, the book has considered in detail how a claimant may establish liability in the tort of negligence. This chapter considers the question of what the claimant wants to recover from the defendant if they are successful in their claim, ie the remedies that they want.

A lawyer in practice needs to be able to analyse the law and determine whether evidence is available to prove each element of the claim. However, the main concern of the lawyer's client is likely to be the remedy they hope to obtain.

In the examples of negligence which have been considered in the book, the kinds of harm the claimants suffered included:

- damage to property, eg a car damaged in a motor accident;
- personal injury, eg a broken leg caused in a tripping accident.

This can be broken down further. For example, a solicitor is acting for a client involved in a road accident who has suffered damage to their car and a broken leg caused by the negligence of the defendant.

In order for the client to be fully compensated for the effects of the accident, the items that would need to be claimed for would include:

- Damage to property – the car damage:
    - cost of repairs or replacement
    - cost of lost use, eg hire of an alternative car.
- Personal injury – the broken leg:
    - compensation for pain and suffering
    - compensation for activities the claimant can no longer do, eg playing football
    - medical expenses, eg prescription charges etc
    - lost wages while unable to work.

This is not an exhaustive list, but it provides some examples of the kinds of loss which a claimant might suffer.

This chapter considers the remedy of damages. In the example above, the claimant suffers an injury (and property damage) but is still alive. It is also necessary to consider the damages which can be awarded where a person dies before they have been compensated for a tort committed against them.

In **Chapters 10** and **11**, two special liability regimes are considered: occupiers' liability and liability for defective products. They are referred to as 'special' regimes because each of them has some particular rules for establishing liability. However, in relation to remedies they are the same as general negligence. Torts in each of these areas could cause the kinds of harm we have looked at above, and the rules on damages are the same.

Chapter 12 considers nuisance, a tort which deals with interference with land. This tort covers kinds of harm which are different from those that have been considered so far. For example, a claim in nuisance is appropriate where a claimant suffers interference with the use and enjoyment of their land, eg unpleasant smells caused by chemical fumes from the defendant's factory. It might be appropriate for the claimant to seek damages to compensate for the interference. However, damages would not always be enough. The claimant in the above situation would probably also want to stop the defendant from carrying on with the harmful activity. To achieve this they would need to ask the court to grant the remedy of an injunction. The remedy of an injunction is considered in **Chapter 12**.

This chapter concentrates on the remedy of damages.

8.2 Compensatory damages: general principles

8.2.1 The measure of damages

The aim of damages in tort is to put the claimant in the same position they would have been in if the tort had not been committed. For example, if the defendant's negligence caused damage to the claimant's bicycle, the defendant would have to compensate the claimant for that loss either by paying for repairs to the bicycle, or by replacing the bicycle.

In some situations it is relatively easy to comply with this principle. Many of a claimant's losses will be easy to quantify in monetary terms, and by paying the claimant money the defendant will be able to restore the claimant to the position they were in before the wrong was committed. For example, with money, the claimant can repair a car, replace a bicycle and have earnings restored.

However, with personal injuries, the payment of damages would not restore the claimant to his previous position. For example, money cannot mend a broken arm or prevent someone suffering post-traumatic stress disorder. Here the damages received are seen as compensation for the injury.

8.2.2 Mitigation of loss

The guiding principle in assessing damages is that claimants should be put back in the position they were in prior to the wrongdoing having been committed. This means that the claimant should be no worse off because of the occurrence – but also no better off. That is, the claimant should not profit from the incident. This principle also means that claimants cannot claim damages for losses which they could have avoided by taking reasonable steps themselves. This is the duty to mitigate. It means that a claimant must take all reasonable steps to keep the losses he is claiming to a minimum.

In practical terms this means that, for example, the claimant who loses their job because of the defendant's wrongdoing, but who is still capable of working, should look for alternative employment. A claimant who needs a vehicle to earn a living and has had their vehicle destroyed by the defendant's tort should replace the vehicle, either by purchasing an alternative or by hiring one. The principle even extends to seeking medical care. A claimant who unreasonably refused medical treatment would not recover damages for harm which the treatment would have avoided.

8.2.3 The one action rule

A claimant can bring only one claim based on one set of facts. This means that when a court assesses the claimant's damages, it must award a single lump sum to cover both losses already suffered up to the time of trial and losses which the claimant is expected to suffer in the future. Future losses could encompass, for example, continuing pain and suffering and loss of earnings.

A judge has to make an assessment of the claimant's future losses. Once an award of damages has been made, a claimant cannot go back to court with a second claim simply because the injury worsens rather than improves. This can cause difficulties for the claimant, the defendant, and even the judge. For example, it is not always possible to predict accurately how far someone might recover, or what that person might have achieved in life if the accident had not occurred. A limited exception to this rule in the case of provisional damages and periodic payments is considered at **8.3.4** below.

8.2.4 General and special damages

A distinction is drawn between special damages and general damages:

- Special damages – those losses which are capable of being calculated precisely at the time of the trial and which are stated in the form of a calculation. This covers financial losses incurred before trial, such as loss of earnings.

- General damages – those losses which are not capable of being calculated precisely and are therefore left to the court to determine. They must still be stated but no definitive figure can be placed on them. This includes pain, suffering and loss of amenity and all losses incurred after the trial.

8.3 Damages for personal injury

The theory behind damages is considered above. The next matter to consider is the actual damages that a successful claimant in the tort of negligence, who has suffered personal injury, might hope to recover.

In considering how the damages will be calculated it is necessary to divide the losses into the two categories of damages which the courts use in awarding compensation: pecuniary and non-pecuniary losses.

The distinction between the two is:

- Pecuniary losses are those which are capable of mathematical calculation in money terms. These losses may have been suffered pre- or post-trial, but can nevertheless be calculated in terms of money. An example of pecuniary losses would be the claimant's loss of earnings and medical expenses.

- Non-pecuniary losses are not capable of being calculated in money terms. The main example of non-pecuniary losses is the claimant's personal injury.

8.3.1 Non-pecuniary losses

The main example of non-pecuniary losses is the claimant's personal injury which is made up of the claimant's pain and suffering and 'loss of amenity' caused by the injury.

⭐ *Example*

A solicitor acts for a client who has fallen off a ladder and suffered a broken leg caused by the negligence of the defendant.

The information required from the client in order to be able to assess the damages which they should receive as compensation for pain and suffering and 'loss of amenity' includes:

- *Full details of the injury suffered – eg type of fracture?*

- *Medical treatment received – eg was the claimant in hospital? For how long?*

- *Pain and suffering – eg how painful was the injury? How long did the effects last?*

- *Drugs and prescriptions – eg did the claimant need pain-killing drugs? How much relief did they give?*

- *Continuing effects – eg does the claimant still suffer pain from the injury?*

- *Future effects – eg will the claimant continue to suffer pain from the injury? How long is that expected to last? (Medical evidence would be required on this last point, and generally in order to support the client's account of their pain and suffering.)*

- *Are there any activities which the claimant can no longer do, eg playing football, or running over rough ground?*

- *What were the claimant's previous interests which they can no longer enjoy, eg playing sports?*
- *Are there any other detrimental effects of the injury? For example, has the claimant been forced to change to a job which they enjoy less?*

The last set of questions above asked about the effects of the injury on the claimant's enjoyment of life. This is what lawyers call 'loss of amenity'.

Damages for pain and suffering and loss of amenity are considered in more detail below.

8.3.1.1 Pain and suffering

This head of damage covers the pain and suffering which the claimant has incurred as a result of the injury. This head of damage covers past, present and future pain, physical and mental anguish, the fear of future surgery, etc.

It also covers the claimant's anguish of knowing that their life expectancy had been shortened because of the accident (Administration of Justice Act 1982, s 1(1)(b)).

The court needs to assess the claimant's pain and suffering to reach a monetary figure for compensation. In general the court will just give one figure, which includes both pain and suffering and loss of amenity. How a figure is reached is dealt with after consideration of loss of amenity.

However, there is one more point to note on damages for pain and suffering. The case of *Wise v Kaye* [1962] 1 QB 638 establishes a subjective test for awarding a sum for this head of damage. This means that the claimant must be aware of the injuries to be able to claim for pain and suffering. If a claimant was unconscious they would not recover damages for pain and suffering for that period because they would not be aware of it and would fail the subjective test. (However, they would still be able to recover for loss of amenity, as discussed below.)

8.3.1.2 Loss of amenity

This head of damage aims to compensate the claimant for the loss of the enjoyment of life, and it therefore covers a wide area of loss, eg loss of freedom of movement, loss of sight, loss of smell, loss of marriage prospects, inability to pursue hobbies, etc.

It therefore follows that a claimant who was very active prior to the accident will receive more under this head of damage than a claimant who was inactive.

Unlike pain and suffering, the test for this head of damage is an objective test (*West v Shephard* [1964] AC 326), and a claimant will be able to recover under this head whether conscious or not.

8.3.2 Quantification of non-pecuniary damages

There is no easy way to assess the value of, say, the loss of a leg. Such a loss would mean different things to different people, depending on age, sex, hobbies, etc. This means that to assess damages for non-pecuniary loss, the courts have to consider the individual facts of each case.

⭐ Example

A litigation solicitor acts for a personal injury client. They would seek to reach an agreed settlement of the claim if possible. The agreement would be based on the likely amount a court would award for the client's injuries.

In practice, lawyers will turn to the Judicial College Guidelines for the Assessment of General Damages in Personal Injury Cases *and* Kemp and *practitioner texts like* Kemp on Damages, *which contains thousands of cases in which damages have been awarded.*

The lawyer then finds those cases which are most like the one under consideration, to obtain a rough guide to the amount of damages the client may be able to recover for the non-pecuniary heads. Even the best, most experienced litigation lawyers are only able to estimate the amount of damages that a claimant might receive.

Non-pecuniary damages for pain and suffering and loss of amenity are, therefore, general damages, because they are not capable of being calculated precisely.

8.3.3 Pecuniary losses

Pecuniary losses are those which are capable of mathematical calculation in money terms. These losses may have been suffered pre- or post-trial, but can nevertheless be calculated in terms of money.

⭐ *Example*

A solicitor acts for a client who has fallen off a ladder and suffered a broken leg caused by the negligence of the defendant.

The information required from the client in order to be able to assess the damages which they should receive as compensation for their pecuniary losses includes:

- *Was the client absent from work as a result of the accident?*
- *Did they lose wages/receive any sick pay?*
- *Are they still off work?*
- *How long do they expect to be off work? (The solicitor would need medical evidence in support of this.)*
- *Did they incur any medical expenses? For example, the cost of private treatment, prescription charges.*
- *Did they incur any other expenses? For example, extra travel costs, costs of nursing care, costs of special equipment.*
- *For how long will those medical and other expenses continue? (The solicitor would need medical evidence here too.)*

These are all examples of pecuniary losses which the client might suffer. How these losses would be quantified is considered below.

8.3.3.1 Medical expenses

The claimant is able to recover any medical expenses that have been incurred. If the expenses are incurred pre-trial, they will be special damages and are calculated simply by adding together all of the expenses.

If they are to be incurred post-trial, they will be general damages. In this case, the court will base its assessment on the annual cost of treatment and the number of years the treatment is likely to continue.

The claimant can claim for any reasonable medical expenses which result from the accident. Examples might include the cost of wheelchairs, adapting the house, special dietary needs, travelling to and from hospital to receive treatment.

If the claimant has received medical treatment from the National Health Service, generally this will be free of charge. This means that the claimant has not incurred any treatment costs to recover from the defendant. (In some circumstances, the defendant may be required to make a payment towards the costs of NHS medical treatment. However, this does not form part of the claimant's damages.)

A claimant may choose to pay for private medical treatment. The effect of s 2(4) of the Law Reform (Personal Injuries) Act 1948 is that a claimant cannot be found to have failed to mitigate their loss by paying for private treatment rather than obtaining free treatment under the National Health Service.

A claimant can recover the reasonable cost of private medical treatment. However, damages are to compensate the claimant for losses actually suffered. This means that although a claimant can recover private treatment costs which he has actually paid (or intends to pay for future treatment), a claimant who is treated by the NHS free of charge cannot recover what it would have cost them to have private treatment.

8.3.3.2 Loss of earnings pre-trial

Loss of earnings pre-trial are relatively easy to calculate. The guiding principle is to put the claimant back in the position they would have been in if the accident had never happened. For any loss of earnings before the trial, this simply means calculating the net earnings for that period.

As this is a loss suffered before trial, and it is capable of precise mathematical calculation, this element of the award would be special damages.

It is necessary to ascertain net earnings, ie after deduction of tax and national insurance contributions, because claimants should receive as compensation the same sum of money they would have taken home with them if they had been able to work. Another deduction that would be made from the claimant's gross earnings would be any pension contributions which are normally deducted at source from wages.

As the payment should put the claimant back in the same position they would have been in if the accident had never occurred, if the claimant regularly earned overtime or bonuses, these should be included in the calculation. Also any perks of the job which the claimant received, eg a company car, reduced rate mortgage, share options, should be included in the calculation.

8.3.3.3 Loss of earnings post-trial

Loss of earnings post-trial are much more difficult for the court to assess. Since they are after the trial, and are not capable of precise mathematical calculation, they are general damages.

The difficulty for the court is that it must make the assessment at the date of trial. However, it is seeking to determine how much the claimant would have been capable of earning in the future, if the accident had not occurred.

In some cases the claimant will never work again. In other cases the claimant is still working, but earning less than prior to the accident. It is also common for a claimant to need several months (or years) off work to recover, after which he will be able to work again. In each case the court has to assess, at the date of the trial, the future loss to the claimant. The court will award one lump sum to compensate for that future loss. The method by which the court could work out a claimant's future loss of earnings is considered below.

⭐ Example

A client falls off a ladder and loses a leg due to the negligence of the defendant. The client is aged 35. They were employed as a window cleaner. They earned £25,000 per annum. Medical evidence suggests that they will be unable to return to work as a window cleaner.

In order to be able to assess the damages which they should receive as compensation for their future loss of earnings, the questions to consider include:

- *How long did the client have left in their working life? If they would have retired at 60, they would have 25 years left to work.*
- *Should their current earnings of £25,000 per year be used to estimate their loss over 25 years?*
- *Could they do some other kind of work which would give them some earnings?*

This is a simplified example, but it illustrates the issues which can now be considered in more detail.

The court applies a formula to enable it to calculate the future loss of earnings of the claimant. Each of the elements of that formula is examined further below.

Multiplicand

The first step in the process of assessing future loss of earnings is for the court to ascertain the claimant's gross annual loss as at the date of the trial. If the claimant would have had an increase in earnings due to, for example, promotion, and that increase was very likely to happen, the court can take that into account in assessing the amount of the claimant's loss. (However, the salary cannot be increased for the effects of inflation. This is because a claimant can counteract the effects of inflation by investing the lump sum compensation they receive and earning interest.)

From the gross salary the court will deduct tax, national insurance, and pension contributions deducted at source. The resulting figure, the net annual loss, is known as the 'multiplicand'.

Multiplier

The court then needs to calculate for how long the claimant will lose this money – the period of future loss. If the claimant is not expected to work again, this period will be based on the claimant's pre-accident working life expectancy, ie the length of time he would have to work until normal retirement age. This period of time is called the 'multiplier'.

Clearly, if the claimant is expected to be able to return to work at some time in the future, a smaller multiplier will be used, which reflects the period for which they are likely to be off work.

In the example above, the client could have worked for a further 25 years, and could have earned £25,000 per year. These figures could be used to calculate a total figure as:

25 years (the multiplier) x £25,000 (the multiplicand) = £625,000

It is an important principle that damages are to compensate the claimant for loss suffered. The claimant should not end up in a better position than they would have been in if the accident had not occurred. For example, a claimant would be over-compensated, the defendant would argue, if they received their full loss of future earnings at the date of the trial. This is because they would be able to invest that whole lump sum and allow it to earn interest. By contrast, if the claimant received salary monthly, as they did when working, that option of investing and having a return of interest would not be available.

On the other hand, the claimant should not be under-compensated. This would be the case if the interest they receive on their damages does not protect them against the effects of inflation. The rate of interest that a claimant is expected to receive when investing their damages (known as the 'discount rate') is, therefore, a crucial consideration.

The Lord Chancellor exercises powers under the Damages Act 1996 to set the discount rate. The current discount rate is minus 0.25%. The justification behind this figure is that claimants should be treated as risk averse investors. The discount rate mirrors the performance of low risk investments that do not protect against the effects of inflation. The concern is that claimants would be under-compensated by assuming that they would invest in better performing, but riskier, investments.

The court uses actuarial tables, called the Ogden tables, in order to find the correct multiplier. Litigation solicitors therefore use the Ogden tables to find the appropriate multiplier based on the client's age and the rate of interest (the discount rate) it is assumed that the claimant could earn on his lump sum.

Applying the current discount rate of minus 0.25% to the example above demonstrates how a claimant's lump sum will be increased. This is because the multiplier is increased:

$$\text{Multiplier (25.2 years)} \times \text{Multiplicand (£25,000)} = \text{Award for future loss of earnings (£630,000)}.$$

The principle remains that a claimant must not be over-compensated. Therefore, the court needs to take into account what might have happened to the claimant in their future working life. One example could be the possibility that the claimant would be made redundant and so lose their income in any event. The courts refer to possibilities like this as the 'contingencies of life'.

It is important to note, therefore, that the court could reduce the basic multiplier figure (obtained from the client's age and the discount rate as above). It would make this reduction in order to take account of future adverse 'contingencies of life'. For example, would the window cleaner client have been at a particular risk in any event of losing their job and being out of work?

The discussion above considers a relatively simple example of a loss of future earnings. In practice, there may be other matters to be taken into account. For example, it was considered above that the window cleaner client might be able to undertake some other, less profitable work. If that were the case, the calculations would need to take into account the money which they could earn. Also, the example deals with the situation where the claimant will never work again. However, often a claimant is expected to be able to return to work after a period of months or years. The same kind of method as above is used to calculate the claimant's loss for that limited period.

8.3.3.4 Loss of earnings – the lost years

In the example above the client recovered damages on the basis that had it not been for the accident, they would have continued to work up to their normal retirement age. What would happen if the client's injury had been so serious that it reduced their remaining life expectancy?

⭐ Example

A solicitor has a client aged 35. Prior to the accident the client was expecting to work to age 60. They had 25 years left to work. However, the medical evidence shows that now, as a result of their injury, they are likely to live and work for only another five years. The client has lost 20 years' earning capacity. These are the 'lost years'.

The issue to be considered is whether it matters to the client that they have lost those earnings? Does the client need those earnings if they are expected to die?

Clearly, this loss of earnings does matter to the client, because they are likely to have dependants, who will rely on those earnings for support. If no award of damages is made for those earnings during the 'lost years', the claimant will be unable to provide for their dependants (or leave the money by will to someone else). The claimant is not, therefore, fully compensated.

The case of *Pickett v British Rail Engineering* [1980] AC 136 established that claimants whose life expectancy had been shortened by the incident could recover loss of future earnings for lost years.

How should the client's damages for future loss of earnings be calculated in that case? If the method set out above is applied, there is a risk that they will be over-compensated. If the claimant were working normally, they would spend part of their earnings on themselves (for food, clothing, etc). Only the balance of their earnings would be left over to support their family. So, when the loss of earnings figure is calculated for the period after the claimant is expected to die, it is necessary to deduct the amount which the claimant would have spent on themselves from the multiplicand. Only the balance of their earnings should be awarded as damages.

That deduction from the multiplicand is generally set at 25% for a person married with dependent children, and at 33% for those with no dependants. These are average deductions though, and different figures can be argued if the evidence is that a particular claimant would have spent more or less on themselves. It is only relevant to make this deduction where the client's life expectancy has been reduced so that they are expected to die during the period for which damages are calculated.

8.3.3.5 Loss of earnings – children

If a child is injured in an accident, and will never be able to work in the future, there is nothing which prevents the courts awarding a sum for future loss of earnings. However, it is difficult for the courts to assess the correct level of the child's future earnings. If a child is very young at the date of the accident, it is virtually impossible to predict what that child's earnings might have been.

There are many ways in which a child's future loss of earnings might be assessed. One way would be to consider what the child's parents earn and assume the child would reach a similar level. Another approach would be to take the national average earnings and base the child's earnings on those figures. If a child has shown any potential in a particular area of future employment, that could be considered in assessing future loss of earnings.

8.3.3.6 Services provided to the claimant

> ⭐ *Example*
>
> *A solicitor is acting for a client who has been seriously injured. The client is about to be released from hospital to go home. The kind of help and services they might need includes:*
>
> - *help with housework/shopping/gardening/laundry etc;*
> - *nursing care.*

The key question for the injured client will be: Can they recover the cost of these services as part of their damages award?

The law does allow the claimant to recover the cost of services of this kind. This was established in the case of *Schneider v Eisovitch* [1960] 2 QB 430. (The claimant has to be able to show that the need for the services follows from the injury caused by the defendant's negligence.)

It is important to note that the need for services is part of the claimant's damage. The third party, who provides the services, cannot claim the value of the services themselves from the defendant. The third party does not have a cause of action against the defendant. The defendant owed a duty of care to the claimant, not to the third party.

The claimant is able to recover the cost of the services because the claimant is being compensated for their need for care – which was caused by the defendant's tort.

Services might be provided by a professional carer. However, very often, this kind of help might be given freely by relatives who may have had to give up work. A claimant can recover damages for the services they need, and it does not matter who renders these services. It might be a relative, a friend, or a paid professional. However, the identity of the carer might make a difference to how much the claimant can recover for the cost of care.

If a claimant has paid for professional nursing care, they can recover the cost of that care. They must show that the costs were reasonable. That is, that they are in accordance with the usual market rate for such services.

Where the claimant's spouse (or any other relative, etc) has given up paid employment to care for them, the claimant can recover the cost of that care. The way in which that cost should be assessed was decided in *Housecroft v Burnett* [1986] 1 All ER 332. The court held that the starting point was the loss of earnings suffered by the carer. However, the costs could not exceed the commercial rate for providing the services.

8.3.3.7 Loss of earning capacity

Another head of pecuniary loss arises where a claimant is injured, and suffers some continuing disability, but is still able to work. The claimant faces the risk that if they lose their job in the near future, they will be disadvantaged on the job market because of their disability. They may find it very difficult to get employment. Alternatively, they may be able to get some employment but find that it is less well paid.

An award of damages can be made to compensate the claimant for this disadvantage. However, it is very speculative. The judge must be satisfied that there is a real risk of the claimant losing their job. The judge must then try to put a money value on the chance of that happening.

This award is also known as the *Smith v Manchester Corporation* award after the case in which this head of damage was established (*Smith v Manchester Corporation* (1974) 17 KIR 1).

Note that this award is relevant where the claimant is currently still working in their original job. It will not be relevant if the claimant can no longer work at all, or if the claimant has already been forced to move to lower-paid work. In these cases, the claimant will simply make a claim for their loss of future earnings in the normal way, as considered above.

8.3.3.8 Other pecuniary expenses

Claimants can recover for any other pecuniary expenses they have incurred due to the incident. For example, the claimant's property might be damaged in the accident. The claimant could recover such costs as, for example, clothing, jewellery, watches, spectacles, bags, shoes, etc. There is no definitive list of these items. Any reasonable loss incurred by the claimant as a result of the accident can be recovered.

8.3.3.9 Deductions from damages and exceptions

The example of a client who loses a leg and is unable to work has been considered. It is also necessary to examine the following further issues:

- What extra financial support might such a person receive? For example: insurance payments, ill-health pensions, charitable payments and State benefits.
- How should that support be taken into account when damages are calculated?

The general principle that a claimant should not be better off as a result of the accident should be taken into account. This might suggest that such payments could be deducted from the claimant's damages. When calculating past and future loss of earnings the net annual loss figure is used (ie gross annual loss less tax and national insurance contributions). This is to ensure that the claimant is not over-compensated. They should not be in a better position than they would have been if the accident had not happened.

However, as an exception to this general principle, there are some payments which a claimant is allowed to keep in full, even though they are an extra benefit which the claimant has received only because of the accident. Thus the following payments are *not* deducted from the damages which the claimant receives:

- insurance payments;
- ill-health pensions;
- charitable payments. (This would include *ex gratia* payments made by the claimant's employer, provided the employer is not the tortfeasor.)

If these sums were deducted, it would discourage people from protecting themselves by insurance, or from making charitable payments, because the benefit would simply go to the defendant.

In the list of possible sources of support above it was also noted that a claimant might recover State benefits. If the claimant receives State benefits as a result of an accident, some account must be taken of the receipt of these benefits. On the one hand, if no account were taken and damages not reduced, the claimant would be over-compensated. On the other hand, if State benefits reduced the damages which the defendant had to pay, the State would be bearing the costs of the defendant's negligence.

The solution is to deduct relevant benefits from the claimant's damages, and then require the defendant to pay that amount back to the State. This is provided for by the Social Security (Recovery of Benefits) Act 1997.

Under the Act, State benefits can be deducted from only certain kinds of damage suffered by the claimant. The three heads of damage affected by the Act are:

- compensation for lost earnings;
- compensation for cost of care;
- compensation for loss of mobility.

No benefits are deductible from the claim for pain and suffering and loss of amenity.

This is a brief summary. A practitioner in this area would need to study the provisions of the Act (and associated regulations) in much greater detail.

8.3.4 Provisional damages and periodic payments

Damages in personal injury claims are awarded in one lump sum at the date of trial, and this should cover past, present and future losses which the claimant might suffer. This may cause problems as the claimant might be under-compensated. On the other hand, the defendant may be ordered to pay compensation at a level which protects the claimant if their condition deteriorates, although it might be the case that this never happens.

The limited alternatives that exist to the lump sum award system are within two statutory provisions which create limited exceptions to the rule that damages should be awarded once and for all in a single lump sum.

1. Section 32A of the Senior Courts Act 1981 allows for an award of provisional damages.

⭐ Example

Mandeep has a 10% chance of loss of sight in one eye. On the basis that loss of sight in one eye would be worth £30,000, if the court awarded her 10% of this, Mandeep would receive £3,000. However, if Mandeep does lose the sight in her eye, she will be under-compensated by £27,000. If Mandeep does not lose sight in her eye, she will have been over-compensated by £3,000.

So, in this situation, because there is a chance of serious deterioration, a provisional damages award would be appropriate. At the trial, the court will assess damages on the basis that Mandeep will not lose the sight in her eye. The judgment will specifically provide that, in the event that Mandeep does lose the sight in her eye in the future, she will be entitled to further damages.

2. In some circumstances, s 2 Damages Act 1996, allows the court to award damages for personal injury as periodic payments rather than as a lump sum.

8.4 Damages on death

This section considers two separate issues:

- the position if a claimant dies before they have received an award of compensation; and
- the damages that can be recovered where the defendant's negligence causes the claimant's death.

It is necessary to understand some of the terminology used when looking at claims following death.

- Estate – all of the property belonging to the deceased person. This includes land and buildings, and personal possessions such as money, shares, jewellery, cars, etc.
- Will – the document in which a person sets out his wishes as to the distribution of their estate on death.
- Intestate – a person who has died without leaving a will.
- Executors – people appointed under the will to administer the distribution of the estate according to the deceased's wishes.
- Administrators – people who administer the distribution of the estate in an intestacy. They are appointed according to statute.
- Personal representatives – this is a generic term and includes the executors if the deceased left a will, or the administrators in the case of an intestacy.
- Beneficiaries – those persons either named in the will or who satisfy the rules of intestacy and who inherit all or part of the deceased's estate.
- Dependants – those persons for whom the deceased used to provide financially.

8.4.1 The Law Reform (Miscellaneous Provisions) Act 1934

This section considers the situation where a claimant dies before they have received an award of compensation.

A claimant could die because of the defendant's negligence. For example, where the defendant causes a fatal road accident, or where the claimant is seriously injured by the defendant and dies of their injuries some time later.

Alternatively, a claimant might die for some reason which is completely unrelated to their claim against the defendant. For example, where the defendant causes damage to the claimant's car and the claimant later dies of an illness while the claim in respect of the car is still pending.

The rules which deal with the effect of death on the claimant's claim are the same in both cases and are found in the Law Reform (Miscellaneous Provisions) Act 1934 (the 1934 Act).

The 1934 Act does not create any new cause of action. It simply allows existing causes of action to continue after death. Under s 1(1) of the 1934 Act, all causes of action (except claims for defamation and bereavement damages (see **8.4.2**)) survive the death of either the claimant or the defendant. A claim by a claimant survives for the benefit of their estate. A claim against a defendant survives against their estate.

Under the 1934 Act, no account is taken of any money received by the estate as a result of the death. Examples would be the receipt of insurance money payable on death, or a lump sum payment from a pension. Such sums do not reduce the damages claimed by the estate.

Also, any money that the estate has had to pay out because of the death will not be taken into account. Here, the important point is the exception: that reasonable funeral expenses can be claimed, provided they have been paid for by the estate.

The rest of this section concentrates on the position of the deceased claimant.

The deceased claimant

The claim may cover the following:

Non-pecuniary losses

- Pain and suffering and loss of amenity. Naturally, these end at the date of death.

Pecuniary losses

- Damage to property, eg clothes or a car damaged in an accident.
- Medical and other expenses. Naturally, these will end at the date of death.
- Loss of income up to the date of death.

Where the claimant's death has been caused by the defendant's tort, the claim for loss of income under the 1934 Act must end at the date of death. If the deceased claimant leaves dependent relatives, they would be compensated by a claim under the Fatal Accidents Act 1976. This is considered at **8.4.2** below.

The claim is brought by the estate, and damages awarded become part of the estate. This means that if the deceased claimant has left a will, the damages will be distributed under the terms of the will. If the deceased claimant died intestate, the damages will pass under the terms of the intestacy.

In practical terms, the 1934 Act can affect court proceedings against a defendant, where the claimant has died. Firstly, the claimant might die before they have begun any proceedings against the defendant. In that case their personal representative will be entitled to commence a claim on behalf of the claimant's estate. Alternatively, the claimant might die during the proceedings. In other words, the claimant has started proceedings but dies before they are completed. In this case his personal representative will be entitled to continue with the claim on behalf of the estate.

What if the claim has already been settled?

Finally, note one situation in which the 1934 Act will not be relevant.

One application of the 1934 Act is where the claimant's death was caused by the defendant's negligence. However, it is possible that a claimant could already have received damages from the defendant before their death. The claimant could have survived for long enough to commence proceedings and receive an award of damages, or the claim could have been settled.

In those circumstances there would, of course, be no possibility of a claim on behalf of the claimant's estate under the 1934 Act after their death. The claimant in this situation has already been compensated in full.

Furthermore, the damages paid to a claimant in this situation should reflect their reduced life expectancy (ie that they are likely to die as a result of the defendant's negligence). They should therefore recover damages for their 'lost years' earnings, as considered at **8.3.3.4** above. Those damages should then be available to support the claimant's dependants after the claimant's death.

8.4.2 The Fatal Accidents Act 1976

The 1934 Act enables the estate to continue or commence a claim on behalf of a deceased claimant. The estate can claim damages for pain and suffering, loss of earnings, nursing care, property damage, travel expenses, etc, up to the date of death. However, the deceased may well leave behind dependants. The compensation under the 1934 Act does not put these people in the same position they would have been if the accident had never happened.

The Fatal Accidents Act 1976 (the 1976 Act) created a new cause of action as it allows dependants to sue for the death of the person on whom they were dependent. A claim under the 1976 Act is usually commenced by the deceased's personal representatives.

A claim under the 1976 Act is dependent on the original cause of action by the deceased person against the defendant. In order to bring a claim under the 1976 Act claimants have to be able to show that, had the deceased survived, the deceased would have been able to bring a claim against the defendant themselves.

Therefore, the defendant must have committed a tort against the deceased. Any defence which was available to defeat the original claim will also defeat the 1976 Act claim. In the case of the defence of contributory negligence, if the deceased's own damages would have been reduced, damages under the 1976 Act will also be reduced.

The nature of the claim under the 1976 Act can be described as being 'parasitic' upon the original claim by the deceased. It follows from that 'parasitic' nature of the claim that there can be no claim under the 1976 Act – for dependency or bereavement – if the deceased person had already completed their claim and received damages from the defendant before they died. If the deceased has already completed their claim, there is no outstanding cause of action to provide the foundation of a claim under the 1976 Act.

There are three possible claims under the 1976 Act, which are considered below:

- A claim on behalf of dependants for loss of dependency.
- A claim for damages for bereavement – limited to certain persons only.
- A claim for funeral expenses – if paid by the dependants.

8.4.2.1 Loss of dependency

In order to claim damages for loss of dependency, a person must satisfy two requirements:

- they must fall within the class of dependants as listed in the 1976 Act (it includes current and former married spouses/ civil partners, cohabitees who have lived together for at least two years, parents, children, siblings; the list is definitive, so that if a person does not fall within it, they cannot make a claim); and
- they must have been actually financially dependent on the deceased (they must show that they had a reasonable expectation of pecuniary benefit from the deceased).

'Pecuniary benefit' does not simply mean provision of money. Dependants can claim for the cost of replacing services which were provided by the deceased. This would cover, for example, child care, DIY, gardening and housework.

Damages are awarded to compensate for the loss of pecuniary benefits from the deceased. In essence, the court needs to look to the future and assess the future pecuniary benefits which the dependants would have received from the deceased. As considered above, future losses are generally calculated by using a multiplicand-multiplier calculation. Loss of dependency under the 1976 Act is calculated in a similar way.

Calculation of dependency

The multiplicand

The multiplicand is based on the deceased's net annual earnings. However, the court will also take into account the fact that, if the deceased were alive, they would have spent part of those earnings on themselves. So, not all of the deceased's salary would have been available to support their dependants. Therefore, in order to avoid over-compensating the dependants, the deceased's own living expenses will be deducted from their earnings. That will leave a reduced figure available as the basis for the dependency claim.

The conventional deduction is 25% for a married person with children and 33% for a married person without children. Where all of the deceased's children were no longer dependent upon them at the time of death, then the conventional deduction would also be 33%.

The deceased might have contributed to the family's wealth by means other than net annual salary. If so, such other contributions should become part of the multiplicand calculation. The contributions which may be taken into account include:

- perks of the job, eg company car, reduced rate mortgage, reduced shopping bills, cheaper holidays, etc;
- services which were provided to the household which will now have to be paid for, eg gardening, decorating, cooking, cleaning, etc.

The multiplier

In a 1976 Act case the multiplier should be based on the period of loss to the dependant, ie on the period for which the dependency might have continued. Clearly, the longest possible period a dependency could continue would be until the deceased would have ceased to work. In the case of a spouse of a deceased wage earner, it is likely that his period of dependency would continue for this full period – until the deceased ceased to work.

However, if a particular claimant would not be dependent on the deceased for so long, a shorter multiplier should be applied to their claim. So, in the case of a child, the period of dependency would be expected to cease when the child reached the age of 18 or ceased full-time education.

Once the basic period(s) for the multiplier have been calculated, they need to be adjusted – in just the same way as for a living claimant. So, in summary, the multiplier in a 1976 Act case would be calculated by taking the period of dependency that the particular dependant might have on the deceased and then converting that into a multiplier by using the Ogden tables.

Example

The deceased is a married man who, prior to his death, worked full-time. His death was caused by the negligence of his employer. He leaves as dependants:

- his wife; and
- his grandmother.

His grandmother lived rent-free and without bills in a granny flat. The basic calculation for the dependency claim under the 1976 Act would be as follows:

The Multiplicand

For the wife – the deceased's net earnings + value of the perks of his job + value of any services he provided.

LESS money he spent on himself

For the grandmother – what it would cost her to pay rent and her bills, etc.

The Multiplier

For the wife – the multiplier would be based on the balance of the husband's working life (unless there was any evidence that either of them would die before that time).

For the grandmother – the multiplier would be based on her life expectancy. Clearly, this is likely to be less than the wife's period of dependency.

There are two factors which are not taken into account when calculating the value of a claimant's lost dependency:

- damages for a dependant spouse do not take into account their remarriage or prospects of remarriage;
- the fact that dependants are likely to inherit money from the deceased (under a will or on intestacy) is not to be taken into account.

8.4.2.2 Damages for bereavement

The only people who can claim damages for bereavement are:

- the wife, husband or civil partner of the deceased;
- the parents (or mother if illegitimate) of a minor who was never married or a civil partner;
- the cohabiting partner of the deceased, who:
    (a) was living with the deceased in the same household immediately before the date of the death; and
    (b) had been living with the deceased in the same household for at least two years before that date; and
    (c) was living during the whole of that period as the wife or husband or civil partner of the deceased.

The amount of bereavement damages is currently £15,120. This is a fixed sum. It is not in the court's discretion. Only one award of £15,120 will be made in respect of the death. So, where both parents are entitled to claim, the award is split between them.

8.4.2.3 Funeral expenses

The third claim permitted by the 1976 Act is a claim for funeral expenses, where they have been paid by the dependants. (Funeral expenses paid out of the deceased's estate will be claimed under the 1934 Act.)

Summary

A person brings a claim in tort because they are seeking a remedy for the harm they have suffered. A lawyer in practice always has to consider two issues when advising a client:

- Which tort deals with the kind of harm this claimant has suffered, and what does the claimant have to prove to establish a claim?
- What remedy can they expect to obtain?

Previous chapters concentrated on the first of these questions – what the claimant must prove to establish a claim. However, this chapter demonstrates that successfully establishing a claim is only half the story. The most important issue from the client's point of view is usually what remedy they can obtain. This chapter focuses on the award of damages as this is the usual remedy for a claim in tort.

In the context of damages for personal injury, this chapter reviews the principles by which damages are assessed. It has considered the pecuniary elements in an award of damages, such as loss of earnings, and distinguishes these from the non-pecuniary elements, such as pain and suffering.

This chapter also considers the awards of damages which are relevant when the victim of the tort has died. The key distinction is between the claims brought on behalf of the estate under the 1934 Act, and the claims brought by dependants under the 1976 Act.

Summary flowchart

Figure 8.1 Remedies: damages for personal injury flowchart

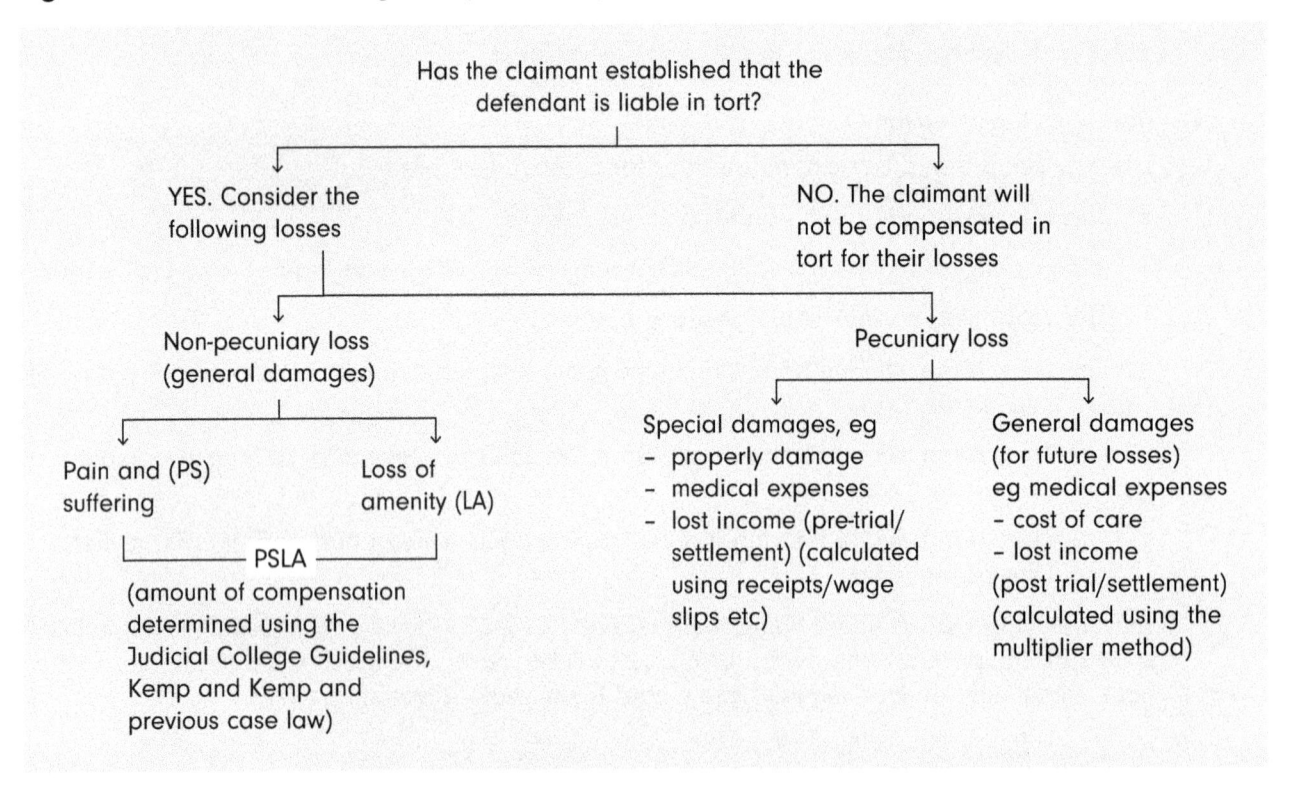

```
Has the claimant established that the
defendant is liable in tort?
            |
    ┌───────┴────────┐
    ▼                ▼
YES. Consider the   NO. The claimant will
following losses    not be compensated in
                    tort for their losses
    |
    ┌───────────────┐
    ▼               ▼
Non-pecuniary loss  Pecuniary loss
(general damages)
    |                   ┌──────────────┬──────────────┐
┌───┴────┐              ▼                              ▼
▼        ▼        Special damages, eg            General damages
Pain and (PS)  Loss of    - properly damage      (for future losses)
suffering     amenity (LA) - medical expenses    eg medical expenses
                           - lost income (pre-trial/  - cost of care
└──── PSLA ────┘             settlement) (calculated  - lost income
(amount of compensation      using receipts/wage      (post trial/settlement)
determined using the         slips etc)               (calculated using the
Judicial College Guidelines,                          multiplier method)
Kemp and Kemp and
previous case law)
```

Principles of Remedies for Personal Injury and Death Claims

Figure 8.2 Remedies: damages on death under the Law Reform (Miscellaneous Provisions) Act 1934

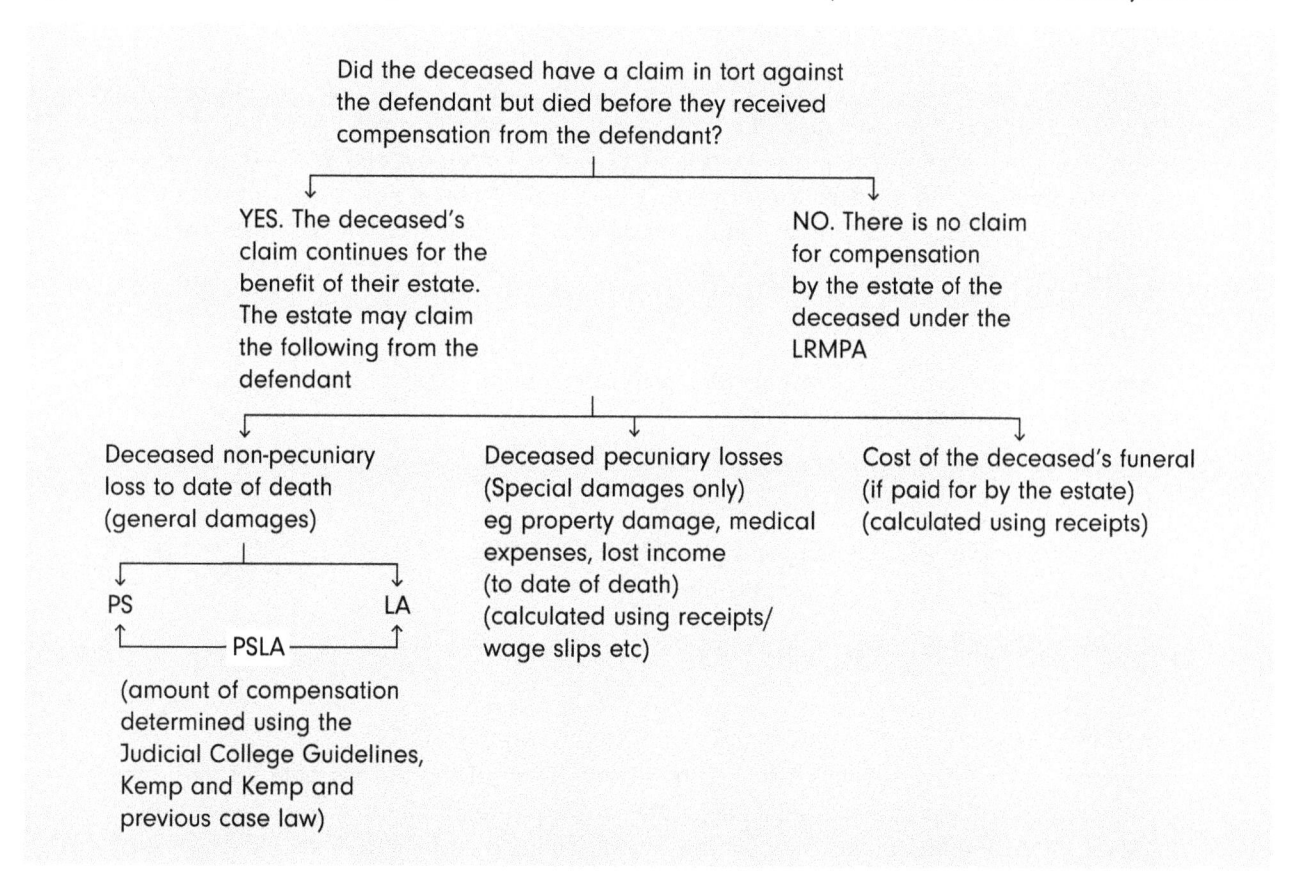

Did the deceased have a claim in tort against the defendant but died before they received compensation from the defendant?

- **YES.** The deceased's claim continues for the benefit of their estate. The estate may claim the following from the defendant
- **NO.** There is no claim for compensation by the estate of the deceased under the LRMPA

Under YES:

- Deceased non-pecuniary loss to date of death (general damages)
  - PS
  - LA
  - —— PSLA ——
  - (amount of compensation determined using the Judicial College Guidelines, Kemp and Kemp and previous case law)
- Deceased pecuniary losses (Special damages only) eg property damage, medical expenses, lost income (to date of death) (calculated using receipts/ wage slips etc)
- Cost of the deceased's funeral (if paid for by the estate) (calculated using receipts)

Figure 8.3 Remedies: damages on death under the Fatal Accidents Act 1976

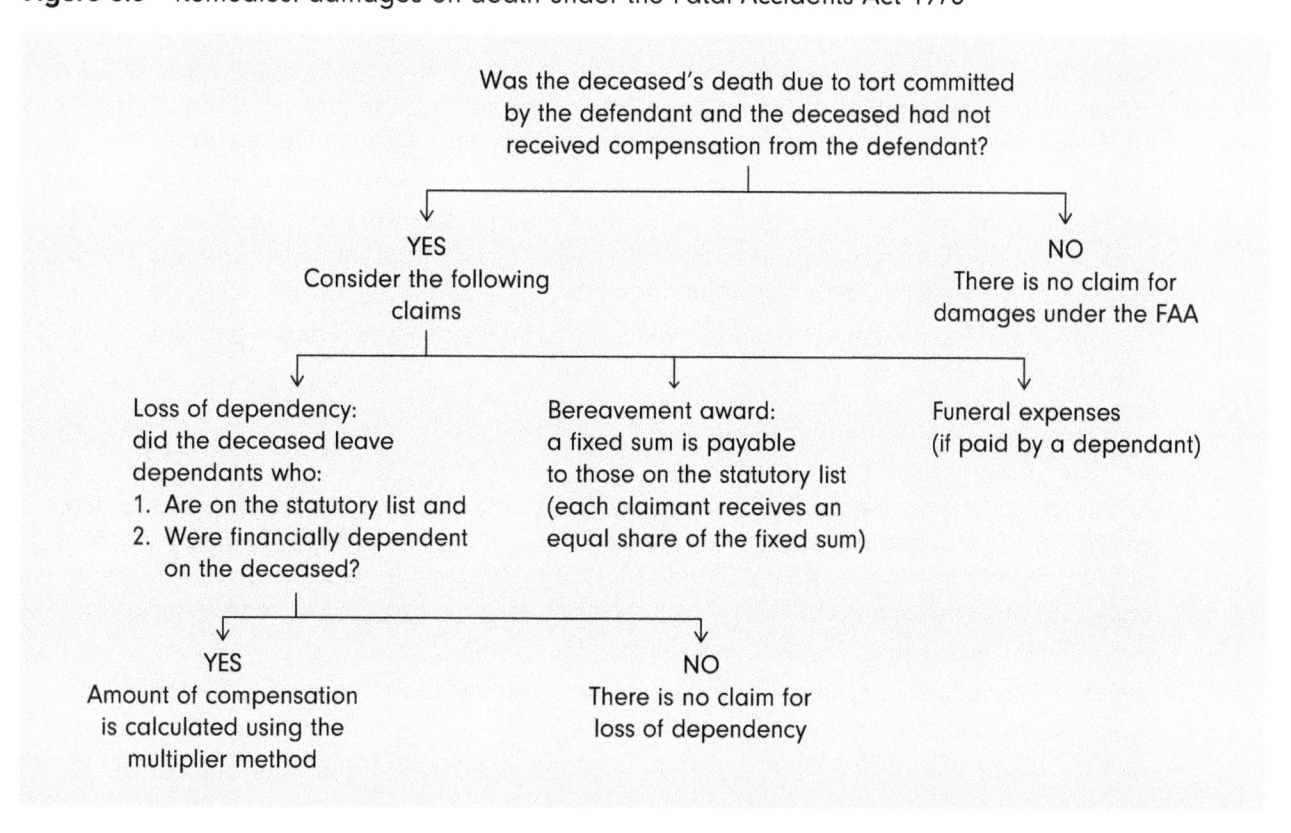

Was the deceased's death due to tort committed by the defendant and the deceased had not received compensation from the defendant?

- **YES** Consider the following claims
- **NO** There is no claim for damages under the FAA

Under YES:

- Loss of dependency: did the deceased leave dependants who:
  1. Are on the statutory list and
  2. Were financially dependent on the deceased?
  - **YES** Amount of compensation is calculated using the multiplier method
  - **NO** There is no claim for loss of dependency
- Bereavement award: a fixed sum is payable to those on the statutory list (each claimant receives an equal share of the fixed sum)
- Funeral expenses (if paid by a dependant)

121

Tort

Sample questions

Question 1

The claimant is a specialist machine tool operator whose hand was crushed in a setting machine. Their employer has admitted liability. The claimant earned £30,000 net prior to the accident with the expectation that they would have been promoted to a position with a salary of £40,000 net. Medical evidence confirms that the claimant will never be able to return to their previous occupation. However, the medical evidence also confirms that they should be able to return to work in a less skilled occupation earning £15,000 net. The claimant is 30 years old and plans to retire at 65.

Which of the following statements best explains how the claimant's claim for future loss of earnings should be calculated?

A   Multiplier (35) x Multiplicand (£25,000 (£40,000 minus £15,000)).

B   Multiplier (35) x Multiplicand (£40,000).

C   Multiplier (35.11) x Multiplicand (£25,000 (£40,000 minus £15,000)).

D   Multiplier (35.11) x Multiplicand (£30,000).

E   Multiplier (35.11) x Multiplicand (£40,000).

Answer

Option C is correct. The multiplier is correct because applying the current discount rate of minus 0.25% will increase the multiplier from 35 (years) to 35.11 using the Ogden tables. (Note, you are not expected to know the actual multiplier, only that it will increase using the current discount rate of minus 0.25%.) The multiplicand is also correct because it takes into account both the claimant's promotion prospects and also the claimant's prospects of doing a less well paid job. The figure of £25,000 is correct as it is the claimant's annual loss of future earnings.

Option A is wrong as the multiplier is based upon the number of years that the claimant will not be able to work in their chosen occupation (here 35 years until they would have retired), but it must be adjusted in accordance with the discount rate using the Ogden tables.

Option B is wrong for the same reason but also because the multiplicand is incorrect. While the multiplicand can be adjusted to take into account the claimant's promotion prospects, it should also take into account the claimant's prospects of doing a less well paid job. This is an aspect of the claimant's duty to mitigate their loss.

Options D and E are incorrect because, while the multiplier is correct, the multiplicands are wrong.

Question 2

A solicitor acts for the estate of a person who was killed when a driver negligently collided into them. The defendant's insurer has admitted liability. The deceased was a single parent of a daughter aged 18 years. The daughter has a place to go to university full-time later in the year. Under the deceased's will they left all of their estate to their daughter. The estate has been valued at £1.5 million.

Which of the following statements best explains whether the deceased's daughter's claim for loss of dependency will be successful?

A   Yes, because the deceased's daughter is on the statutory list of people who can claim.

B   Yes, because the daughter was clearly financially dependent on the deceased.

C   Yes, because the deceased's daughter is on the statutory list of people who can claim and they were clearly financially dependent on the deceased.

D   No, because the daughter is aged 18 and, therefore, an adult.

E   No, because the daughter is due to inherit £1.5 million and cannot, therefore, be said to be financially dependent upon the deceased.

Answer

Option C is correct as it sets out the two criteria that must be satisfied for a successful claim for dependency under the Fatal Accidents Act 1976 – they must be both on the statutory list of people who can claim and be financially dependent on the deceased. The daughter satisfies both criteria as a child of the deceased who was financially dependent on the deceased (see below).

Options A and B are wrong as they do not set out both criteria.

Option D is wrong because, while generally a child's period of dependency ends when they reach the age of 18, it is extended where the child is in, or as here, expected to be in full-time education.

Option E is wrong as any moneys a dependant is due to inherit from the deceased are disregarded under the Fatal Accidents Act 1976.

Question 3

A solicitor acts for the estate of a mother who was negligently killed in a workplace incident. The defendant's insurer has admitted liability. The deceased had a spouse and twin children aged 6 months.

Which of the following statements best explains whether the deceased's children's claim for damages for bereavement will be successful?

A   Yes, the children have clearly suffered sorrow and grief as a result of their mother's death. The amount will be determined by the court.

B   Yes, the children have clearly suffered sorrow and grief as a result of their mother's death. The amount of damages is a fixed sum.

C   Yes, because the children are on the statutory list of people who can claim. However, the damages will be split between the children and the deceased's spouse.

D   No, because the award of damages for bereavement is a matter of the discretion of the court and, because of their age, it cannot be said that the children have suffered sorrow and grief as a result of their mother's death.

E   No, because the children are not on the statutory list of people who can claim.

Answer

Option E is correct: the children will not receive the award because they are not on the statutory list of people who can claim. The spouse will receive the award (in full) as they are on the statutory list.

Option A is wrong because the criteria for a claim is not whether the claimant has suffered sorrow and grief as a result of the death. It is also incorrect that the amount will be determined by the court.

Option B is correct in so far as the award is a fixed sum (currently £15,120), but states the wrong criteria for a claim.

Option C is wrong as children are not on the statutory list of people who can claim. It is incorrect, therefore, that the award would be shared with the deceased's spouse. The spouse would receive the whole award (it is correct that, if there were more than one person who was entitled to the award, it would be split between them).

Option D is wrong because it states the wrong criteria and because the court has no discretion on whether the claimant should receive the award or not.

9 Vicarious Liability

9.1	Introduction	126
9.2	Requirements for vicarious liability	126
9.3	Employer's indemnity	130

SQE1 syllabus

This chapter will enable you to achieve the SQE1 Assessment Specification in relation to Functioning Legal Knowledge concerned with the core principle of vicarious liability in the context of an employer's liability for the torts of their employees.

Note that for SQE1, candidates are not usually required to recall specific case names or cite statutory or regulatory authorities. Cases are provided for illustrative purposes only.

Learning outcomes

By the end of this chapter you will be able to apply relevant core legal principles and rules appropriately and effectively, at the level of a competent newly qualified solicitor in practice, to realistic client-based and ethical problems and situations in the following areas:

- the principle of vicarious liability;
- the requirements to be satisfied for an employer to be vicariously liable for the tort committed by its employee.

9.1 Introduction

Vicarious liability is not a tort; it is a principle under which a person is liable for the torts committed by another. While other, less common, situations of vicarious liability exist, this chapter concentrates on the most common situation of an employer's liability for the action of their employees.

Under the principle of vicarious liability, it is not a requirement that the employer has committed a tort themselves. Their liability is a form of secondary liability in that it derives from a tort committed by their employee.

The employer is liable in addition to (not instead of) its employee. They are jointly liable. This means that a claimant can sue either the employer (as vicariously liable), or the employee (as primarily liable) or both of them (as jointly liable). This is demonstrated by Figure 9.1.

Figure 9.1

```
         Watt & Co (Employer)
            │        ↖
            │          ↘ Ashraf (Injured party)
            ↓        ↙
         James (Employee)
```

⭐ Example

James is employed by Watt & Co in their factory. One day he negligently loses control of the drill he is using to carry out his work, and Ashraf, a fellow employee, is injured.

Ashraf can sue either Watt & Co, or James, or he can sue both of them.

If Watt & Co pay compensation to Ashraf, they may, in certain circumstances, claim this back from James. This is known as a right of indemnity and is considered below.

9.2 Requirements for vicarious liability

The three essential elements for vicarious liability to exist on the part of an employer are:

- The worker must be an employee (or in a relationship akin to employment).
- The employee must have committed a tort.
- The employee's tort must have been committed in the course of his employment.

Before vicarious liability can exist the employee must have committed a tort. This is often negligence, but the employee could have committed any other tort. It is logical to start by considering whether the facts of a case do suggest an underlying tort by the employee. If they do not then there is nothing for the employer to be vicariously liable for. Other chapters consider this second requirement, eg the claimant's claim against the employee in negligence. This chapter concentrates on the other two requirements that are needed for vicarious liability.

9.2.1 Who is an employee?

For vicarious liability to exist, there must be a relationship of employer and employee (or a relationship akin to employment). The important distinction is between an employee (employed under a contract of service) and an independent contractor (employed under a contract for services). This distinction is important because employers cannot be held to be vicariously liable for the acts of independent contractors.

The principal differences between an employee and an independent contractor are, first, that an employee performs a service for just one person (the employer). An independent contractor, on the other hand, provides services to several people. Secondly, an independent contractor is self-employed and therefore is in business on their own account. An employee, on the other hand, receives a wage, but it is the employer who has the business interest.

Factory workers, airline pilots and shop assistants are all examples of employees. Self-employed plumbers, builders and electricians are examples of independent contractors.

In many cases, it will be easy to decide whether a worker is an employee or an independent contractor. However, in marginal cases, it can be a difficult distinction to draw. Over the years, the law has developed a number of tests to try to distinguish employees from independent contractors. The scope of vicarious liability was considered by the Supreme Court in *Various Claimants v Catholic Child Welfare Society and Others* [2012] UKSC 56, which dealt with a relationship akin to employment.

The Supreme Court set out five criteria that are relevant to determine whether there is a relationship of employment or 'akin to employment', such that it may be fair, just and reasonable to impose vicarious liability on an employer:

(i) The employer is more likely to have the means to compensate the victim than the employee and can be expected to have insured against that liability;

(ii) The tort will have been committed as a result of activity being taken by the employee on behalf of the employer;

(iii) The employee's activity is likely to be part of the business activity of the employer;

(iv) The employer, by employing the employee to carry on the activity will have created the risk of the tort being committed by the employee;

(v) The employee will, to a greater or lesser degree, have been under the control of the employer.

The next requirement, which is that the employee must commit a tort in the course of their employment, is considered below.

9.2.2 Employee must act 'in the course of employment'

An employer is vicariously liable for an employee's torts only if they were committed 'in the course of the employee's employment'. This is therefore clearly an important concept, and one which often causes difficulty for the courts.

The classic definition of acts committed in the course of an employee's employment (which the employer may be vicariously liable for) are:

- wrongful acts which it has authorised;
- wrongful and unauthorised modes of carrying out an authorised act.

⭐ Example 1

An off-duty employee pushes away a man he sees trying to steal from his employer's market stall.

It is likely this would be within the course of the employee's employment. This is based on *Poland v Parr* [1926] All ER Rep 177. Here the court felt that as the man was protecting his employer's property, he had implied permission to push away the thief. The employer therefore authorised the tort (battery) the employee committed. In contrast, in *Warren v Henleys Ltd* [1948] 2 All ER 935 an employee, who was insulted by a customer and punched him in the face to retaliate, was not acting in the course of his employment. The retaliation was a personal act not authorised or connected with his employment.

⭐ Example 2

An oil tanker driver decides to have a cigarette while unloading his tank of oil at a garage forecourt. He throws away the match he uses to light the cigarette, which causes a fire.

This is likely to be within the driver's course of employment. He is doing an authorised act (unloading oil) in an unauthorised way (while smoking). This is based on the case of *Century Insurance v NI Road Transport Board* [1942] 1 All ER 491.

⭐ Example 3

An employee in high spirits and larking about loses control of a wheelbarrow he is pushing, which then collides with a colleague injuring him.

Here the employee is doing his job (pushing the wheelbarrow) but in a careless way. This is likely to fall within his course of employment. This scenario is based on the case of *Harrison v Michelin Tyre Co Ltd* [1985] 1 All ER 918.

The classic definition is a good starting point when considering 'course of employment'. However, there are some areas of difficulty which have caused the courts to develop the concept of course of employment beyond the classic explanation, starting with acts which the employer has prohibited.

9.2.3 Acts expressly prohibited by the employer

The classic explanation of 'course of employment' would suggest that acts done in express contravention of a prohibition from an employer would fall outside the employee's course of employment. However, an analysis of the two cases below demonstrates that this is not always true.

> In Rose v Plenty [1976] 1 All ER 97, the defendant milkman was expressly prohibited by his employers from engaging young persons to assist in the performance of his duties. Nonetheless the defendant engaged the 13-year-old claimant to assist in the collection and delivery of milk bottles. The claimant was injured while riding on the back of the milk float due to the defendant's driving.
>
> The Court of Appeal held that the defendant's employer was vicariously liable. The prohibited act was done to further the employer's business (the claimant was helping with the deliveries). Lord Denning stated that in considering whether a prohibited act is within the course of the employment, 'it depends very much on the purpose for which it is done. If it is done for his employer's business, it is usually done in the course of his employment, even though it is a prohibited act'.

If the claimant had not been helping with the deliveries it is likely that, in disobeying the employer's instructions, the milkman would have been acting outside the course of his employment. The prohibited act (giving the claimant a lift) would not then be done to further the employer's business.

> In Twine v Bean's Express (1946) 202 LT 9, a van driver gave a lift to a hitch-hiker despite being prohibited by his employer from giving lifts. The passenger then died in an accident caused by the van driver's negligence. Lord Greene MR, in deciding that the negligence of the driver was outside his course of employment, asked: 'Was the driver, Harrison, in giving a lift to the deceased man acting within the scope of his employment? The answer is clearly, No. He was doing something that he had no right whatsoever to do ...'

In *Twine* the prohibited act did not further the employer's business at all. In contrast, in *Rose v Plenty* the prohibited act did further the employer's business. Cases like *Rose v Plenty* are often referred to as being examples of where the prohibition relates to the manner (or mode) of doing the job rather than determining the scope of the job (as in the *Twine* case).

9.2.4 Intentional torts

Intentionally committed torts are often also criminal acts (eg fraud). The classic definition suggests it is unlikely an employer would be vicariously liable for such acts, as they would neither be authorised acts nor unauthorised ways of doing authorised acts.

Despite this, there are cases where an employer has been found vicariously liable. For example *Lloyd v Grace, Smith & Co* [1912] AC 716, where a conveyancing clerk used his position to fraudulently transfer property into his own name. The court found the fraud stemmed from an act that his employer had authorised him to do (transfer property) and so it fell within his course of employment.

The issue of whether intentionally committed torts can be within an employee's course of employment was considered by the House of Lords in *Lister and others v Hesley Hall Ltd*.

In Lister and others v Hesley Hall Ltd *[2001] 2 All ER 769, the defendant ran a school for boys with emotional and behavioural difficulties. A warden employed by the defendant subjected the claimants to systematic sexual abuse.*

The House of Lords held that an employer can be vicariously liable for an intentional wrongful act committed purely for an employee's own purposes, without any benefit to the employer, where there is a sufficient close connection between the work he had been employed to do and the acts in question. On the facts of the case the warden had been employed to care for children, and there was therefore a sufficient connection between his job and the acts of abuse in question. The sexual assaults had been committed at the employer's premises while the employee was caring for the children in performing his duties.

The requirement for a *close connection* between the work an employee is employed to do and the tort they commit is often referred to as the *Lister* principle.

The Supreme Court in *Mohamud v WM Morrison Supermarkets plc* [2016] UKSC 11 provided guidance on the *Lister* principle. First, the court must ask what function or field of activities has been entrusted by the employer to the employee (ie what was the nature of their job). Secondly, the court must decide whether there was a sufficient connection between the position in which they were employed and their wrongful conduct to make it fair and just for the employer to be held liable.

9.2.5 'Frolic' cases

If an employee is acting outside of their course of employment when they commit a tort, they are often said to be 'on a frolic of their own'. Many of the cases concern employees whose work involves driving and who commit a tort while deviating from the route authorised by their employers.

✪ Example 1

Amy is employed to deliver garden furniture to customers of Gardenware Ltd. Between her second and third deliveries of the day, Amy departs from what would be the normal route and an accident occurs due to her negligent driving.

The factors that will be relevant in determining whether Amy is 'on a frolic of her own' at the time of the accident include:

- *The extent to which Amy has deviated from her authorised route. Is it a major departure (a new journey), or just a minor detour (a new route)?*

- *The purpose of her departure from the authorised route. If she was still going about her employer's business at the time of the accident, she will not be 'on a frolic of her own'.*

⭐ Example 2

Having made the morning's deliveries, instead of reporting back to his employer's premises to collect further deliveries, a van driver sets off in the opposite direction to visit a relative in hospital.

The employee cannot be said to be going about his employer's business. The employee is not doing anything he was employed to do.

⭐ Example 3

A sales representative drives three miles off his route to get some lunch.

Stopping for lunch is reasonably incidental to the employee's work.

Therefore, it will be a question of degree in each case whether an employee's departure from their authorised route is sufficient to put them 'on a frolic of their own' and consequently outside the course of their employment. This involves considering two issues – geographical divergence and departure from the task set. The greater the degree of departure from one or both of these, the more likely it is that an employee will be 'on a frolic of their own'.

The section below considers the position of an employer who has been found vicariously liable and who has had to pay damages to someone as a result.

9.3 Employer's indemnity

Where an employer (or usually the employer's insurers) has paid out compensation to someone, having been found vicariously liable, the case of *Lister v Romford Ice & Cold Storage Co Ltd* [1957] 1 All ER 125 is authority for the fact that the employer has a right at common law to claim an indemnity (ie its full loss) from the employee who actually committed the tort. The employer and employee are jointly liable, and because of this there is also now a similar right contained within the Civil Liability (Contribution) Act 1978.

However, employers' liability insurers have entered into an informal agreement not to pursue such claims for an indemnity unless there is evidence of collusion or wilful misconduct on the part of an employee.

Summary

Vicarious liability is an important principle in practice as frequently claims are brought against an employer for torts committed by its employees. The concept of 'course of employment' is crucial because it determines the scope of an employer's vicarious liability.

It is important to be able to understand the overlaps and differences between a claim by an employee against their employer in negligence and a claim against the employer using vicarious liability. (The personal duty of care owed by an employer to its employees is considered in **Chapter 6**.)

Summary flowchart

Figure 9.2 Vicarious liability

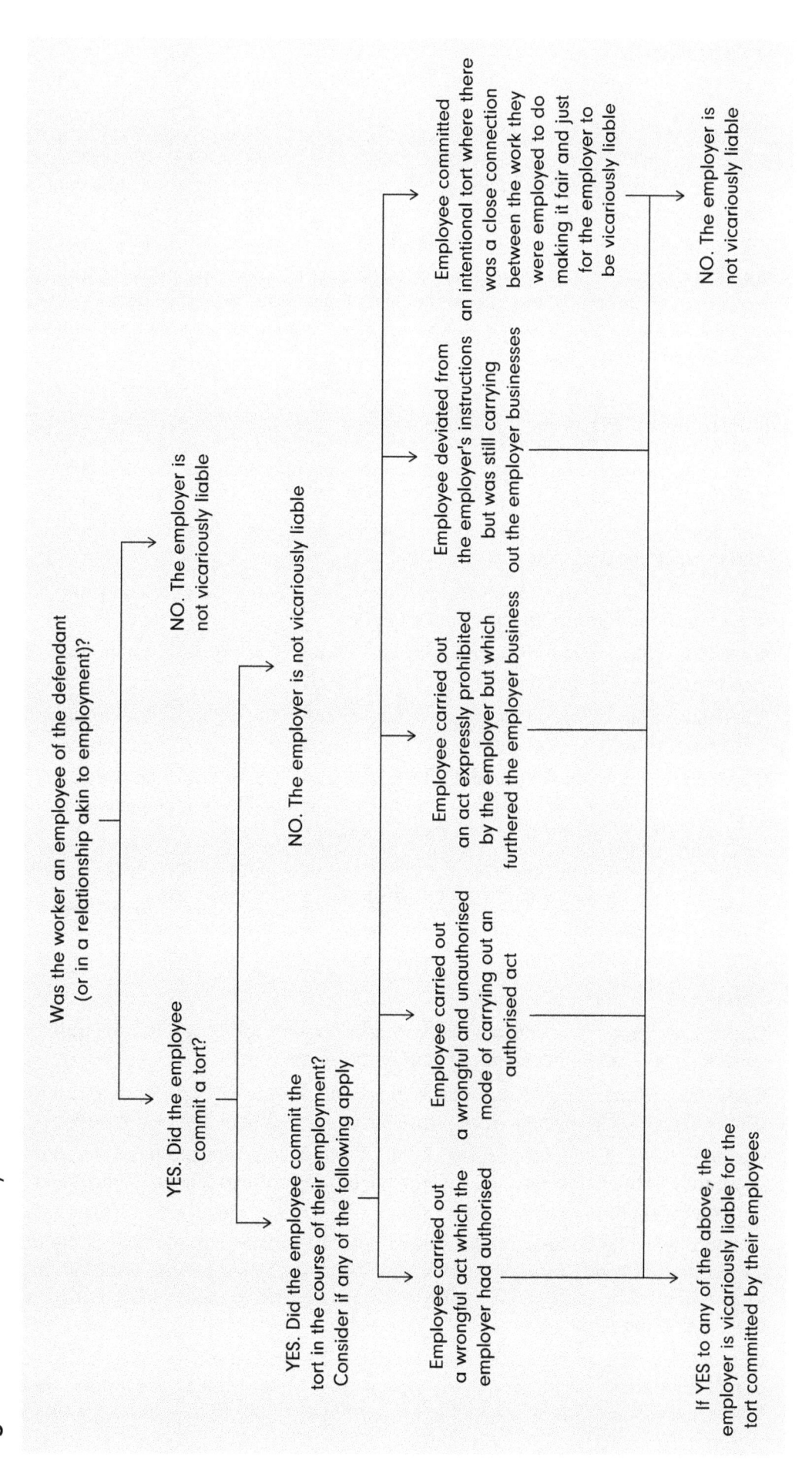

Was the worker an employee of the defendant (or in a relationship akin to employment)?

→ NO. The employer is not vicariously liable

YES. Did the employee commit a tort?

→ NO. The employer is not vicariously liable

YES. Did the employee commit the tort in the course of their employment? Consider if any of the following apply

- Employee carried out a wrongful act which the employer had authorised
- Employee carried out a wrongful and unauthorised mode of carrying out an authorised act
- Employee carried out an act expressly prohibited by the employer but which furthered the employer business
- Employee deviated from the employer's instructions but was still carrying out the employer businesses
- Employee committed an intentional tort where there was a close connection between the work they were employed to do making it fair and just for the employer to be vicariously liable

If YES to any of the above, the employer is vicariously liable for the tort committed by their employees

NO. The employer is not vicariously liable

Tort

Sample questions

Question 1

A solicitor's client is an employee of a plastics company and worked in its factory as an operator of a machine that makes plastic cups. The plastics company has contracted with a maintenance company for the maintenance of its plant and equipment.

The maintenance company had installed a fence to guard the dangerous moving parts on the plastic cup machine. When the client first began to use the machine, they discovered that the safety guard could easily be moved to one side. The client developed the habit of moving the safety guard to one side when they were working on the machine because they could work more quickly.

Another employee, the supervisor in charge of the client's work, had noticed this practice. At first the supervisor told the client that they must only use the machine with the fence in place. However, the client ignored this instruction and continued to move the fence. Eventually, the supervisor gave up ordering the client to replace the fence when using the machine.

One day the client caught their hand in the machine and suffered severe injury, necessitating the amputation of their hand.

Which of the following statements best explains why the plastics company may be held to be vicariously liable for the client's injuries?

A   Because the maintenance company was negligent in carrying out the task of maintaining the equipment.

B   Because the plastics company was negligent by breaching its duty to provide a safe system of work.

C   Because the supervisor breached the duty of care they owed the client. This breach caused a loss to the client that was not too remote. This employee was therefore negligent during the course of their employment.

D   Because, while the supervisor breached the duty of care they owed the client, the supervisor is unlikely to have the funds to compensate the client.

E   Because the plastics company is insured to cover the client's loss.

Answer

Option C is correct as it sets out all three requirements for vicarious liability, ie an employee must commit a tort in the course of their employment.

Option A is wrong because the maintenance company is an independent contractor. Employers can only be held vicariously liable for the acts of their employees.

Option B is wrong because it sets out one of the reasons why the plastics company may be personally liable to the client in negligence. It does not explain why it may also be held to be vicariously liable.

Option D is wrong because, while it does partially explain one element of the requirement for vicarious liability (a tort must have been committed), it does not deal with all three of the requirements. The fact that the supervisor may not have the funds to compensate the client is irrelevant to the legal issue.

Option E is wrong for similar reasons to option D – while the availability of insurance may be one of the general justifications for the principle of vicarious liability, it does not explain why the plastics company may be held to be vicariously liable to this particular claimant.

Question 2

A solicitor is instructed by an employee of a company which wishes to commence a claim for damages for a personal injury they suffered while at work. The company supplies and erects scaffolding for the construction of buildings.

The company's Operations Manager carried out a training session with all employees to remind them of the safe methods to be used when dismantling and lowering the scaffolding to the ground.

However, after this training some employees still often dropped pieces of scaffolding down to other employees while dismantling the scaffolding. They usually made sure the other employees were looking up at them at the time. Another employee who was the client's supervisor was aware of this practice but ignored it even though it was contrary to the Manager's training. They did this because the practice saved time and, therefore, money.

The client's injuries occurred when a fellow employee was dismantling scaffolding and dropped a large pole from above and it struck the client heavily.

Which of the following statements best explains whether the scaffolding company will be vicariously liable for the injury to the client?

A No, because the company trained their employees in the safe method of dismantling and lowering the scaffolding and was not, therefore, at fault in any way.

B No, because the supervisor and the fellow employee were acting outside of the course of their employment by acting contrary to their express instructions.

C Yes, because the actions of the supervisor and the fellow employee benefitted the company's business.

D Yes, because the negligent actions of the supervisor and the fellow employee benefitted the company's business.

E Yes, because the actions of the supervisor and the fellow employee were clearly negligent.

Answer

Option D is correct as it sets out the full reason why the company would be vicariously liable for the client's injury. The supervisor and the fellow employee have both been negligent and, while they were acting contrary to their express instructions, they were still acting in the course of their employment because their negligent actions furthered their employer's business ('they did this because the practice saved time and, therefore, money').

Option A is wrong because the imposition of vicarious liability does not depend upon the employer having been at fault in any way. It is irrelevant for vicarious liability whether the company may or may not have breached their personal duty of care to the client by ensuring training took place.

Option B is wrong because employees can still be held to be acting within the course of their employment even if they act in a way that is contrary to their express instructions.

Options C and E are wrong because they only correctly state some elements of the requirements for vicarious liability (option C, that an employee who acts contrary to their express instructions will nevertheless be acting in the course of their employment if their actions further the employer's business, and option E, that the employee must have committed a tort).

Tort

Question 3

A solicitor is instructed by a supermarket in relation to a claim for damages for personal injury that one of its customers is bringing against it.

One of the supermarket's employees was employed to collect up shopping trolleys from the supermarket car park. As the employee was pushing a long row of trolleys they lost control of them. They crashed into a car owned by the customer's daughter.

The customer of the supermarket witnessed these events. They went to the store supervisor and reported what they had seen, making it clear that the accident was the employee's fault. The employee overheard this conversation and became very angry. As the customer left the store the employee followed them out and attacked them in the car park. The employee pushed the customer violently causing them to fall to the floor and then kicked him, breaking the customer's wrist.

Which of the following statements best explains whether the supermarket will be vicariously liable for the injury to the customer?

A Yes, because the employee committed a tort during the course of their employment; there was a sufficiently close connection between the employee's job and the tort they committed.

B Yes, because the employee committed a tort during the course of their employment; there was a sufficiently close connection between the employee's job and the tort they committed to make it fair and just for the employer to be held liable for the employee's actions.

C No, because, while the employee committed the tort during the course of their employment, the employee's actions were intentional and employers can only be held vicariously liable for the negligent acts of their employees.

D No, because the employee committed an intentional tort which did not benefit the employer's business and it would not be fair or just to impose liability on the employer.

E No, because, while the employee committed the tort during the course of their employment, it would not be fair or just to hold the employer vicariously liable for an act which did not benefit the employer's business.

Answer

Option B is the correct answer as it sets out all the elements that are required before an employer will be held vicariously liable for the intentional acts of their employees.

Option A is wrong as it omits the element of the 'course of employment' requirement that it must be fair and just to impose liability on the employer.

Option C is wrong because an employer will be held liable for *any* torts committed by their employees during the course of their employment. This includes intentional torts (in this case, the tort of trespass to the person).

Option D is wrong because it is not a requirement that the tort must benefit the employer's business. Employers can be vicariously liable for employees' intentional torts that only benefit the employees as long as the tort is carried out during the course of their employment.

Option E is wrong for the same reason as option D. In addition, if the employee *did* act in the course of their employment, then it will have been decided that it was fair and just to impose liability on the employer as this is an element of the course of employment requirement.

10 Occupiers' Liability

10.1	Introduction	136
10.2	Liability of occupiers to visitors	136
10.3	Liability of occupiers to trespassers	144

SQE1 syllabus

This chapter will enable you to achieve the SQE1 Assessment Specification in relation to Functioning Legal Knowledge concerned with the core principles of the law regulating occupiers' liability for losses which occur on their premises.

Note that for SQE1, candidates are not usually required to recall specific case names or cite statutory or regulatory authorities. Cases are provided for illustrative purposes only.

Learning outcomes

By the end of this chapter you will be able to apply relevant core legal principles and rules appropriately and effectively, at the level of a competent newly qualified solicitor in practice, to realistic client-based and ethical problems and situations in the following areas:

- the claim a visitor may bring against an occupier of premises under the Occupiers' Liability Act 1957;
- the claim a trespasser may bring against an occupier of premises under the Occupiers' Liability Act 1984.

10.1 Introduction

'Occupiers' liability' is sometimes referred to as a 'special liability' regime because statutory regulation combines with common law negligence to produce a package of obligations imposed on, in this case, the occupier of premises. Although claims against occupiers are brought within the framework of negligence, statute (namely the Occupiers' Liability Act 1957 (the 1957 Act) and the Occupiers' Liability Act 1984 (the 1984 Act)) has intervened to provide some of the applicable law. The 1957 Act governs an occupier's duties to 'visitors', and the 1984 Act governs an occupier's duties to others (mostly trespassers).

10.2 Liability of occupiers to visitors

Someone seeking to prove an occupier's liability to a visitor must establish a number of important factors. To fall within the 1957 Act a claimant would need to:

- establish that they have suffered loss due to the state of the premises;
- identify the occupier;
- prove that they are a visitor;
- establish that the occupier failed to take reasonable care for the visitor's safety.

The next section considers who would constitute an occupier for these purposes.

10.2.1 Who is an occupier?

Under both the 1957 and 1984 Acts, the duties owed are imposed on the 'occupier' of the premises. Neither Act provides a definition of an occupier. It is necessary, therefore, to look at case law for assistance.

> In the case of Wheat v E Lacon & Co Ltd [1966] 1 All ER 582, the managers of a public house were allowed by the defendants, the owners, to take paying visitors, who were accommodated in part of the premises labelled 'Private' of which the managers were the licensees. The claimant's husband, while a paying visitor, was killed by a fall from a staircase on the 'private' part.

The case establishes that the most important characteristic of an occupier is the element of control they have over the premises. An occupier is defined as someone who has 'a sufficient degree of control over premises'.

Given that the test is one of control, someone who is not an owner of the premises can still have sufficient control over them to be an 'occupier' for the purposes of the Acts. In *Wheat v E Lacon & Co Ltd*, the managers of the pub were only lodgers in the rooms above, and yet they were found to be occupiers for the purposes of the 1957 Act.

Where a landlord lets flats in a block, but retains control of the common staircase, the landlord will be regarded as 'occupier' of that staircase. The landlord will have sufficient control over the common staircase to be an 'occupier' of it.

There can be more than one occupier of the same premises, as *Wheat v E Lacon & Co Ltd* illustrates. Both the defendants (the brewery company) and the managers were held to be occupiers of the relevant part of the premises where the accident occurred.

An independent contractor, working on another person's premises, could also constitute an 'occupier' while on the premises (along with the owner of the premises), having the required degree of control over the area where it is working.

To summarise, therefore, the definition of an 'occupier' is widely interpreted, and the test which the courts will apply is one of occupational control. However, the control need not be exclusive – there may be more than one occupier of the same premises, eg contractors undertaking a large building development would be occupiers for the duration of the building work. Whether a contractor, like a decorator painting a house, would have sufficient control to constitute an 'occupier', would be a question of degree.

10.2.2 Who is a 'visitor'?

The 1957 Act imposes a duty on occupiers towards their 'visitors'. Under the 1957 Act, visitors are those persons who have express or implied permission to be on the occupier's land. For the avoidance of doubt, the 1957 Act makes it clear that this includes persons who enter under the terms of a contract and persons who enter in order to exercise any right conferred by law.

A visitor who exceeds his express or implied permission becomes a trespasser and will potentially fall under the Occupiers' Liability Act 1984, which deals with entrants who do not have permission.

> ### ✪ Example 1
>
> Guests who are invited to dinner by a friend.
>
> The dinner guests are lawful visitors because they have the occupier's express permission to be on the premises.
>
> ### ✪ Example 2
>
> A sales representative who walks up the front drive to a house, ignoring a large sign at the gate which states: 'No canvassers or salespeople please.'
>
> A person who enters to communicate with the occupier normally has the occupier's implied permission to enter. However, the occupier here has revoked permission by displaying the sign at the gate. The sales representative is, therefore, a trespasser.
>
> ### ✪ Example 3
>
> A hotel guest who enters a door marked 'Staff Only'.
>
> The hotel guest has exceeded the occupier's permission by entering a part of the premises where they are expressly forbidden to go. The hotel guest is, therefore, a trespasser when entering the door.
>
> ### ✪ Example 4
>
> A police officer who enters premises to conduct a search. They have a valid search warrant.
>
> The police officer is a visitor under the 1957 Act if they enter in the exercise of a right conferred by law.
>
> ### ✪ Example 5
>
> A customer in a shop who goes behind the counter to steal from the till.
>
> In going behind the counter, the customer has exceeded the occupier's permission. The occupier's permission extends neither to this part of the shop nor to this purpose.
>
> ### ✪ Example 6
>
> A teenager who has managed to see a film at a cinema without paying.
>
> The teenager is a trespasser because the occupier has permitted the teenager to be on the premises only if they have paid the entrance fee.

In some of these cases (eg Example 5) the entrant would start as a visitor, and therefore fall within the 1957 Act. Once they exceed their permission their status would change. If loss or injury resulted, any claim would then need to be brought under the 1984 Act.

10.2.3 Premises

The definition of premises under the 1957 Act is very wide. It includes open land as well as fixed or moveable structures. It also specifically includes vessels, vehicles or aircraft.

10.2.4 The common duty of care

The duty owed by an occupier to visitors under the 1957 Act is called the 'common duty of care'. (Note that this is because the duty is the same for all visitors and not a reference to the common law.)

The duty is to take such care as is reasonable in all the circumstances to see that the visitor is reasonably safe in using the premises for the purpose for which they are permitted to be there. You should note that the duty is directed towards the visitor's reasonable safety rather than towards the safety of the premises.

10.2.5 Breach of the common duty of care

The occupier owes the visitor the 'common duty of care', ie to take such care as is 'reasonable'. This means that the standard of care expected of an occupier is the same as that in an ordinary claim in negligence, ie an occupier must reach the standard of the reasonable occupier and will, therefore, be in breach of duty if they have failed to reach this standard. All the circumstances of the case must be considered in deciding what 'reasonable care' is.

Given the similarity with a claim in negligence, a court will take into account similar factors when assessing the standard of care expected of the 'reasonable occupier'. These factors include:

- nature of the danger;
- purpose of visit;
- seriousness of injury risked;
- magnitude of risk;
- cost and practicability of steps required to avoid the danger;
- how long the danger had been on the premises;
- any warning of the danger;
- type of visitor.

The type/nature of the visitor is specifically mentioned in the 1957 Act as a factor which is relevant in determining the standard of care expected of an occupier. In addition, the 1957 Act singles out two types of visitor for 'special' treatment.

Child visitors are singled out as requiring a higher degree of care from the occupier than other visitors. They cannot be expected to appreciate dangers which would be obvious to an adult. (This is, of course, also true in negligence claims.)

The other category of special visitor singled out by the 1957 Act is visitors coming onto the premises to exercise their skills. The effect of the 1957 Act is that in the case of skilled visitors, an occupier can reasonably expect them to appreciate and guard against any risks which are part and parcel of their job. This has the effect of lowering the standard of care expected of the occupier in relation to such visitors.

The next two sections consider these special categories of visitor in more detail.

10.2.5.1 Children

An occupier must be prepared for children to be less careful than adults. In some situations involving children there are other specific considerations which may be relevant in assessing the standard of care. The role of 'allurements' and parental responsibility are considered in the cases below.

In Glasgow Corporation v Taylor [1922] 1 AC 44, the father of a boy, aged 7, who died from eating the berries of a poisonous shrub growing in some public gardens in Glasgow, sued the Corporation as the proprietors and custodians of the gardens for damages for the death of his son. The father argued that the defendant knew that the berries were a deadly poison, but took no precautions to warn children of the danger of picking the berries of the shrub or to prevent them from doing so; and that there was no adequate notice in the gardens warning the public of the dangerous character of the shrubs.

The court held that the poisonous berries represented a concealed danger to a 7-year-old. It was decided that, because the shrub was a temptation ('allurement') to such a young child, the occupier should have taken additional precautions. The defendant should have adequately warned of the danger, or fenced off the shrub.

The standard of care would have been lower as regards an adult, who would be expected to be aware of the dangers posed by red berries from an unidentified shrub. As a result, the occupier might not have been in breach of duty as regards an adult.

Where the danger is an allurement, an occupier must therefore do even more to safeguard a child's safety than where it is not. This has the effect of further increasing the standard of care.

In the case of very young children, even the most innocuous objects can represent a potential danger. However, the courts have considered that parental responsibility can reduce or eliminate the liability of occupiers for the harm suffered to very young children.

In Phipps v Rochester Corporation [1955] 1 QB 450, a boy, aged five, while out blackberry picking with his sister, aged seven, walked across a large open space of grassland, part of a building site on which a housing estate was being developed by the defendants. A long deep trench had been dug in the grassland for the purpose of laying a sewer. The boy fell in the trench and broke his leg. The children lived, with their parents, in a house in a road adjacent to the open grassland. Children were in the habit of using the land, and the defendants had taken no steps to prevent them from so doing, but there was no evidence that little children frequently went there unaccompanied.

The court held that the crucial issue was the boy's age and the role of parental responsibility. On the facts it was held that a prudent parent would not have allowed two small children to go alone to the building site. The defendant corporation was entitled to assume that parents would not behave in this way and, therefore, the corporation escaped liability as it had reached the standard to be expected of a reasonable occupier in all the circumstances (ie the premises would have been reasonably safe for a very young child accompanied by an adult).

The principle laid down in the *Phipps* case is important. Occupiers will have complied with their duty to a very young child visitor if they make their premises reasonably safe for a child who is accompanied by the sort of guardian by whom the occupier is entitled, in all the circumstances, to expect the child to be accompanied.

10.2.5.2 Skilled visitors

In the case of skilled visitors, the occupier's duty is modified slightly by the 1957 Act, in that the occupier is entitled to expect such a visitor to appreciate and guard against any special risks which are part of the visitor's job.

⭐ *Example 1*

Woyjeck, a window cleaner, is injured in a fall while cleaning the outside of Harriet's windows. A window handle, which he is using to support himself, is loose and comes off in his hand.

The risk of such a fall was a special risk ordinarily incidental to the work of a window cleaner. Harriet could, therefore, reasonably expect Woyjeck to appreciate and guard against such a danger.

⭐ *Example 2*

James, a window cleaner, is injured on a defective stair when going upstairs in Harriet's house to clean the inside of her windows.

In this situation, the relevant risk is not one that is ordinarily incidental to the job of a window cleaner and, therefore, the occupier is not entitled to expect such a visitor to appreciate and guard against it.

10.2.5.3 Escaping breach by warnings

An adequate warning will mean that the occupier has complied with their common duty of care. The occupier will not, therefore, be in breach of duty. However, to have this effect, the warning must be 'adequate'.

The mere fact that a warning was given will not necessarily suffice to enable the occupier to escape liability. The crucial issue is whether the warning given by the occupier was sufficient to enable the visitor to be reasonably safe. This will be a question of fact.

The most important factors for a court to consider in deciding the adequacy or otherwise of a warning are:

- The nature of the warning, ie how specific it was. Did it actually mention by name the relevant danger, or was it just a general warning? For example, compare 'Danger – Slippery Floor' with 'Danger'. The former type of warning is more likely to be adequate than the latter.
- The nature of the danger, ie whether it was a hidden or an obvious danger. If a hidden danger, the warning will need to be more specific. A general warning (eg 'Danger') is unlikely to be adequate in such a case.
- The type of visitor, ie whether the injured visitor is an adult or a child. A written warning to a child may not be enough to enable him or her to be reasonably safe.

⭐ *Example 1*

Alice owns an old stately home which she opens to the public during the summer months.

The steps leading down to the dungeons are steep and slippery, and there is no handrail. A warning notice is displayed at the top of the steps stating 'Danger'. Bill, an American tourist, slips on a step and is injured when he falls.

The warning should have been more specific as to the nature of the danger. Given the lack of any handrail, it was not sufficient to enable Bill to be reasonably safe. (Even if the warning had mentioned the particular danger, it probably would not have enabled Bill to be reasonably safe due to the absence of the handrail in any event.)

⭐ *Example 2*

Boris, a Russian tourist, is injured in the armoury room of Alice's stately home when he touches a display of armour and it falls on him. A notice by the display reads 'Do not touch'.

The notice does not expressly warn of any danger. It is simply an instruction to visitors. Even if the notice had contained a warning, could Boris read English? If not then, without a translation, the notice would not allow Boris to be reasonably safe, no matter how clearly expressed in English.

As Alice opens her stately home to the public then the first question is whether she should reasonably anticipate Russian tourists who cannot read English. The answer has to be yes. So having only a written notice in English might not be sufficient. This does not necessarily mean that the occupier must have a warning in every language, but if it was in all the major languages then reasonable care might have been taken. More likely the occupier would have a picture/illustration that warns about touching the exhibits (a hand with a cross through it etc); or a physical barrier (a rope around truly dangerous exhibits).

⭐ Example 3

Doris visits the ladies' toilets of Alice's stately home and is scalded by the water from the hot tap when washing her hands. There is a sign on each washbasin clearly stating 'DANGER VERY HOT WATER'. Although Doris noticed the sign, she could not be bothered to put on her reading glasses, and therefore could not read what it said.

The warning would appear to be adequate. Doris, having seen the sign, should have put on her glasses to read what it said. Had she done so, she would have been safe. The warning was, therefore, sufficient to enable her to be reasonably safe.

An adequate warning of a danger will enable an occupier to escape liability to a visitor injured by the danger. However, an occupier need not warn of every danger – for example, there is no obligation to warn of a danger which would be obvious to the particular visitor (eg the danger of drowning in a pond would be obvious to an adult visitor).

It is necessary to distinguish between a warning notice on the one hand, and a notice which purports to restrict or exclude an occupier's liability on the other. Consider the two notices below, both of which relate to refurbishment work which is taking place in a hotel.

⭐ Example 1

'The management accepts no liability for any injury or loss sustained by a visitor as a result of the current refurbishment of the hotel lobby.'

⭐ Example 2

'Notice to all visitors. The lobby of the hotel is currently being refurbished. We request you to take extra care when crossing the lobby as the floor may be rough and uneven.'

The notice in Example 1 is an exclusion notice; the notice in Example 2 is a warning notice. The significance of this distinction is that an occupier may comply with their common duty to a visitor by a warning notice. In such a case the visitor will be unable to prove breach of duty. In contrast, an exclusion notice may operate as a potential defence to a claim once the visitor has established breach of the common duty of care. Exclusion notices are considered in the section covering defences below.

10.2.5.4 Independent contractors

Often an occupier may engage an independent contractor (such as an electrician) to carry out work on the occupier's premises. In such cases, provided the occupier satisfies the three requirements to be found in the 1957 Act, the occupier will have discharged their common duty of care. If injury then results from the faulty workmanship of the contractor, the occupier is not liable (instead the visitor must look to the contractor for recompense).

The three requirements under the 1957 Act are, if in all the circumstances, the occupier had acted reasonably in:

- entrusting the work to an independent contractor; and
- had taken such steps (if any) as they reasonably ought in order to satisfy themselves that the contractor was competent; and

- had taken such steps (if any) as they reasonably ought in order to satisfy themselves that the work had been properly done.

This ability to discharge the occupier's duty of care does not apply to all types of work done by an independent contractor. The 'work' must be 'work of construction, maintenance or repair'.

It will be rare for a court to find that an occupier has acted unreasonably in employing an independent contractor. In a modern society there are very few tasks that you would expect an occupier to have to carry out personally. The more technical the work, the more reasonable it will be to employ an independent contractor.

The practical steps occupiers can reasonably take to satisfy themselves that their contractors are competent include obtaining references and making enquiries locally and of Trade Associations to ascertain the contractor's competence.

The requirement that the occupier must have taken reasonable care to check that the contractor's work was done properly is considered below.

In Haseldine v Daw & Son Ltd *[1941] 3 All ER 156, the landlord of a block of flats engaged a highly reputable firm of hydraulic engineers to maintain the lifts. A visitor was injured when a lift malfunctioned due to the contractor's negligent maintenance.*

The court found that the servicing of a lift was work of a technical nature which an occupier could not reasonably check themselves. Accordingly, the occupier would discharge their duty by entrusting the work to the contractor without the need to check the work for themselves.

In Woodward v The Mayor of Hastings *[1945] KB 174, a child at a school was injured when they slipped on a step which a cleaner had negligently left in an icy condition.*

An occupier is only expected to make such checks as are reasonable in all the circumstances of the case. Since no specialist knowledge was required to recognise that an icy step is dangerous, by not checking the contractor's work the occupier had not discharged their duty of care and was held liable.

In summary, where an occupier employs an independent contractor, the key question is whether the occupier has done all that reasonable care requires of them. If they have then they will not be in breach of duty.

10.2.6 Causation and remoteness of damage

Having considered the issue of duty of care and breach of duty, the issues of causation (including intervening acts) and remoteness apply to all torts, and a claim under the 1957 Act is no exception. The rules covering these issues are considered in **Chapter 3**.

10.2.7 Defences

There are a few arguable defences open to an occupier who has breached their common duty of care.

10.2.7.1 Consent (voluntary assumption of risk/*volenti non fit injuria*)

The 1957 Act preserves the common law defence of consent.

Example

A notice displayed by an occupier at the entrance to their premises reads:

'ALL VISITORS ENTER AT THEIR OWN RISK.'

A court will apply exactly the same principles as for consent under the common law (considered in **Chapter 7**) in deciding whether the notice should succeed under the 1957 Act. The claimant must therefore know of the precise risk that causes the injury and show by their conduct that they willingly accepted the legal risk.

The wording of this notice is not specific enough to enable the occupier to rely on it. It does not make visitors aware of the precise nature of any risk before they encounter it.

10.2.7.2 Exclusion of liability

Occupiers may discharge the common duty of care owed to their visitors by adequately warning of the relevant danger on their premises. The situation under consideration here, however, is the case of an occupier who has not discharged the duty (ie who has breached the common duty of care) and who is seeking to rely on an exclusion clause or notice to escape liability.

The 1957 Act permits an occupier to exclude their liability but is subject to the same requirements as those considered in **Chapter 4**. They are:

- Reasonable steps must have been taken to bring the exclusion notice to the claimant's attention before the tort was committed.
- The wording of the notice must cover the loss suffered by the claimant.

The ability of a defendant to exclude liability is further limited by the Unfair Contract Terms Act 1977 (UCTA) and the Consumer Rights Act 2015 (CRA).

UCTA controls attempts by business occupiers to exclude or restrict their liability for negligence to non-consumers (ie other businesses). The definition of 'negligence' for the purposes of UCTA includes a breach of the common duty of care imposed by the 1957 Act. Private occupiers, however, are not subject to the provisions of UCTA or CRA. CRA controls attempts by traders to exclude or restrict liability for negligence (defined under CRA to include the common duty of care under the 1957 Act) to consumers. Consumers are defined under CRA as individuals acting for purposes that are wholly or mainly outside the individual's trade, business, craft or profession.

The 1957 Act must, therefore, be read subject to the provisions of UCTA and the CRA where business occupiers or traders are concerned.

✪ Example 1

A business delegate at a conference centre sustains personal injury when a defective shutter falls on her.

✪ Example 2

A business delegate's car is damaged in a conference centre car park when a dangerous wall falls on to it.

✪ Example 3

A business delegate's car is damaged in a conference centre car park when a dangerous wall falls onto it, and the owner of the car is killed when the wall collapses on the car.

✪ Example 4

A business delegate's valuables are stolen from a conference centre safe because a conference centre employee carelessly leaves the door to the safe open.

Any exclusion of liability as regards situations in Example 1 and Example 3 is subject to UCTA, given that the conference centre is a business occupier and the claimants are non-consumers. In accordance with UCTA, any attempt to exclude liability for negligence causing death or personal injury is void. Consequently, the conference centre would be unable to exclude its liability for the business delegate's injuries in Example 1 and the business delegate's death in Example 3.

As regards situations in Example 2 and Example 4, and in Example 3 for the damage to the car, an occupier can exclude liability under UCTA for other loss, provided it is reasonable, in all the circumstances, for the occupier to rely on the exclusion term/notice. In considering the issue of reasonableness the court would have regard to the factors, such as bargaining power and the practical consequences for the parties, as set out in Smith v Eric S Bush, *considered in* **Chapter 4**.

To conclude on the issue of exclusion, business occupiers will be subject to the control of UCTA and will be unable to exclude their liability for a non-consumer visitor's death or personal injury. They may, however, be able, under UCTA, to exclude liability for damage to a visitor's property if a court considered it was fair and reasonable to allow them to do so. Traders will be subject to the controls under the CRA and will be unable to exclude liability for a consumer visitor's death or personal injury. They may exclude liability for damage to a consumer visitor's property if they can satisfy the fairness test under CRA.

Private occupiers, on the other hand, are not subject to the control of UCTA or CRA. Ordinary householders can, therefore, display a prominent notice at the entrance to their property excluding their liability to visitors.

10.2.7.3 Contributory negligence

Where visitors suffer loss due partly to an occupier's breach of the common duty of care and partly due to their own carelessness, their damages will be reduced for contributory negligence. The normal principles of this partial defence will apply (considered in **Chapter 7**).

10.3 Liability of occupiers to trespassers

The common duty of care owed by an occupier under the 1957 Act is owed only to 'visitors', a term which excludes trespassers as 'non-visitors'. The law relating to trespassers is to be found in the Occupiers' Liability Act 1984 (the 1984 Act).

The 1984 Act, where it applies, replaces the previous common law duty owed by an occupier to trespassers which was very limited. This common law duty remains valid for any claims by trespassers which fall outside the scope of the 1984 Act.

The duty laid down by the 1984 Act is, as with the 1957 Act, imposed on an 'occupier' of 'premises', and both these terms have the same meaning as for the 1957 Act.

10.3.1 To whom is the duty owed?

The duty under the 1984 Act is owed to people other than visitors. Under the 1957 Act, a visitor is someone who has the occupier's express or implied permission to be on the premises. The 1984 Act therefore applies to persons who do not have such permission, ie trespassers. As being a trespasser is determined by whether the entrant does in fact have express or implied permission, it does not matter that the entrant is unaware that they are trespassing.

⭐ Example

Bryan is out for a walk in the country. He inadvertently strays onto land belonging to Janice. Bryan is a trespasser as he does not have Janice's permission to be on Janice's land. It is irrelevant that Bryan may believe that he is still on a public path.

An entrant can initially enter premises as a 'visitor' but then become a 'trespasser', either by going onto a part of the premises to where their permission does not extend, or by doing something outside the scope of their permission.

In addition to trespassers, the 1984 Act covers three other types of entrants. They are:

- people entering under an access agreement or order under the National Parks and Access to the Countryside Act 1949;

- people who enter land pursuant to the Countryside and Rights of Way Act 2000 (the duty owed to this category of person is limited by the 1984 Act);
- people who exercise private rights of way over land.

Under the 1984 Act, a person using a public right of way (a highway) is excluded from protection under the Act. Such persons are not within the definition of a visitor for the purposes of the 1957 Act either, and therefore are outside the statutory framework of occupiers' liability altogether. Some highways are, however, maintained at public expense. Users of such highways are protected by a duty of care imposed by the Highways Act 1980.

Trespassers are clearly the most significant of these categories, and therefore the remainder of this section will use the term 'trespasser' when referring to the person to whom the duty is owed under the 1984 Act.

10.3.2 Existence of the duty

In contrast to the 1957 Act, the duty owed by an occupier to a trespasser does not arise automatically but is subject to certain conditions. The conditions are that an occupier must:

- be aware of the danger or has reasonable grounds to believe that it exists;
- know or has reasonable grounds to believe that the trespasser is in the vicinity of the danger concerned or that they may come into the vicinity of the danger; and
- be reasonably expected to offer the other some protection against the risk (considering all the circumstances of the case).

The words 'has reasonable grounds to believe' require actual knowledge of facts which would lead a reasonable occupier to be aware of the danger or presence of the trespasser.

The court will look at all the circumstances of the case in assessing whether it is reasonable to expect the occupier to have offered the trespasser some protection. The following information will be particularly important:

- The nature and extent of the risk. This will largely depend on what the danger is, ie is it an obvious or a hidden danger? Could the trespassers be killed or seriously injured by it, or do they just risk minor injury? The more serious the risk, the more likely it will be that the court will consider some protection 'reasonable'.
- The type of trespasser. Are the trespassers adults or children? Are the trespassers deliberate (ie they know they have no permission to be on the land) or inadvertent? The requirement is more likely to be satisfied in the case of a child or an inadvertent trespasser.
- The cost and practicality of precautions (ie how difficult would it be to remove the danger or at least reduce the risk from it). If the cost is low, this would also point to it being 'reasonable' for the occupiers to offer some protection.

10.3.3 Scope of the 1984 Act duty

The 1984 Act contains three conditions, all of which must be satisfied before the occupier owes a duty to the trespasser.

In addition to the three conditions, there are two other issues that limit the duty under the 1984 Act.

In Tomlinson v Congleton Borough Council *[2003] 3 All ER 1122, the claimant suffered serious personal injuries when he dived into the shallow water at the edge of a lake and struck his head on the bottom. Swimming in the lake was prohibited and the local authority had erected notices and distributed leaflets warning of the dangers of swimming in the lake.*

The principal reason for the failure of the claimant's claim was that no duty was owed to him under the 1984 Act. The shallow nature of the lake into which he dived was a natural and obvious feature of the premises. The only risk was in diving in. As this arose out of the claimant's own conduct, it could not be attributed to the state of the premises.

This case confirms, therefore, that (like the 1957 Act) the 1984 Act is concerned with liability due to the state of the premises. Another case that demonstrates this point is *Revill v Newbery* [1996] 2 WLR 239. In this case the defendant fired a shotgun towards a trespasser intending to frighten him off. The trespasser was injured. The Court of Appeal held that the provisions of the 1984 Act were not applicable on these facts. The trespasser was injured by an 'activity', not the state of the premises, and as the 1984 Act did not regulate the 'activity' duty the trespasser had to look to common law negligence for a remedy.

The second limit on the scope of the duty of care is that the duty is owed only in respect of 'injury'. The 1984 Act defines injury as 'anything resulting in death or personal injury' (personal injury covers both physical and mental impairments). This means that the duty under the 1984 Act does not cover damage to a trespasser's property.

10.3.4 Breach of duty

If the three conditions considered above are all satisfied, the occupier owes a duty to the trespasser under the 1984 Act. Under the 1984 Act the duty is to take such care as is reasonable in all the circumstances to see that the trespasser does not suffer injury on the premises by reason of the danger concerned. This means that, like the duty under the 1957 Act, the occupier will not be liable unless they have fallen below the standard of the reasonable occupier.

In deciding what constitutes 'reasonable care' for the purposes of judging whether an occupier has breached the duty owed to a trespasser, the court will consider all the circumstances of the case, but the following factors will be relevant:

- The nature of the danger (ie hidden or obvious and the degree of danger).
- The age of the trespasser (ie adult or child).
- The nature of the premises (ie how dangerous are they? A private house? An electrified railway line?).
- The extent of the risk (ie is there a high or low risk of injury?).
- The cost and practicability of precautions (ie how easy would it be to remove or reduce the risk and what would such measures cost?).
- The nature and character of the entry (eg burglar, child trespasser or adult inadvertently trespassing).
- The gravity and likelihood of injury.
- The foreseeability of the trespasser (ie the more likely people are to trespass, the more precautions must be taken).

10.3.4.1 Warnings

Just as an occupier can discharge the common duty of care owed to lawful visitors by adequately warning of the danger, the same is true in the context of trespassers.

A warning will often be inadequate for children. If the warning is on a notice, a child may be too young to read and/or fully to appreciate the danger.

The 1984 Act mentions discouragements as well as warnings. Where a warning would be inadequate to protect a trespasser from danger, an occupier should therefore put an obstacle (eg a barrier which is too high for a child to climb) round the danger to prevent the trespasser coming into physical contact with the danger.

10.3.4.2 Children

The cases of *Glasgow Corporation v Taylor* [1922] 1 AC 44 (allurements) and *Phipps v Rochester Corporation* [1955] 1 QB 450 (parental responsibility) were considered above in relation to an occupier's liability for children under the 1957 Act. It is generally considered that they are equally applicable under the 1984 Act as they are under the 1957 Act.

10.3.5 Causation and remoteness

Having determined that a duty of care exists which the occupier has breached, the issues of causation (including intervening acts) and remoteness should then be considered. These issues are determined in the same way as for common law negligence.

10.3.6 Defences

10.3.6.1 Consent (voluntary assumption of risk/*volenti non fit injuria*)

The common law defence of consent is preserved for claims under the 1984 Act.

In *Ratcliff v McConnell and another* [1999] 1 WLR 670, the claim failed because the defendants were able to establish that the claimant was aware of the risk of diving into a partly drained swimming pool with very shallow water and willingly accepted it. They were, therefore, able to rely on the defence of consent under the 1984 Act and consequently escaped liability.

10.3.6.2 Exclusion of liability

The 1984 Act is silent as to whether or not liability can be excluded. This contrasts with the 1957 Act, which expressly states that liability can be excluded or restricted.

As the 1984 Act does not expressly state that the occupier can exclude liability, this could be interpreted to mean that the occupier cannot exclude liability. This interpretation is consistent with the view that Parliament intended the 1984 Act to be a 'safety net' form of protection for trespassers. Such an intention would be thwarted if occupiers could evade the obligations of the 1984 Act by a carefully worded notice. If, however, it is possible to exclude liability then, irrespective of whether the occupier is a private, business or trade occupier, the provisions of UCTA or CRA do not apply to liability under the 1984 Act.

10.3.6.3 Contributory negligence

Trespassers who are injured partly due to their own carelessness and partly due to an occupier's breach of duty under the 1984 Act will find their damages reduced for contributory negligence. The usual principles apply (see **Chapter 7**).

10.3.6.4 Illegality

Although trespass is not in itself a crime, some trespassers will enter onto land for some criminal purpose (for example to commit burglary). If such a trespasser is injured in their attempt to commit a serious crime and the occupier is found to have breached a duty owed under the 1984 Act, if the defence of illegality applied, it would deprive the trespasser of a remedy.

This issue was addressed in *Revill v Newbery*. In this case the Court of Appeal took the view that it would thwart Parliament's intention, which was to provide safety net protection to trespassers (some of whom clearly would be trespassing for a criminal purpose), were this defence to be available in relation to liability under the 1984 Act.

Summary

Statute regulates the liability of an occupier of premises to visitors and trespassers. The statutory provisions of the Occupiers' Liability Acts 1957 and 1984 interact with and complement the common law of negligence. Claims under these Acts are structured and analysed in the same way as claims in negligence are analysed.

A duty of care under the Occupiers' Liability Act 1957 is owed automatically by an occupier to a visitor. The duty is to make the visitor reasonably safe, not the premises safe. The standard of care is the same as that in negligence (that of a reasonable occupier), but the 1957 Act provides some additional considerations that should be taken into account.

A duty under the Occupiers' Liability Act 1984 does not arise automatically but is subject to conditions. In practice, it can be difficult for a trespasser to satisfy them. If a duty is owed, the standard of care is, as with the 1957 Act, determined in the same way as at common law (standard of a reasonable occupier). However, the duty under the 1984 Act covers only injury to the trespasser, not any property damage.

Summary flowcharts

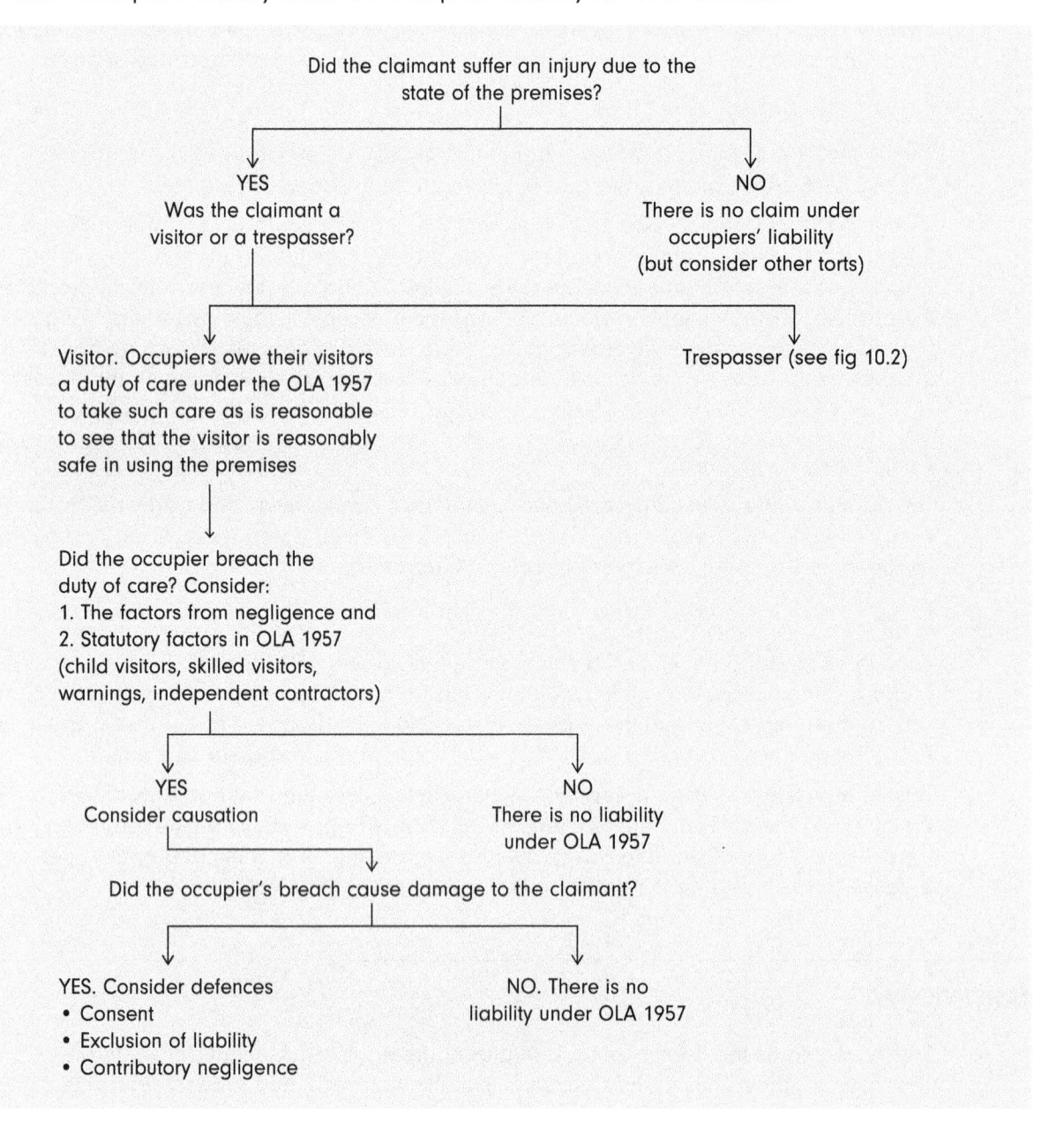

Figure 10.1 Occupiers' liability under the Occupiers' Liability Act 1957 flowchart

Did the claimant suffer an injury due to the state of the premises?

YES — Was the claimant a visitor or a trespasser?

NO — There is no claim under occupiers' liability (but consider other torts)

Visitor. Occupiers owe their visitors a duty of care under the OLA 1957 to take such care as is reasonable to see that the visitor is reasonably safe in using the premises

Trespasser (see fig 10.2)

Did the occupier breach the duty of care? Consider:
1. The factors from negligence and
2. Statutory factors in OLA 1957 (child visitors, skilled visitors, warnings, independent contractors)

YES Consider causation

NO There is no liability under OLA 1957

Did the occupier's breach cause damage to the claimant?

YES. Consider defences
- Consent
- Exclusion of liability
- Contributory negligence

NO. There is no liability under OLA 1957

Figure 10.2 Occupiers' liability under the Occupiers' Liability Act 1984 flowchart

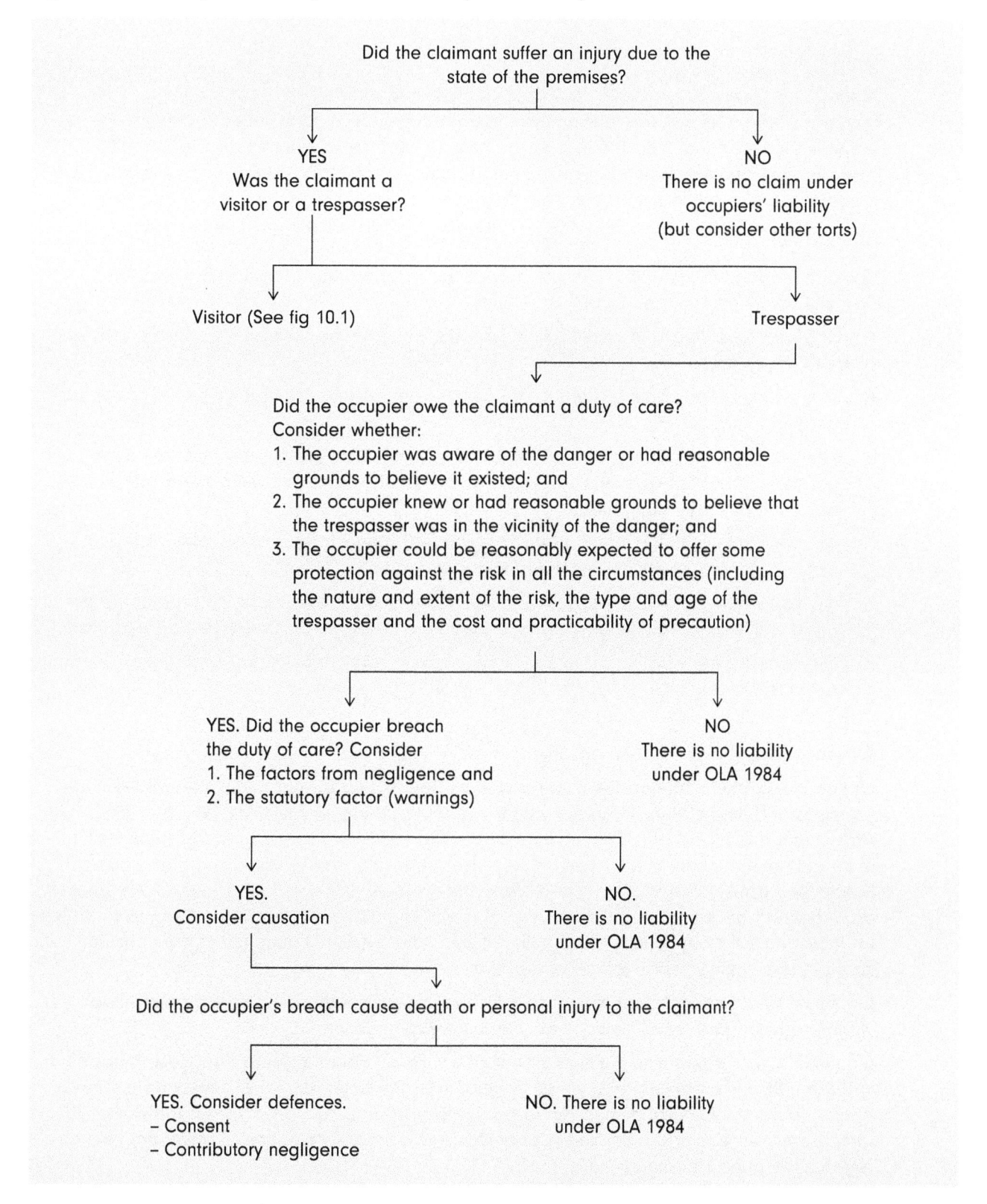

```
                Did the claimant suffer an injury due to the
                         state of the premises?
                    │                           │
                    ▼                           ▼
                   YES                          NO
            Was the claimant a          There is no claim under
            visitor or a trespasser?      occupiers' liability
                                        (but consider other torts)
              │              │
              ▼              ▼
      Visitor (See fig 10.1)   Trespasser
                                   │
                                   ▼
              Did the occupier owe the claimant a duty of care?
              Consider whether:
              1. The occupier was aware of the danger or had reasonable
                 grounds to believe it existed; and
              2. The occupier knew or had reasonable grounds to believe that
                 the trespasser was in the vicinity of the danger; and
              3. The occupier could be reasonably expected to offer some
                 protection against the risk in all the circumstances (including
                 the nature and extent of the risk, the type and age of the
                 trespasser and the cost and practicability of precaution)
                    │                           │
                    ▼                           ▼
          YES. Did the occupier breach         NO
          the duty of care? Consider     There is no liability
          1. The factors from negligence and   under OLA 1984
          2. The statutory factor (warnings)
                    │                           │
                    ▼                           ▼
                   YES.                        NO.
             Consider causation          There is no liability
                    │                      under OLA 1984
                    ▼
      Did the occupier's breach cause death or personal injury to the claimant?
                    │                           │
                    ▼                           ▼
         YES. Consider defences.         NO. There is no liability
         – Consent                          under OLA 1984
         – Contributory negligence
```

Sample questions

Question 1

A solicitor's client owns and runs a hotel. Their in-house maintenance team have been repairing a leak in the fountain that is in the hotel foyer. To access the leak, the maintenance team have had to remove a marble slab from the surface of the floor which exposed a large hole. A hotel guest, running to catch the lift in the hotel foyer and carrying a heavy suitcase, fell into the hole, breaking their pelvis as a result. There is a large notice at the reception desk, at the entrance to the foyer, stating: 'Warning Fountain Repair Work: The hotel management apologises for any inconvenience caused by repair work being carried out in the hotel foyer but accepts no responsibility for any injury, loss, or damage howsoever caused to guests.'

Which of the following statements best explains whether the hotel will be liable for the injury to the guest?

A Yes, because the warning did not enable the guest to be reasonably safe as it was too general in nature.

B Yes, because the warning did not enable the guest to be reasonably safe as it was too general in nature. However, it is likely that the guest's damages will be reduced as they were contributory negligent.

C No, because, while the warning did not enable the guest to be reasonably safe as it was too general in nature, the hotel have excluded their liability.

D No, because reasonable steps have been taken to bring the risk of the problem to the guest's attention and the wording of the warning covers the loss suffered by the guest.

E No, because the warning enabled the guest to be reasonably safe as the hole was an obvious danger.

Answer

Option B is correct. The guest is a visitor who has been injured due to the state of the hotel premises and their claim will be governed by the Occupiers' Liability Act 1957 (the 1957 Act). Under the 1957 Act, a warning will not discharge the occupier's duty of care unless it is adequate, ie it enables the guest to be reasonably safe. This warning is too general in nature as it does not alert visitors to the specific problem with the floor. However, the guest's damages will be reduced as they were contributory negligent on the facts. They were careless for their own safety by running for the lift etc and not paying full attention to the floor. This carelessness contributed to the injury that they suffered.

Option A is not the best answer as it fails to take account of the fact that the hotel's liability will be reduced due to the defence of contributory negligence.

Option C is wrong because the exclusion notice will be void as against the guest. It appears that the notice is prominent and so, at common law, the hotel has taken reasonable steps to draw it to the attention of guests. However, it will be subject to the Consumer Rights Act 2015 because the hotel is a 'trader' and the guest is a consumer. The notice is, therefore, void as regards the guest's personal injury.

Option D is wrong because it incorrectly states the test for when a warning will be adequate under the 1957 Act (these are the common law requirements for an exclusion notice).

Option E is wrong because the fact that it may, or may not have been an obvious danger did not, in itself, make the warning adequate under the 1957 Act.

Question 2

A solicitor's client owns and runs a clothes shop. They contracted with a known and reputable company to supply and fit new stairs to the second floor of the shop. The work was carried out one evening while the shop was closed to customers. The next day a customer trod on a long protruding nail in the middle of the bottom step, causing a severe injury to their foot.

Which of the following statements best explains whether the shop owner will be liable for the injury to the customer?

A No, because the shop owner used a reputable company to carry out the work and is therefore not at fault in any way. The customer should bring their claim against the company that installed the stairs.

B No, because the shop owner used a reputable company to carry out the work and it was not reasonable for the shop owner to check the stairs before opening the shop to the public. The customer should bring their claim against the company that installed the stairs.

C Yes, because the customer was injured due to a breach of the duty of care the shop owner owes their visitors.

D Yes, because the customer was injured due to a breach of the duty of care the shop owner owes their visitors. The shop owner cannot delegate this duty of care to the company that installed the stairs.

E Yes, because, despite the fact that the shop owner used a reputable company to carry out the work, it was reasonable to expect the shop owner to check the stairs before opening the shop to the public.

Answer

Option E is the correct answer as it considers the requirements under the 1957 Act and correctly applies the facts of the question.

Option A is wrong because it fails to consider all elements of the requirement that the occupier, who employs an independent contractor to carry out work on their premises, must have done all that reasonable care requires of them under the 1957 Act. Entrusting the work to an independent contractor is generally accepted to be reasonable. The fact that the independent contractor is 'reputable' meets the requirement that steps were taken to ensure that the contractor was competent. However, it fails to consider whether the occupier had taken such steps (if any) as they reasonably ought in order to satisfy themselves that the work had been properly done. Without considering this final requirement, it is not possible to state that the occupier was not at fault.

Option B is wrong because, while it does consider the final requirement, it is incorrect on the facts of the question. The fitting of a new staircase is work of a technical nature. However, no specialist knowledge was required to see that a nail was sticking out of one of the steps by checking the contractor's work. The shop owner had not, therefore, discharged their duty of care.

Option C is wrong as it is an oversimplification of the breach issue. It does not consider the requirements under the 1957 Act (set out above), so is not the best explanation of why the shop owner will be liable.

Option D is wrong for the same reason as C. In addition, it is wrong because, if an occupier meets all the requirements under the 1957 Act (set out above), it can, in effect, delegate its duty of care by employing independent contractors.

Tort

Question 3

A solicitor is instructed by a client who broke their leg and damaged an expensive watch when they fell while attempting to break into a factory by climbing over one of the ten-foot-high perimeter walls. Following several recent break-ins, the factory owner had installed an electrified wire along the top of all the perimeter walls. The factory owner accepts that there is not a notice warning of the wire's presence on the wall. The solicitor's client fell upon touching this wire.

There is a prominent notice at the entrance to the factory which reads: 'The owner accepts no liability for any injury or damage suffered by anyone, howsoever caused, on these premises.'

Which of the following statements best explains whether the client will be successful in their claim against the factory owner?

A   Yes, because, the factory owner was clearly aware of the danger, knew that trespassers could come within the vicinity of the danger and the danger of touching an electrified wire was a hidden hazard. The factory owner was, therefore, expected to offer some protection against the risk of falling off the wall, eg a warning sign. The breach of this duty of care caused the client's injuries and property damage.

B   Yes, because, the factory owner was clearly aware of the danger, knew that trespassers could come within the vicinity of the danger and the danger of touching an electrified wire was a hidden hazard. The factory owner was, therefore, expected to offer some protection against the risk of falling off the wall, eg a warning sign. The breach of this duty of care caused the client's injuries and property damage. However, the client will not be able to claim for their damaged watch.

C   No, because the factory owner can rely upon the defence of illegality to defeat the claim.

D   No, because the client was a trespasser and will not be owed a duty of care by the factory owner. While the factory owner was clearly aware of the danger and knew that trespassers could come within the vicinity of the danger, the danger of falling off the wall was an obvious hazard. The factory owner was not, therefore, expected to offer any protection against the risk of falling off the wall.

E   No, because the factory owner can rely upon the defence of exclusion of liability to defeat the claim.

Answer

Option B is the correct answer as it correctly sets out why the client would be owed a duty of care by the factory owner under the 1984 Act.

Option A is wrong because, while it also sets out why the client is owed a duty of care, it does not deal with the fact that property damage is not a loss covered by the 1984 Act.

Option C is wrong because the defence of illegality does not apply to claims under the 1984 Act.

Option D is wrong because, while the height of the wall is an obvious danger, the electrified wire is not. The client would, therefore, be owed a duty of care.

Option E is wrong because the most likely interpretation of the 1984 Act is that an occupier's liability cannot be excluded.

11 Product Liability

11.1	Introduction	154
11.2	Negligence	154
11.3	Consumer Protection Act 1987	158

SQE1 syllabus

This chapter will enable you to achieve the SQE1 Assessment Specification in relation to Functioning Legal Knowledge concerned with the core principles on negligence and the Consumer Protection Act 1987 that cover liability for defective products in tort.

Note that for SQE1, candidates are not usually required to recall specific case names or cite statutory or regulatory authorities. Cases are provided for illustrative purposes only.

Learning outcomes

By the end of this chapter you will be able to apply relevant core legal principles and rules appropriately and effectively, at the level of a competent newly qualified solicitor in practice, to realistic client-based and ethical problems and situations in the following areas:

- the tort of negligence as it applies to a product liability claim;
- the statutory tort created by the Consumer Protection Act 1987.

11.1 Introduction

This chapter considers the liability for damage caused by defective products. A cause of action for defective products may lie in one of three areas of law. The two areas considered in this chapter are:

- the tort of negligence; and
- under the Consumer Protection Act (CPA) 1987.

The third area of law which might be of use in claims arising from defective products is contract law. Although this chapter focuses on tortious liability, the possibility of suing in contract where a buyer has suffered injury or loss as a result of a defective product should always be borne in mind. However, in many cases this will not be an option, eg where the claimant was not the buyer of the product (and does not come within the Contracts (Rights of Third Parties) Act 1999), or where the supplier has gone out of business. In these situations, the only causes of action that are open to the claimant are in tort.

11.2 Negligence

In order to succeed in a negligence claim, the claimant must show that the defendant owes a duty of care which has been breached, causing damage to the claimant which is not too remote. These issues remain the same for a claim concerning defective products, but case law has established some special rules.

11.2.1 Duty of care: the narrow rule in *Donoghue v Stevenson*

In **Chapter 1**, the case of *Donoghue v Stevenson* [1932] All ER Rep 1 was considered in the development of a test for duty of care in 'novel' situations. Lord Atkin formulated the well-known 'neighbour principle' in this context, which is often known as the 'wide rule' from *Donoghue v Stevenson*.

The case itself was about a bottle of ginger beer containing the remnants of a dead snail. On its facts it was a case concerning a defective product (the ginger beer). Having laid down the neighbour principle/ wide rule, Lord Atkin went on to consider the circumstances in which a manufacturer of a product would owe a duty of care to the consumer. This is usually known as the 'narrow rule' in *Donoghue v Stevenson*.

To show a duty of care under the narrow rule the claimant must establish that:

- the defendant is a 'manufacturer';
- the item causing damage is a 'product';
- the claimant is a 'consumer'; and
- the product reached the consumer in the form in which it left the manufacturer with no reasonable possibility of intermediate examination.

Each of these constituent elements is considered in turn below, starting with the meaning of 'manufacturer'.

11.2.2 Who is a 'manufacturer'?

Liability is imposed on the 'manufacturer' of a product. The word 'manufacturer' for the purposes of the narrow rule is widely interpreted by the courts. Case law has extended this to include any person who works in some way on a product before it reaches the consumer. This includes, for example, repairers of products (*Haseldine v Daw & Son Ltd* [1941] 3 All ER 156), installers of products (*Stennett v Hancock* [1939] 2 All ER 578) and even, on rare occasions, suppliers of products (*Andrews v Hopkinson* [1957] 1 QB 229).

⭐ Example

Tessa has her car serviced by her local garage and a new boiler installed in her home by a firm of heating engineers. Both the local garage and the heating engineers would fall within the scope of a 'manufacturer' for the purposes of the narrow rule, and would owe a duty in negligence to Tessa.

A supplier can be within the scope of 'manufacturer' for the purposes of the narrow rule. In *Andrews v Hopkinson* [1957] 1 QB 229, the supplier was found liable because a car's defective steering could easily have been discovered by a competent mechanic. The supplier was under a duty to check the steering because of the car's age (the defect being a common one in cars of its age) and because of the potentially serious consequences of allowing a car with defective steering to be driven on the road.

Suppliers, therefore, may owe a duty under the narrow rule if the circumstances are such that they ought reasonably to inspect or test the products which they supply (eg because the manufacturer has asked them to do so). They could also owe a duty if they actually know of a defect/ danger.

11.2.3 What is a 'product'?

The case of *Donoghue v Stevenson* concerned a drink, but the word 'product' covers almost any item which is capable of causing damage.

In addition, as Lord Atkin talked about an absence of care in the preparation of or 'putting up' of the product, it is clear that the duty also extends to items supplied with the product, eg packaging, containers, labels, instructions for use.

11.2.4 Who is a 'consumer'?

This term includes not only the ultimate user of the product, but also anyone whom the defendant should reasonably have in mind as likely to be injured by the defendant's negligence (ie 'neighbours' in *Donoghue v Stevenson* terms).

⭐ Example

Mrs Smith is driving her daughter, Pamela, and Pamela's friend, Sandra, to school one day when she brakes approaching a bend in the road. Unfortunately, the brakes fail to function as they are defective (having been negligently manufactured). Mrs Smith's car mounts the pavement, injuring William, a pedestrian. The car then ploughs into the wall of a house owned by Jennifer. Mrs Smith, Pamela and Sandra are badly injured.

The term 'consumer' would cover all four people injured in the accident: Mrs Smith, Pamela, Sandra and William. It would also cover Jennifer whose house is damaged in the incident. They are all people whom the manufacturer of the brakes ought reasonably to have had in mind as likely to be injured by any failure to take reasonable care on its part. Cars are driven on roads adjacent to buildings and pavements, and cars are driven by people who may well be carrying passengers.

11.2.5 Intermediate examination

The ginger beer in *Donoghue v Stevenson* was contained in a sealed, opaque bottle. There was therefore no likelihood of anyone examining the contents before they were consumed. However, if there is a reasonable possibility of intermediate examination then the 'manufacturer' of the product will not owe a duty under the *Donoghue v Stevenson* narrow rule. This does not necessarily mean an injured party will be without a cause of action as the duty may be owed instead by the party having the opportunity to examine the product.

> *In* Kubach v Hollands *[1937] 3 All ER 907, the claimant was a schoolgirl who was carrying out a chemical experiment with chemicals supplied by the teacher of the chemistry class, when an explosion occurred and she was severely injured. The teacher had purchased the chemicals from the second defendants. The chemicals were wrongly labelled, leading to them being unsuitable for the experiment. The second defendants had purchased the wrongly labelled chemicals from a third party, whose invoice stated: 'The above goods are accurate as described on leaving our works but they must be examined and tested by user before use. The above goods are not invoiced as suitable for any purpose but they are of the nature and quality described.' The second defendants had not carried out a test on the chemicals and had not advised the teacher that an examination or test would be advisable. The second defendants knew that the powder would be used for the purpose of school experiments, but they had not told the third party that the powder might be so used.*
>
> *The manufacturer escaped liability in* Kubach v Hollands *because the chemical was provided with an express warning that it was to be tested before use. Such a test would have revealed the problem. As the manufacturer expected the test to be carried out, there was a 'reasonable possibility' of an intermediate examination and so no duty arose under Lord Atkin's narrow rule.*
>
> *The school escaped liability in* Kubach v Hollands. *Although the school, through the chemistry teacher, had supplied the chemical to the injured girl, it did not owe a duty as a supplier (under Lord Atkin's narrow rule) as it had not been warned of any problem with the chemical or of the need to test before use.*
>
> *The court held that the second defendant, as the intermediate supplier of the chemical to the school, because of its knowledge of the need to test before use, owed a duty to the injured girl. It had breached this duty and so had to compensate for the girl's injury.*

Although Lord Atkin in *Donoghue v Stevenson* talked about a 'reasonable possibility', it is clear from *Kubach v Hollands* that a mere opportunity or possibility of intermediate examination will not be enough to exonerate a manufacturer. The manufacturer must believe there is a likelihood of such an examination taking place.

Note that if an examination by a third party (eg a supplier), or by the consumer himself, would not have revealed the defect (eg because it is a hidden defect), the manufacturer will not be exonerated.

11.2.6 Scope of the duty owed under the narrow rule

It is necessary to consider what types of loss are within the scope of the duty.

Example

Amanda buys a new toaster. Unfortunately, due to negligence in the manufacturing process, it fails to eject the toast from the toaster when it is cooked. As a result the toast catches fire. The fire spreads to Amanda's kitchen curtains which are badly damaged. Amanda also suffers burns to her hands. Her toaster will need replacing and her kitchen redecorating.

Lord Bridge in *Murphy v Brentwood District Council* (considered in **Chapter 4**) said that a duty under *Donoghue v Stevenson's* narrow rule in respect of products would cover any injury to persons or damage to property done by the defect in the product. However, he said that if the only loss is the defective quality of the product itself, the reduction in value of the product, or the cost of repairing the defect or of replacing the product would not be covered by the duty of care. The reason for this is that he classified these losses, stemming purely from the defective quality of the item, as pure economic loss.

Therefore the losses due to Amanda's burns and the damage to the curtains are recoverable since they fall within the scope of the narrow rule, being injury and property damage respectively. The cost of replacing the faulty toaster is regarded as being pure economic loss and is not, therefore, recoverable in negligence. The cost of redecorating the kitchen is recoverable because this results from damage to property other than the defective product itself.

11.2.7 Breach of duty

In all cases the duty of care in negligence is to exercise reasonable care. The standard of care required would, for example, be: the reasonable ginger beer manufacturer, the reasonable garage or the reasonable hydraulic engineer.

As in all claims in negligence, the actual standard of care expected of the reasonable person in each case will be determined by looking at all the circumstances, including the magnitude of the foreseeable risk, the gravity of potential injury, and the costs and practicalities of precautions.

In addition, a manufacturer may be able to comply with its duty of care by adequately warning the consumer of any danger connected with the product. Warnings may also be relevant in the context of the 'intermediate examination' element of the narrow rule (see *Kubach v Hollands*).

11.2.8 Proof of breach

As with any claim in negligence, the onus of proving the duty has been breached lies with the claimant. The claimant's task is not an easy one. How does the claimant produce evidence of what went wrong in the manufacturing process when the claimant was not present in the factory at the relevant time?

Usually in negligence, where the facts are beyond the knowledge of the claimant, the claimant can be assisted in proving breach of duty by the maxim *res ipsa loquitur*. However, Lord Macmillan in *Donoghue v Stevenson* said that this maxim should not be relied on in cases of product liability.

The problem faced by claimants is demonstrated by the case of *Daniels v R White & Sons* [1938] 4 All ER 258. Despite the presence of carbolic acid in their lemonade, the claimant failed to show that there was any problem with the manufacturing process. The court confirmed that the duty under *Donoghue v Stevenson* is only a duty to take reasonable care. As the defendant had apparently taken reasonable care, it was not in breach of duty.

Despite Lord Macmillan's dictum in *Donoghue v Stevenson*, other cases have been prepared to 'infer' breach of duty from facts that the claimant is able to prove. An example of this is the Privy Council decision in *Grant v Australian Knitting Mills* [1936] AC 85. Here the claimant suffered severe dermatitis due to the presence of sulphur in some underwear which the defendant had supplied. The claimant could prove the presence of the chemical in the factory and in the underwear, but could not show any specific problem in the manufacturing process. Nonetheless, the Privy Council inferred that the chemical would not have been present in the underwear had the defendants taken reasonable care, ie it inferred breach of duty. This approach was followed more recently in *Carroll v Fearon* [1998] PIQR P416.

This inference differs from *res ipsa loquitur* in that it does require the claimant to prove some facts on which the court can base its inference. However, once the inference arises then, as with *res ipsa loquitur*, the court will infer breach of duty unless the defendant can rebut the inference of breach of duty by proving that the defect was not due to the defendant's lack of care but to some later problem, for example the claimant's own misuse of the product.

Tort

11.2.9 Causation and remoteness

The claimant must prove that the defendant's breach caused their loss in the normal way (ie the 'but for' test applies). This is illustrated in the context of product liability by the case of *Evans v Triplex Safety Glass Co Ltd* [1936] 1 All ER 283. Here the windscreen of the claimant's car shattered some 12 months after it was fitted by the defendants. A shard of glass injured the claimant. Due to the lapse of time the claimant could not establish any causal link between the alleged negligence by the defendant and the disintegration of their windscreen.

If factual causation is established, the court will then consider any intervening acts and also the issue of remoteness, ie whether the claimant's loss is of a reasonably foreseeable type (*The Wagon Mound* test).

11.2.10 Defences

11.2.10.1 Consent (voluntary assumption of risk/*volenti non fit injuria*)

If a claimant is aware of a defect in a product and nonetheless decides to continue with the use of the product then there is scope for the defendant to argue the defence of consent. However, knowledge of a risk is not on its own enough to amount to consent. The claimant's conduct must also indicate a willing acceptance of the risk. This is difficult to show.

11.2.10.2 Exclusion of liability

Liability in negligence for death or personal injury cannot be excluded at all (Unfair Contract Terms Act 1977 (UCTA) and Consumer Rights Act 2015 (CRA 2015)) where liability arises in the course of a business or trade. However, liability to non-consumers in negligence for other loss or damage can be excluded if the reasonableness test is satisfied (UCTA) or the fairness test if the claimant is a consumer (CRA 2015).

11.2.10.3 Contributory negligence

If the circumstances are not enough to show consent, the defendant may alternatively rely on the partial defence of contributory negligence.

> ⭐ *Example*
>
> *Mike buys a new hammer to do some odd jobs around the house. When he uses it for the first time, he notices that the head is rather loose, but thinks he must have imagined it since it is, after all, brand new. He therefore continues to use it. On the third such occasion, when Mike is knocking a nail into a wall, the head of the hammer falls off and injures his foot. It is unlikely that Mike's conduct is sufficiently foolhardy to equate to him consenting to run the risk of the hammer head falling off. However, any damages Mike recovers in a negligence claim against the manufacturer would be reduced on account of his contributory negligence in continuing to use the hammer once he became aware of the danger.*

11.3 Consumer Protection Act 1987

A claim under the CPA 1987 provides an additional cause of action to a claim in negligence (but the claimant cannot recover damages twice over for the same loss).

11.3.1 Who can sue?

Anyone who can establish the following can sue under the CPA 1987:

- that they have suffered damage
- caused by

- a defect
- in a product.

The class of claimants is, therefore, very wide. It is not just confined to the buyer, or even a direct user, of the defective product. In contrast to a claim in negligence under the narrow rule, neither need the claimant be a foreseeable victim.

The following sections examine the meaning of each of the requirements listed above.

11.3.2 'Damage'

'Damage' is defined in the CPA 1987. In summary:

- claims for death and personal injury are without limit. Personal injury is defined as including 'any disease and any other impairment of a person's physical or mental condition'.
- Damage to private property must exceed £275 before a claim for it can be brought. Provided the loss of or damage to private property exceeds £275, the full amount of the loss or damage is recoverable.
- Damage caused by a defective product to business property is outside the scope of the CPA 1987.
- The cost of repairing or replacing the defective product itself is not recoverable. This is regarded as being pure economic loss.

⭐ Example

Clive works from home. The contents of his study include a portable television set, an antique clock worth over £1,000 and a computer. He uses the computer predominantly for his business. One day the television explodes due to a mechanical defect. The resulting fire destroys the contents of Clive's study. Clive is taken to hospital suffering from burns and the effects of smoke inhalation.

The damage to the television itself is pure economic loss and not recoverable. The cost of replacing the clock is recoverable as this is damage to private property exceeding £275. The damage to the computer is damage to business property. The computer may be used for home purposes as well as business use. Under the CPA 1987, the property damage is excluded if 'not ... used mainly for his own private use'. As the facts state that the computer is used predominantly for business purposes, it would not be recoverable. Clive's personal injury is recoverable. If Clive loses income because of his burns, ie economic loss consequential on physical damage or on personal injury, it is likely that he would be able to recover this applying the ordinary principles for assessing liability in tort (the CPA 1987 is silent on the point).

If Clive chose to sue in negligence instead of under the CPA 1987, he would be able to recover for the loss of his computer in negligence, which he could not recover for under the CPA 1987. Damage to business property (assuming it is foreseeable) is recoverable in a negligence claim. In neither claim, however, can he recover for the damage to the television set (pure economic loss).

11.3.3 'Caused by'

A claimant needs to establish the causal link between the claimant's damage and the defect in the product. As with a claim in negligence, the claimant has the burden of proving causation, and the usual 'but for' test applies. However, under the CPA 1987 the claimant must show that the defect caused the damage. In negligence the claimant must show that the defendant's breach of duty caused the damage.

(The issue of remoteness is not addressed in the CPA 1987. It may be, therefore, that if a claimant can establish damage caused by a defect, the defendant will be liable for that damage without limit. If the rules on remoteness do apply, however, then, as this is a tort of strict liability, the 'direct consequences test' from *Re Polemis* [1921] All ER 40 would probably govern the issue rather than the *Wagon Mound* test.)

11.3.4 'Defect'

Claimants suing under the CPA 1987 must prove that they have suffered damage caused wholly or partly by a defect in a product.

'Defect' as defined by the CPA 1987 effectively means 'unsafe', ie that the safety of the product is not such as persons generally are entitled to expect. The CPA 1987, therefore, applies to products which are unsafe as opposed to products which are simply defective. This limitation does not apply to claims in negligence, but in essence a similar position is achieved, as under the narrow rule the duty only covers damage to property and personal injury and not pure economic loss.

To decide the level of safety persons generally are entitled to expect, the CPA 1987 sets out some circumstances to be taken into account, including:

- the whole get-up and presentation of the product (including packaging, instructions, warnings);
- what the expected use of the product is;
- the age of the product in question.

In *A v National Blood Authority* [2001] 3 All ER 289 the court decided that consumer expectations for blood products were that the blood would be free from viruses (such as hepatitis C). This meant the blood was defective within the meaning of the CPA 1987 even though the defendants showed that the risk of such a viral infection in blood was unavoidable at the time as there were no tests then available for this. This is much more onerous than the duty in negligence which is satisfied where a defendant takes all reasonable care.

11.3.5 'Product'

The defect must exist in a 'product'. Under the CPA 1987, 'product' is widely defined. It means 'any goods or electricity and... includes a product which is comprised in another product whether ... a component ... or raw material'. This would, therefore, include component parts like an engine in a car. It also includes 'blood' (*A v National Blood Authority* [2001] 3 All ER 289).

11.3.6 Who is liable?

Under the CPA 1987, the four categories of potential defendant are:

- The producer of the product (ie the manufacturer).
- An 'own-brander'.
- An importer.
- A supplier, but only in limited circumstances outlined under the CPA 1987.

11.3.6.1 The producer (manufacturer)

The manufacturer of the 'product' will be the usual defendant.

The definition of 'product' includes components as well as finished products. This means, therefore, that if a component part is faulty, both the manufacturer of the part and the manufacturer of the whole product are liable.

⭐ Example

An aircraft crashes due to faulty landing gear. Both the manufacturer of the aircraft and the manufacturer of the landing gear could be sued.

11.3.6.2 The 'own-brander'

This is the person who, by putting their name or trademark on the product, holds themselves out as being its producer.

⭐ Example

Many large retail stores in the UK (eg Marks & Spencer, Tesco) put their own brand name on goods produced by others.

11.3.6.3 An importer

This is a person who imported the product into the UK from outside of the UK in order to supply it to another person.

11.3.6.4 A 'forgetful supplier'

Under the CPA 1987, a supplier (eg retailer) is liable only where they are unable to meet a victim's request to identify any of the people involved in the chain of supply (eg the wholesaler or the manufacturer). Suppliers are otherwise not liable under the CPA 1987.

11.3.7 Nature of liability

The CPA 1987 merely requires the claimant to show that they have suffered damage caused by a defect in a product. It does not require a claimant to prove that the defect resulted from any fault or carelessness on the defendant's behalf. In other words, liability is strict under the CPA 1987 in that the defendant will be liable without proof of any fault on his part.

A v National Blood Authority demonstrates the strict liability nature of the CPA 1987. The fact that the defect in the product was unavoidable was not an argument the defendant could put forward.

Strict liability under the CPA 1987 is advantageous for claimants when compared with a claim in negligence based upon proving fault. Under the narrow rule in *Donoghue v Stevenson*, the claimant has to establish that the defendant had failed to reach the standard of care of the reasonable person in their position in order to prove breach of duty (and therefore negligence) on the defendant's part.

11.3.8 Defences

Once a claimant establishes a defect, causation and damage, the onus shifts to the defendant to establish one of the defences under the CPA 1987. The availability of these complete defences means that although the defendant's liability is strict, it is not absolute.

11.3.8.1 The defect was attributable to compliance with legal requirements

Compliance with a legal requirement will absolve a producer from liability only if the defect was an inevitable result of compliance.

11.3.8.2 The defendant did not supply the product to another

✪ Example

A thief breaks into a factory and steals a batch of toys which contain defects. A child of the thief is subsequently injured when playing with the toy. The manufacturer has not supplied the toy to the thief (or to the child) and therefore could rely on this defence.

11.3.8.3 The defendant supplied the product otherwise than in the course of business

✪ Example

A defective product is sold by one friend to another.

11.3.8.4 The defect did not exist when the defendant supplied the product

If a defendant could therefore show that the defect was caused by misuse of the product or by fair wear and tear, this defence will succeed.

11.3.8.5 A manufacturer of component parts is not liable for a defect in the finished product which is wholly attributable to the design of the finished product or to compliance with the instructions given by the manufacturer of the finished product

11.3.8.6 'Development risks' (or 'state of the art')

This defence is particularly relevant in the area of drugs, medicines and pharmaceutical products.

To rely on the development risks defence, a defendant must prove that the state of knowledge, at the time the product was supplied, amongst producers of the product in question, was not such as to allow a producer of the product to discover the defect.

Case law has confirmed that when considering this defence the producer in question should be judged against the highest standard of knowledge that is accessible anywhere in the world. A producer would only be able to rely on this defence, therefore, if they could show that they could not have discovered the defect via any information accessible anywhere in the world. This considerably curtails the scope of this defence.

In addition, the case of *A v National Blood Authority* [2001] 3 All ER 289 also confirms that the defence only applies to defects/risks that could not have been foreseen. It did not therefore help the defendant in that case, as the risk of blood infection was known but nothing could be done about it.

11.3.8.7 Contributory negligence

In addition to the complete defences considered above, the CPA 1987 also retains the partial defence of contributory negligence. The defence of contributory negligence applies where the claimant is partly responsible for their loss or damage. In such cases the defendant may rely on contributory negligence in the usual way (considered in **Chapter 7**).

✪ Example

Bethan buys a new electric blanket and leaves it switched on in her bed one evening when she goes out to visit a friend. The blanket has been negligently manufactured and, as a consequence, catches fire. Bethan returns home to find her house has been destroyed in the resulting fire. It is likely that the blanket is defective under the CPA 1987, but there would be a finding of contributory negligence against Bethan in these circumstances, to the extent that her carelessness has caused or contributed to the damage she has suffered.

11.3.8.8 Exclusion of liability

Under the CPA 1987, a defendant cannot exclude, limit or restrict their liability in any way.

Summary

- This chapter considers how the law of negligence operates in the field of product liability. Under *Donoghue v Stevenson* the duty of care owed by a manufacturer to a consumer is subject to certain conditions. The scope of this duty has also been expanded by the courts beyond the literal interpretation of 'manufacturer' and 'consumer'.
- In terms of case analysis, the other elements of a claim in negligence in this context are the same as were considered in **Chapters 2** and **3**.
- Liability under the Consumer Protection Act 1987 is a statutory tort of strict liability, subject to the applicability of defences under the Act.
- Having studied the two torts that are potentially relevant to product liability, the various advantages and disadvantages of each should be apparent. The facts of any scenario can then be analysed in order to advise accurately on the claims that may be available.

Summary flowcharts

Figure 11.1 Product liability: negligence flowchart

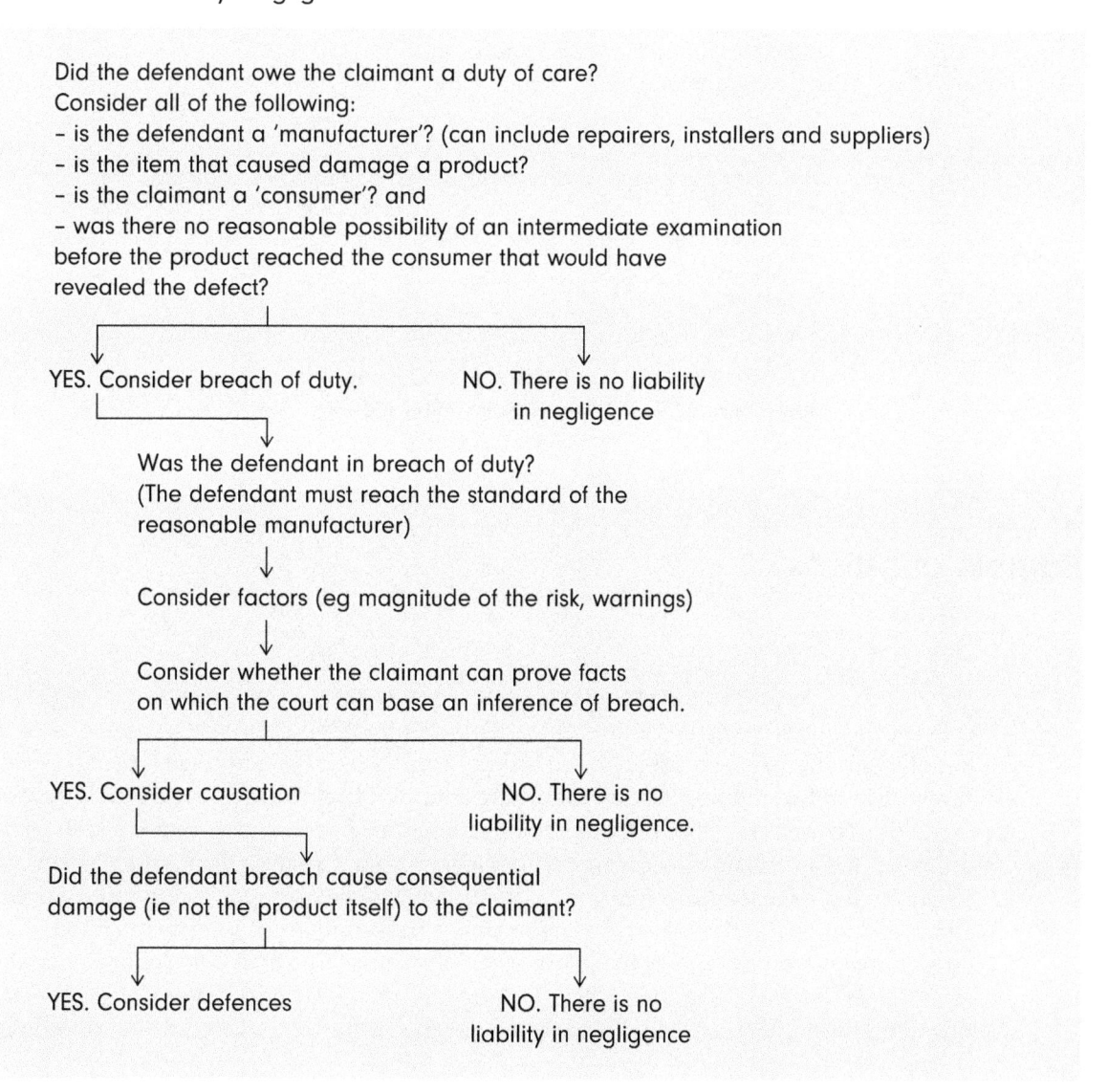

Did the defendant owe the claimant a duty of care?
Consider all of the following:
- is the defendant a 'manufacturer'? (can include repairers, installers and suppliers)
- is the item that caused damage a product?
- is the claimant a 'consumer'? and
- was there no reasonable possibility of an intermediate examination before the product reached the consumer that would have revealed the defect?

YES. Consider breach of duty. → NO. There is no liability in negligence

Was the defendant in breach of duty?
(The defendant must reach the standard of the reasonable manufacturer)

↓

Consider factors (eg magnitude of the risk, warnings)

↓

Consider whether the claimant can prove facts on which the court can base an inference of breach.

YES. Consider causation → NO. There is no liability in negligence.

Did the defendant breach cause consequential damage (ie not the product itself) to the claimant?

YES. Consider defences → NO. There is no liability in negligence

Figure 11.2 Product liability: Consumer Protection Act 1987 flowchart

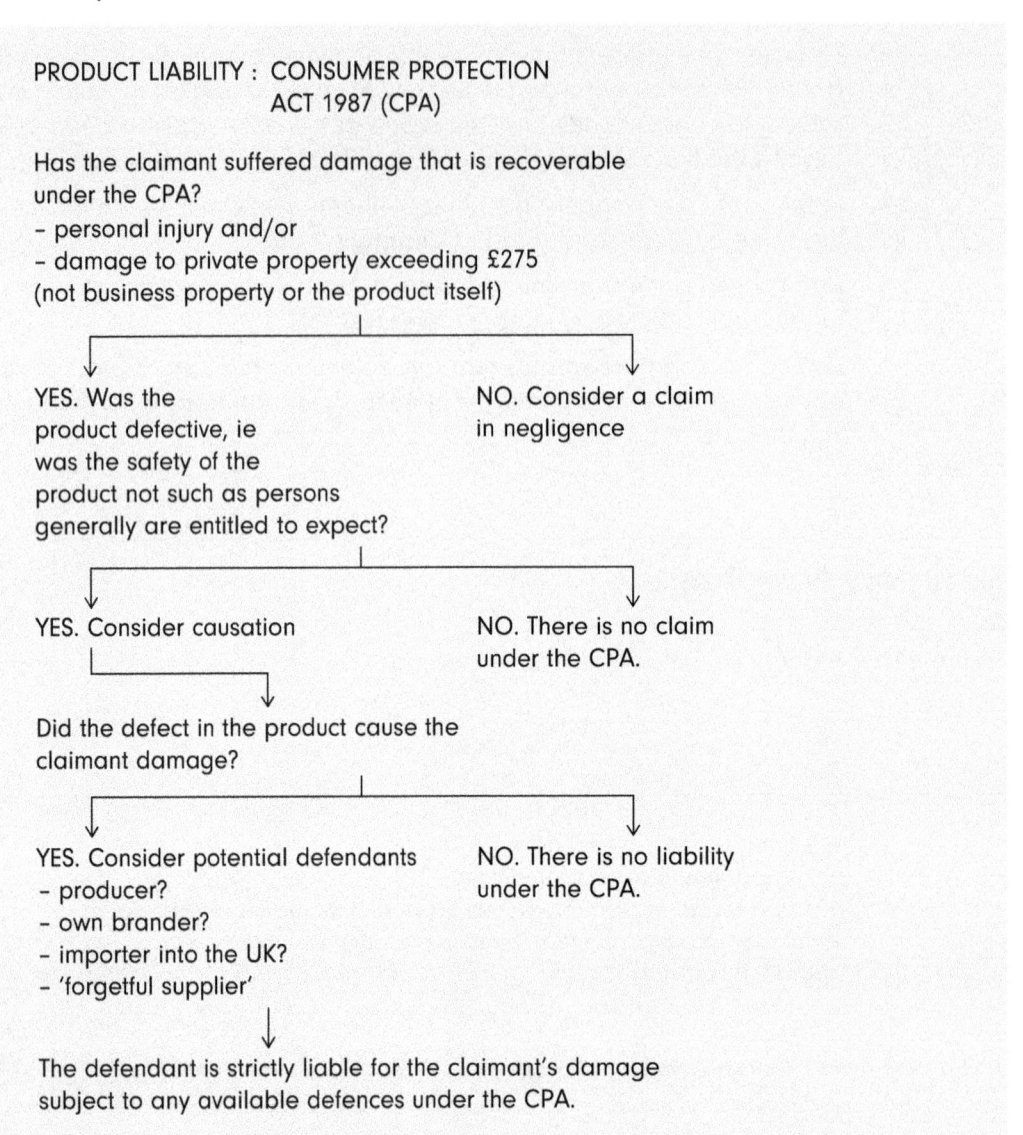

```
              PRODUCT LIABILITY : CONSUMER PROTECTION
                         ACT 1987 (CPA)

      Has the claimant suffered damage that is recoverable
      under the CPA?
      - personal injury and/or
      - damage to private property exceeding £275
      (not business property or the product itself)
                             |
              ┌──────────────┴──────────────┐
              ↓                             ↓
      YES. Was the                  NO. Consider a claim
      product defective, ie         in negligence
      was the safety of the
      product not such as persons
      generally are entitled to expect?
              |
      ┌───────┴──────────────┐
      ↓                      ↓
      YES. Consider causation    NO. There is no claim
              |                   under the CPA.
              ↓
      Did the defect in the product cause the
      claimant damage?
              |
      ┌───────┴──────────────┐
      ↓                      ↓
      YES. Consider potential defendants   NO. There is no liability
      - producer?                          under the CPA.
      - own brander?
      - importer into the UK?
      - 'forgetful supplier'
              ↓
      The defendant is strictly liable for the claimant's damage
      subject to any available defences under the CPA.
```

Sample questions

Question 1

A solicitor is instructed by a manufacturer of exercise bikes. They have been notified of a claim by a customer. The details of the claim are that the customer bought one of the top-of-the-range exercise bikes from a sports shop that has subsequently ceased trading. They took the bike home, opened the packaging that the bike was supplied in by the manufacturer and read the instruction booklet carefully before using it for the first time. The customer is a professional violinist and decided to practise their violin at the same time as trying out the exercise bike. After a couple of minutes the seat post on the bike collapsed. The customer fell off the bike, broke their arm, smashed their glasses worth £150, and caused extensive damage to their very expensive violin. The customer wants compensation for all these losses and also the cost of a replacement bike. The customer has had the bike inspected by an expert who believes that the seat post collapsed due to insufficient welding on the bike. The expert believes that this defect would not have been apparent on a visual inspection of the bike.

All the manufacturer's products are sold subject to an exclusion of liability clause for all losses, howsoever caused.

Which of the following statements best explains whether the manufacturer may be liable for the customer's losses in negligence?

A   No, because the manufacturer did not owe a duty of care to the customer. The duty of care was owed by the sports shop.

B   No, because the customer will not be able to prove breach of duty of care by the manufacturer.

C   No, because the manufacturer will be able to rely on its exclusion of liability for all the customer's losses.

D   Yes, because the customer is likely to succeed in proving liability for all their losses except the cost of the bike.

E   Yes, because the customer is likely to succeed in proving liability for all their losses except the cost of the replacement bike and the damage to the very expensive violin.

Answer

Option E is correct.

Option A is wrong because the duty of care will be owed by the manufacturer. Shops and other suppliers will rarely owe a duty of care in negligence to their customers. The exception to this is where the shop is expected to carry out an intermediate examination of the goods. There is nothing to suggest that the manufacturer expected the sports shop to do this. In fact, the bike appears to have been supplied in packaging by the manufacturer and, according to the expert, an inspection of the bike would not have revealed the defect in any event.

Option B is wrong because, on the facts given, it cannot be said that the customer will definitely not be able to prove breach of duty. There are facts on which the court can base its inference of breach of duty, ie an expert who believes that the seat post collapsed due to insufficient welding on the bike. The court will infer breach of duty unless the manufacturer can rebut the inference of breach of duty by proving that the defect was not due to the defendant's lack of care but to some later problem, for example the claimant's own misuse of the product. This is unlikely to be the case on the facts. If the bike had been safe then the claimant's actions would probably not have been unreasonable – just a little unusual.

Option C is wrong because the manufacturer cannot exclude liability for the personal injury due to the Consumer Rights Act 2015 and they will only be able to exclude liability for the other losses if the exclusion is deemed fair under the Act.

Option D is wrong, because, while the customer may succeed in negligence for all their losses excluding the cost of the bike (as it is pure economic loss), a court may consider that the damage to the violin is too remote. It may not be reasonably foreseeable that a person would be playing a violin on an exercise bike.

Question 2

A solicitor is instructed by a manufacturer of exercise bikes. They have been notified of a claim by a customer. The details of the claim are that the customer bought an exercise bike from a sports shop. They took the bike home, opened the packaging that the bike was supplied in by the manufacturer and read the instruction booklet carefully before using it for the first time. After a couple of minutes the seat post on the bike collapsed. The customer fell off the bike, broke their arm, and smashed their glasses worth £150. They also caused extensive damage to their very expensive violin that was near the bike at the time. The customer is a professional violinist and wants compensation for all these losses, their income lost as a result of not being able to play the violin and the cost of a replacement bike.

The manufacturer has made thousands of this particular exercise bike without any complaints of this nature. They have investigated their production records and are confident that they are not at fault in any way.

All the manufacturer's products are sold subject to an exclusion of liability clause for all losses, howsoever caused.

Which of the following statements best explains whether the manufacturer may be liable for the customer's losses under the Consumer Protection Act 1987?

A   Yes, because the manufacturer will probably be held liable for all the losses except the cost of the replacement bike and the cost of the glasses.

B   Yes, because the manufacturer will probably be held liable, but only for the personal injury and the customer's lost income.

C   No, because the customer should be bringing a claim against the sports shop in contract.

D   No, because the manufacturer will be able to rely on its exclusion of liability for all the customer's losses if the clause is fair.

E   No, because the customer will not be able to prove that the manufacturer was at fault.

Answer

Option B is correct. The customer suffered 'damage' for the purposes of the CPA 1987 as they have broken their arm, and their consequential lost earnings, due to their inability to play the violin with a broken arm. They will not be able to claim for the cost of repairing or replacing the bike as damage to the defective product itself is excluded by the Act. Neither will they be able to recover the cost of the damaged violin if it is regarded as 'business' property. The cost of replacement glasses will not be recoverable as they are worth less than £275. The customer's recoverable losses were caused by a 'defect' as the safety of the bike was not such as persons generally were entitled to expect in all the circumstances. The bike is clearly a 'product' for the purposes of the CPA 1987. The customer will be able to claim against the manufacturer of the bike as the producer of the product.

Option A is wrong as it fails to consider that the violin will not be recoverable as it is business property.

Option C is wrong because, while the customer would also have a claim in contract against the shop, this does not mean that the customer is barred from bringing an alternative claim against the manufacturer under the CPA 1987 and/or negligence.

Option D is wrong because it is not possible to exclude liability under the CPA 1987; the question of whether the exclusion is fair is irrelevant.

Option E is wrong because liability under the CPA 1987 is strict. It is irrelevant, therefore, that the manufacturer may have evidence that they are not at fault (subject to the defence that the defect did not exist when the defendant supplied the product).

Product Liability

Question 3

A client has sought advice of a solicitor arising from the following events. The client lives in a ground floor flat. The client works from home as an IT consultant and their very expensive laptop, which they use for their work, has been damaged beyond repair. This was caused by water from a washing machine in the flat upstairs leaking into their flat. The owner of the upstairs flat's washing machine was brand new and was installed by an independent contractor. It appears that the contractor had forgotten to correctly tighten one of the hoses on the washing machine and this is why the water leaked into the client's flat.

Which of the following statements best explains whether the client may be successful in a claim for the cost of their laptop against the independent contractor under both the Consumer Protection Act 1987 (CPA 1987) and negligence?

A   No, because it is not generally possible for a claim to be commenced under both the CPA 1987 and negligence; claimants must choose between the two claims.

B   No, because, while a claim under the CPA 1987 may succeed as the washing machine was defective, the claim in negligence is bound to fail as the independent contractor was not a manufacturer.

C   No, because the claim under the CPA 1987 is bound to fail as the independent contractor is not a potential defendant under the CPA 1987. The claim under negligence may succeed.

D   Yes, because liability under the CPA 1987 is strict and the claim under negligence may also succeed.

E   Yes, because the independent contractor is a potential defendant under the CPA 1987 and liability under the CPA 1987 is strict. The claim in negligence may also succeed.

Answer

Option C is correct. The CPA 1987 claim is bound to fail as the independent contractor is not one of the potential defendants under the CPA 1987 as they are not a producer of the product, an 'own-brander', an importer or a 'forgetful' supplier. (It is also questionable whether the washing machine itself was 'defective' because, if it was unsafe, this was due to the actions of the installer.) The negligence claim is likely to succeed. The independent contractor is a 'manufacturer' who owes a duty to the client as a 'consumer' (it is reasonably foreseeable that the client would be affected by the contractor's actions and there is nothing to suggest that an intermediate examination of the contractor's work would be expected). The contractor's breach of duty by failing to tighten a hose has caused reasonably foreseeable harm to the client.

Option A is wrong because it is generally possible for a claim to be commenced under both the CPA 1987 and negligence. The claimant cannot, however, recover damages twice over for the same loss.

Option B is wrong because the claim under the CPA 1987 is bound to fail for the reasons discussed above. Option B is also wrong because the term 'manufacturer' (under the narrow rule from *Donoghue v Stevenson*) has been interpreted to include installers. The independent contractor is, therefore, a potential defendant in negligence.

Option D is wrong because, while liability under the CPA 1987 is strict, the independent contractor is not one of the potential defendants under the CPA 1987.

Option E is incorrect for the same reason as option D.

12 Nuisance

12.1	Introduction	170
12.2	Private nuisance	170
12.3	The rule in *Rylands v Fletcher*	183
12.4	Public nuisance	185

SQE1 syllabus

This chapter will enable you to achieve the SQE1 Assessment Specification in relation to Functioning Legal Knowledge concerned with the core principles on private nuisance, the rule in *Rylands v Fletcher* and public nuisance.

Note that for SQE1, candidates are not usually required to recall specific case names or cite statutory or regulatory authorities. Cases are provided for illustrative purposes only.

Learning outcomes

By the end of this chapter you will be able to apply relevant core legal principles and rules appropriately and effectively, at the level of a competent newly qualified solicitor in practice, to realistic client-based and ethical problems and situations in the following areas:

- private nuisance;
- the rule in *Rylands v Fletcher*;
- public nuisance.

12.1 Introduction

If a claimant's complaint relates to something which is happening or has happened in relation to land, there are several potential torts which the claimant may use. The most important of these in practice is private nuisance. This chapter will, therefore, concentrate on this tort. Another tort considered in this chapter is the tort known as the rule in *Rylands v Fletcher*. This is a specialised form of private nuisance which has its own rules. This chapter also briefly considers public nuisance. This is a crime which, in some circumstances, may be used by individuals who have suffered harm to claim damages in the civil courts.

12.2 Private nuisance

There are two types of nuisance at common law: private nuisance and public nuisance. Public nuisance is considered later in this chapter. However, it is important, by way of background and contrast to private nuisance, to appreciate the scope of public nuisance.

Public nuisance, as the name suggests, exists predominantly to protect the public in the exercise of public rights (for example, the right to use the highway without obstruction). Although individuals can sometimes sue in public nuisance, usually cases are brought by the Attorney General on behalf of the public. Public nuisances are also crimes.

In contrast, the law of private nuisance exists to protect an individual in their enjoyment of their own property.

Many of the issues are the same for private nuisance and public nuisance, and in many cases both types of nuisance will be relevant.

Many of the cases referred to below consider both areas of law.

12.2.1 Definition of private nuisance

A judicially approved definition of private nuisance is an 'unlawful interference with a person's use or enjoyment of land, or some right over, or in connection with it'.

This definition requires the claimant to show:

- that there is an interference with the claimant's use and enjoyment of land or some rights they enjoy over it; and
- that the interference is unlawful.

12.2.2 Interferences

In *Hunter v Canary Wharf* [1997] AC 655, three types of interferences within private nuisance were identified:

'(1) nuisance by encroachment on a neighbour's land;

(2) nuisance by indirect physical injury to a neighbour's land; and

(3) nuisance by interference with a neighbour's quiet enjoyment of his land.'

The last type of interference (often known as an interference with personal comfort or loss of amenity) is potentially very wide, encompassing, for example, smells, dust, vibration and noise. It will also include interferences with rights enjoyed over land (such as a right to light acquired by prescription). However, the courts are generally slower to find actionable nuisances based on personal discomfort than where actual damage to property or encroachment is concerned.

To be actionable in nuisance the interference must be something that materially interferes with 'ordinary comfort', not 'elegant or dainty modes ... of living' (Walter v Selfe (1851) 4 De G & Sm 315). It has been held, following this, that loss of prospect (a view) from a home is not an actionable interference (Aldred's Case (1610) 9 Co Rep 57b).

In Hunter v Canary Wharf [1997] AC 655, the House of Lords decided that disruption to TV reception caused by a new building was not an actionable interference in private nuisance. The reasoning in this case could equally apply to other modern 'luxuries' such as satellite reception.

12.2.3 Unlawful interference

The interference must be unlawful to be a private nuisance. The word that best describes 'unlawful' is 'unreasonable'. It does not usually mean criminal (although in some cases the defendant's conduct will also constitute a crime).

The qualification 'unlawful' is necessary because not all interferences will constitute actionable nuisances.

People are expected to tolerate a certain amount of noise, smells, etc as part and parcel of everyday life. However, people are not expected to tolerate substantial and unreasonable (excessive) interferences. Unlawful therefore means 'substantial and unreasonable'.

In *Sedleigh-Denfield v O'Callaghan* [1940] 3 All ER 349, it was said that:

> A balance has to be maintained between the right of the occupier to do what he likes with his own [land], and the right of his neighbour not to be interfered with. It is impossible to give any precise or universal formula, but it may broadly be said that a useful test is perhaps what is reasonable according to the ordinary usages of mankind living in society, or more correctly in a particular society.

The courts will therefore attempt to balance the right of one person to do what they lawfully are entitled to on their land against their neighbour's right to enjoy their land free from interference. However, the courts find encroachment onto a neighbour's land (eg overhanging tree branches) to be unlawful without any further consideration.

12.2.4 Relevant factors

There are various factors that are relevant in deciding whether an interference is substantial and unreasonable and therefore 'unlawful'. These are considered below. However, none of them are conclusive of the issue. The court is attempting to 'balance interests' and all factors will be taken into account in reaching a decision on unlawfulness.

It should be noted that, in deciding whether an interference is substantial and unreasonable (ie unlawful), the court is not concerned with whether the defendant's conduct is itself unreasonable (ie below the standard of care of a reasonable person). The reasonable person test, although central to negligence, has no part to play in the analysis of whether the interference is unreasonable. A defendant may have acted unreasonably, but this is not the key issue. The relevant control mechanism is found within the principle of reasonable user, ie has the defendant's use of their land unreasonably interfered with the claimant's reasonable use of their land.

12.2.4.1 Duration and frequency

The overall duration of an interference will be a very important factor. The longer the interference has lasted, the more likely it is that the court will consider the interference unreasonable. On the other hand, if the interference is only short term then the claimant will generally be expected to put up with it.

A related issue is the frequency of the interference.

⭐ Example

Harriet lives next door to her village cricket club. The cricket club was established 50 years ago. Each summer cricket is played at the club every Saturday afternoon. In an average year two balls are hit by batsmen into Harriet's garden. This is unlikely to be unlawful interference. Although cricket has been played for 50 years, the frequency of the interference into Harriet's garden would not be enough for this to be unreasonable. If, however, 10 balls are hit every Saturday into Harriet's garden, she might be able to show a sufficient degree of regularity to form the basis of a nuisance claim.

Some degree of continuity and frequency is required for an interference to be unlawful. It therefore follows that generally an isolated incident is unlikely to give rise to liability in private nuisance. An isolated happening will only constitute an actionable nuisance if it emanates from some continuing state of affairs on the defendant's property.

12.2.4.2 Excessiveness of conduct/extent of the harm

In determining whether an interference is unlawful, the courts will have regard to how excessive the defendant's conduct is (ie, how far removed it is from 'normal' behaviour). This is viewed objectively.

⭐ Example

Jeff lives next door to Anna. Jeff, a student, likes loud music and plays his powerful music system at maximum volume most afternoons. Objectively, the louder Jeff's music is, the more likely it is that the interference to Anna will be unreasonable.

However, the courts will also look at the extent of the harm (ie the impact on the claimant). This will be viewed subjectively. If, in the example above, Anna does not usually return home from work until late each evening, she would be unable to show that the loud music has much impact on her use and enjoyment of her home.

An interference which causes physical damage to the claimant's land is likely to be considered excessive. This factor will therefore tip the balance in the claimant's favour meaning such an interference is unlawful (unless the damage is trivial).

12.2.4.3 Character of the neighbourhood

The courts will sometimes take into account the character of locality in order to decide whether a particular interference is unlawful.

The courts have distinguished between an interference which causes physical (material) injury to property and an interference which causes only personal discomfort and inconvenience. The character of the neighbourhood is only relevant to an interference which causes personal discomfort and inconvenience.

If the claimant has suffered interference with personal comfort but not physical damage, whether the interference is unreasonable will be judged in relation to the degree and types of interference which can be expected in that particular locality. Each area will have its own standards. For example, a person who lives in London can expect to have to tolerate more noise from traffic, etc than a person who lives in a rural village in Wales. Conversely, the smells attributable to farm life are more appropriate to a rural location than a city centre.

In the case of *Coventry v Lawrence* [2014] UKSC 13, the Supreme Court clarified the law in relation to assessing the character of the locality. The court should start from the proposition that the defendant's activities are taken into account when making such assessment. However, such activities should only be considered to the extent to which they would not cause a nuisance to the claimant.

Therefore, if the activities cannot be carried out without creating a nuisance, such activities will have to be entirely discounted when assessing the character of the locality. Also, if the activities are in breach of planning permission, they will not be taken into account when assessing the character of the locality.

12.2.4.4 Public benefit

A defendant may often argue that their activity is reasonable as it benefits the public (for example, by providing a valuable source of hot food to the local community – a 'smelly' chip shop in *Adams v Ursell* [1913] 1 Ch 269). However, the courts consistently take the view that the interests of the public should not deprive an individual of their private rights. Public benefit, therefore, is not a relevant factor in deciding whether the defendant's use is unreasonable. (It may, however, be relevant when the court is deciding whether or not to grant an injunction (considered below).)

12.2.4.5 Malice

The extent to which any malice (ie spite or improper motive) on the defendant's part will be relevant in deciding whether an interference is unreasonable was addressed in the case of *Hollywood Silver Fox Farm v Emmett* [1936] 2 KB 468. In *Hollywood Silver Fox Farm*, the sole purpose of the defendant's shooting of a shotgun near to the claimant's countryside property was to annoy the claimant and, more particularly, to upset the claimant's silver foxes during breeding time. The interference, as carried out with malice, could not be regarded as a reasonable one.

Malice is a factor that is likely to tip the balance in the claimant's favour, potentially making an interference unlawful that would have been reasonable (and lawful) if done without malice.

12.2.5 Abnormal sensitivity

> In Robinson v Kilvert *(1889) LR 41 Ch D 88, the claimant occupied the ground floor of a warehouse. The defendants occupied the cellar below the claimant and manufactured paper boxes, which required heat and dry air. The defendant put up pipes to heat their cellar. The heat went up to the floor of the claimant's room, and damaged the claimant's stock of brown paper by drying it and preventing it from acquiring weight.*
>
> *The claim failed because the claimant's paper was abnormally sensitive as it was sold by weight. The hot, dry conditions reduced its weight and hence its value. 'Normal paper' (not sold by weight) would have been unaffected by the defendant's interference.*

If normal paper had been affected (even if to a lesser extent), then a nuisance could have been established. The defendant's use of the cellar would have been unreasonable and the claimant would have successfully recovered for all their loss.

So, when deciding whether an interference is unlawful the courts will look at its impact on the normal user of neighbouring land, ignoring any abnormal sensitivity of the claimant. However, if the claimant can show that the interference is unlawful when judged against the normal user of their land, they can then recover for all their loss even if greater (due to their sensitivity) than the normal user. This is an application of the 'egg-shell skull rule' discussed in **Chapter 3**. This is illustrated well by the case of *McKinnon Industries v Walker* [1951] 3 DLR 577. Here the claimant grew sensitive orchids. The defendant's business emitted fumes which damaged the orchids. The fumes would have damaged ordinary, more robust plants. The claimant could, therefore, establish an actionable nuisance and recover for the damage to the orchids.

12.2.6 Who can sue in private nuisance?

According to the House of Lords in *Hunter v Canary Wharf* [1997] 2 All ER 426, only a person with the right to exclusive possession of land can sue in private nuisance (a right to exclusive possession means a right to exclude everyone else). An owner-occupier of land has the best right to exclusive possession through the proprietary interest that they enjoy. A tenant of land also enjoys the right to exclusive possession through their proprietary interest in the leasehold title. Therefore, both owner-occupiers and tenants can sue in private nuisance as they have the right to exclusive possession deriving from their proprietary interest.

Children of the owner-occupier do not have a right to exclusive possession and cannot therefore bring a claim. The same applies to anyone staying in property legally owned by another person as their guest. For example, hotel guests do not have the right to exclusive possession of their rooms. They simply have a right to use their rooms.

In summary, therefore, according to the *Hunter* case, to be able to sue in private nuisance a claimant must have a proprietary interest in the land. A person who has exclusive possession of the land does have such an interest. A person who occupies land but does not have the right of exclusive possession cannot sue in nuisance.

12.2.7 Who is liable in private nuisance?

There are three potential defendants:

- The creator of the nuisance.
- The occupier of the land from which the nuisance originates (whether or not the occupier also created it).
- The landlord.

12.2.7.1 The creator of the nuisance

The original creator of the nuisance remains liable for it even if the land is now occupied by someone else.

The creator did the first wrong, and therefore it is fair that they remain responsible for any damage (subject to the rules on remoteness of damage).

★ Example

Five years ago, Tanya installed a water feature in her garden near the boundary between her land and that of her neighbour, Roger. Tanya moved house two years ago. Roger has just discovered that the pipes connected to this feature have been leaking and the escaping water has damaged the foundations of his house. Roger could sue Tanya as creator of the nuisance. It is immaterial that she no longer owns the house.

However, if the creator can no longer be found or is not financially worth suing, the claimant must look to the current occupier of the land for a remedy.

12.2.7.2 The occupier

The current occupier of land is the usual defendant. The occupier will be liable for nuisances they have created (whether by positive acts, or by failing to take steps, eg failing to repair a roof that becomes dangerous).

In addition, the occupier may also be liable for nuisances that are created by other persons in the following circumstances:

- Where the nuisance was created by an employee acting in the course of their employment (the occupier is liable under the normal principles of vicarious liability, as considered in **Chapter 9**).

- Where the nuisance is created by an independent contractor, provided the nature of the work carried a special danger of the nuisance being created (for example, where the risk of a nuisance is inevitable due to the substantial alteration work being carried out by a contractor).
- Where the nuisance is created by a visitor, predecessor in title or trespasser, or arises through some natural occurrence, provided the occupier has adopted the nuisance or continued it.

The third situation was considered in the case below.

In Sedleigh-Denfield v O'Callaghan *[1940] 3 All ER 349, the defendant's land had a ditch in which a pipe or culvert for carrying off rain water was laid without the knowledge or consent of the defendant, ie trespassers. The defendant, however, subsequently became aware of the pipe's existence and they in fact used it for the draining of their fields. To prevent leaves or other matter blocking the opening of the pipe a grating was placed on the top of the pipe. The consequence of this was that during a heavy rainstorm the pipe became choked with leaves, so that the water overflowed and caused damage to the claimant's property.*

The claimant succeeded because the defendant was aware of the nuisance and failed to take any reasonable steps. The court held that an occupier is liable for a nuisance created by a trespasser if:

- *the occupier has either 'adopted' or 'continued' the nuisance;*
- *occupiers 'adopt' a nuisance if they make use of the thing which constituted the nuisance;*
- *occupiers 'continue' a nuisance if, once they know or ought reasonably to know of its existence, they fail to take reasonable steps to end the nuisance.*

Although case law has not categorically decided the point, it is thought that when considering what are 'reasonable steps' for the purposes of ending a nuisance, the courts will take into account the defendant's actual financial resources.

Although the *Sedleigh-Denfield* case concerned a nuisance created by a trespasser, the same approach has been used in cases where the nuisance is created by visitors, predecessors in title and natural events.

12.2.7.3 The landlord

Where a nuisance arises on premises which are let to a tenant, the general rule is that the landlord is not liable. The tenant is the proper defendant because the tenant is in occupation.

There are, however, some situations where the landlord could still be liable.

The landlord will be liable where he has expressly or impliedly authorised the nuisance, ie the nuisance is the inevitable result of the letting. An example of this is the case of *Tetley v Chitty* [1986] 1 All ER 663. Here a local council let a piece of land to a go-kart racing club for use as a racing track. The court found that the inevitable consequence of this letting was the creation of a noise nuisance to neighbours. The landlord was therefore liable.

Another situation where a landlord will be liable is where the nuisance existed at the start of the letting and the landlord knew or ought reasonably to have known of it.

The final situation where a landlord will be liable arises where the landlord has covenanted (ie promised) to repair the premises, or has the right to enter to do so, and, in either case, fails to make the repairs, giving rise to the nuisance. This, however, does not exonerate the tenant, who may also be liable as occupier.

12.2.8 Damage

The claimant must prove that they have suffered damage.

12.2.8.1 Types of damage recoverable

Given that the tort is an interference with land, physical damage to land or buildings is clearly recoverable. (Crops/plants growing in the land are treated as part of the 'land'.)

In *Hunter v Canary Wharf*, the House of Lords stated that it was inappropriate to use private nuisance to claim for personal injury. The appropriate cause of action is in negligence. This relates to the fact that private nuisance is a tort against land and not against the person.

Nuisance is a tort against land. So interference with the quiet enjoyment of the land clearly comes within its scope even though it is not 'tangible' damage in the sense required by negligence.

Given the reasoning in the *Hunter* case, damage to personal property (eg personal belongings) is probably outside the scope of private nuisance. The appropriate cause of action would be negligence. However, this point was not specifically dealt with in *Hunter*, and other cases have allowed recovery on the basis that such losses flow as a consequence of the personal discomfort caused by the nuisance.

In *Hunter*, it was stated that where the claimant can prove recoverable damage (damage to property and/or personal discomfort) then the defendant would be liable for any consequential losses flowing from this as well. A good example of this would be loss of profits where a nuisance prevents a business from operating normally.

12.2.8.2 Causation and remoteness of damage

The claimant must prove that the unlawful interference caused their damage. The usual tests for causation apply (the 'but for' test and the rules on intervening acts considered in **Chapter 3**).

In *Cambridge Water Co v Eastern Counties Leather plc* [1994] 2 AC 264, it was decided that the same test for remoteness of damage (the *'Wagon Mound'* test) applies as in negligence. What the court must decide, therefore, is whether the kind of damage which occurred was reasonably foreseeable to someone in the defendant's position at the time the relevant acts were done.

12.2.9 Defences

It is necessary to distinguish between 'effective' and 'ineffective' defences. The former will enable the defendant to escape liability, whereas the latter, although often argued, will not.

12.2.9.1 Effective defences

(a) Prescription

The defence of prescription arises if the defendant can show that they have been continuing the nuisance for a period of at least 20 years against the claimant. The effect of prescription is that the defendant has 'acquired' the right to commit the nuisance.

The defence is rarely available, however, as the interference must have been actionable by the particular claimant for at least 20 years.

> ⭐ *Example*
>
> *For five years Anita has lived next door to a factory which has regularly emitted noxious fumes and a nauseating smell. The same factory has been operating at the site for 30 years. If Anita sues the factory's owner in private nuisance the defence of prescription will not apply as the nuisance has been actionable by Anita for only five years.*

⭐ *Example*

Mrs Ali has, for more than 20 years, made sweets in the back of her premises. This involves using large pestles and mortars (utensils for pounding and mixing the ingredients). Dr Khan, a medical consultant, owns a house, the garden of which runs down to Mrs Ali's premises. The noise and vibration caused by using the large pestles and mortars do not affect the doctor's enjoyment of his property until he builds a consulting room at the end of his garden. He then discovers that the noise and vibration substantially interfere with his practice. He sues Mrs Ali in private nuisance.

Mrs Ali would not be able successfully to rely on the defence of prescription because, although her activities have been continuing for 20 years, they have not been an actionable nuisance for this period. They have been actionable only since Dr Khan built his consulting room. (This example is based on the case of Sturges v Bridgman *(1879) 11 Ch D 852.)*

(b) **Statutory authority**

Sometimes a statute will permit a defendant to commit a nuisance. In such cases, the defendant may be able to rely on the defence of statutory authority if it can show that the nuisance was an inevitable result of doing what the statute authorised. This can be a defence to any tort, but it most commonly arises in relation to nuisance claims. It is unlikely to be available to private individuals, and is of most use to public authorities acting under statutory powers.

⭐ *Example*

An oil company is authorised by an Act of Parliament to construct an oil refinery in a particular location. Local residents complain about the noise and vibrations emitted from the refinery. The oil company is likely to be able successfully to plead statutory authority as a defence on the basis that the operation of the refinery is implicitly authorised by the Act of Parliament and the nuisances are, therefore, inevitable. (This example is based on the case of Allen v Gulf Oil Refining Ltd *[1981] AC 1001.)*

(c) **Contributory negligence**

This partial defence is available to claims in private nuisance. The usual principles which are considered in **Chapter 7** apply.

(d) **Consent**

If the defendant can show that the claimant has specifically agreed to accept the interference, the claimant's claim in nuisance will fail.

⭐ *Example*

Mike and Anne are neighbours. As a favour, Mike agrees to let Anne put her garden rubbish on his bonfire each week. If the smoke from Mike's bonfires blows across Anne's garden to such a degree as to constitute a nuisance, she would probably be met with the defence of consent.

(e) **Act of God or nature**

This is not strictly a defence but an operation of the law concerning the circumstances in which an occupier can be liable for natural events on their land. Where an interference on the defendant's land results from a 'secret unobservable process of nature' (eg subsidence under or near the foundations of the defendant's house) or from an act of God (eg lightning) then the defendant will not be liable in nuisance unless they adopt or continue the nuisance.

(f) Necessity

The two elements of the defence of necessity are:

- a situation of necessity exists because of an imminent danger to life and limb (or, in very limited circumstances, a threat to property); and
- that the defendant's actions were reasonable in all the circumstances.

The defence most often arises in the context of intentional torts such as trespass to the person and trespass to land (both outside of the scope of this book). The defence cannot be used if the circumstances giving rise to necessity were of the defendant's own making. For this reason, the defence cannot be relied upon if the defendant was negligent, ie at fault in any way.

The defence has been successfully relied upon in the context of private nuisance. In the case of *Southport Corporation v Esso Petroleum* [1956] AC 218, the defendant's oil tanker ran aground and there was a danger that she might break up with the probable loss of the ship and the loss of the lives of her crew. In order to prevent this, the master discharged 400 tons of oil into the sea. The river estuary was polluted and the claimant corporation alleged that the deposit of oil on the foreshore gave rise to a claim in nuisance. The House of Lords held that a nuisance had been committed but that the defence of necessity succeeded. The defendants were absolved of liability because life and limb were at risk.

12.2.9.2 Ineffective defences

This section considers the arguments which a defendant will not be successful in raising as potential defences to claims in nuisance.

(a) Claimant 'came to the nuisance'

⊛ Example

Richard buys a house next to a factory. Considerable noise from the machinery and noxious fumes emanate from the factory. He can still sue in private nuisance for the noise and the fumes, even though he knew about them when he bought the house. The factory owner cannot successfully defend the claim by claiming 'You bought the house with your eyes open'.

(The justification for this rule is that one landowner could, in effect, potentially block the sale of adjoining property if their unreasonable use of land were unchallengeable. This would restrict the property market and not be in the public interest. Even if the adjoining land did change hands, its use could be curtailed if a neighbour could argue 'I got here first' with their particular use.)

In *Coventry v Lawrence* [2014] UKSC 13, the Supreme Court held that, provided a claimant in private nuisance uses their property for essentially the same purpose as their predecessors before the nuisance started, the defendant cannot rely on the defence that the claimant 'came to the nuisance'. However, where a claimant builds on their land or changes the use of the property after the defendant had initially commenced the activity then the claimant's claim for nuisance could fail.

Although it is generally no defence for a defendant to argue that the claimant came to the nuisance, a court may consider it a relevant factor in deciding whether or not to grant the claimant an injunction (see below).

(b) Public benefit

The fact that the defendant's activity is beneficial to the public will not afford them a defence. However, the court may take this fact into account when deciding whether or not to grant an injunction (see below).

(c) Contributory actions of others

It is no defence that the nuisance results from the separate actions of several people. In other words, a defendant cannot argue that their act alone would not constitute an actionable nuisance.

✪ Example

There are many stalls at a fair which have music playing. The combined effect of the music from all the stalls is to create a nuisance. Each stallholder who has music playing will be liable in nuisance.

(d) Planning permission

The view of the courts is that only Parliament can take away private rights to sue (by primary or secondary legislation). Therefore, the mere grant of planning permission (which is granted by local authorities and not Parliament) does not legitimise a nuisance. For example, in the case of *Wheeler v Saunders* [1995] 2 All ER 697, a farmer obtained planning permission to build a pig unit on their land. The owners of some holiday cottages on adjacent land complained of the smell and noise emitting from the pig unit. The farmer was not allowed to claim in their defence that they had planning permission.

However, the grant of planning permission can operate to change the character of the neighbourhood, which is a consideration when deciding whether an interference with personal comfort is unlawful. For example, in *Gillingham BC v Medway Docks Co Ltd* [1992] 3 WLR 449, the planning authority granted planning permission for a former naval dockyard to be converted into a busy container port. Local residents complained about the noise and vibration from the heavy lorries using the port. When deciding whether this amounted to an unlawful interference, the court said you had to consider the character of the neighbourhood as it was after the grant of the planning permission and not as it was before. The residents now lived in an area that was a container port – in this context the level of noise, etc was not unlawful.

In *Coventry v Lawrence* [2014] UKSC 13, the Supreme Court held that, where planning permission stipulates limits as to the frequency and intensity of noise, then such conditions within a planning permission may be relevant in assisting the claimant's action in private nuisance.

12.2.10 Remedies

The two principal remedies are damages and an injunction.

✪ Example

Jeremy owns a house opposite an oil depot. He complains about the following problems which have been occurring for five years:

- *Acid smuts from a boiler in the depot have damaged plants in his garden.*
- *An unpleasant smell from the oil.*
- *Noise from the boilers at the depot at night.*
- *Noise from lorries at the depot at night. Jeremy intends to sue in private nuisance.*

Jeremy will be seeking monetary compensation (damages) to compensate him for these interferences with the use and enjoyment of his land. He will also ask the court to make an order regulating the oil depot's activities. Such an order is known as an injunction.

(This example is based on the case of Halsey v Esso Petroleum Co *[1961] 1 WLR 683.)*

12.2.10.1 Damages

Damages will be awarded for any loss which the claimant has already suffered by the date of trial. The court also has a limited power to award damages for future loss.

(a) **Physical damage to the claimant's land**

Where the nuisance damages the claimant's land (including buildings on it and plants growing in it), a claimant will generally be awarded damages to reflect the cost of repairing the damage or, if this is not possible, the loss in value of the land in question.

(b) **Personal discomfort**

Where the claimant has suffered an interference with their personal comfort, the value of the claim is more difficult to assess. In *Hunter v Canary Wharf*, it was suggested that personal discomfort should be valued by looking at the loss of amenity value of the land in question (ie the land with the nuisance being worth less than the land without the nuisance).

In many nuisance cases the claimant will want damages to compensate for the defendant's conduct to date, but where the interference is continuing, they will also want an injunction to regulate the defendant's future conduct.

12.2.10.2 Injunctions

An injunction is an order of the court which restrains the commission of or continuance of some wrongful act in the future.

Injunctions are available in many areas of tort, including nuisance, where claimants often seek an injunction to stop the defendant's unlawful interference from continuing. (An injunction is not available in negligence. A claim brought in negligence always relates to an event which is finished, ie it is in the past. As such, there is no scope for an injunction and damages are the appropriate remedy.)

The types of injunction available are briefly considered below.

(a) **Prohibitory injunction**

This type of injunction forbids the defendant from persisting in some wrongful act, ie it stops the defendant from acting in a particular way.

(b) **Mandatory injunction**

By this type of injunction the court orders the defendant to take some positive action to rectify the consequences of what they have done. As the court is requiring the defendant to act positively, such injunctions are granted less readily than prohibitory injunctions.

(c) **A '*quia timet*' injunction**

Normally, either of the types of injunctions considered above will be granted once the tort has been committed. For nuisance this means that the claimant must have suffered damage before seeking an injunction. However, exceptionally, the courts are prepared to grant either a prohibitory or a mandatory injunction *quia timet*, ie in anticipation of the commission of the tort by the defendant, in order to prevent the claimant suffering any damage. In order to obtain such an injunction the claimant will have to show:

- they are almost certain to incur damage without the injunction; and
- such damage is imminent; and
- the defendant will not stop their course of conduct without the order of the court.

An injunction is an equitable and therefore discretionary remedy, which means that although a claimant can seek an injunction, whether or not to grant the injunction is the decision of the court, having regard to all the circumstances of the case.

One crucial point to appreciate about all types of injunction is that they will not be awarded where damages would be an adequate remedy. However, damages can only be awarded for past breaches which have already occurred. Where a claimant seeks to prevent future breaches, damages will not be an adequate remedy. Only an injunction is adequate in those circumstances.

Assuming the claimant has made out a prima facie case for grant of an injunction, the court must then decide how to exercise its discretion whether or not to grant the injunction. If, in the exercise of its discretion, the court decides not to grant the injunction, it has the power to grant damages instead. Damages granted in lieu of an injunction can cover future breaches. The claimant receives the damages as compensation for future interference with their rights, instead of an injunction preventing such interference.

Guidelines were given in the case of *Shelfer v City of London Electric Lighting Co* [1895] 1 Ch 287 on how the court should exercise its discretion to refuse the injunction and grant damages instead. Essentially, where the claimant has made out a prima facie case for grant of an injunction, the court may exercise its discretion to refuse an injunction and grant damages instead where:

- the harm suffered by the applicant is:
    - small; and
    - capable of being quantified in financial terms; and
    - capable of adequate compensation by damages; and
- it would be oppressive to the defendant to grant the injunction.

In other words, if a sum of money will adequately compensate the claimant, the court will not grant an injunction halting or restricting the defendant's activity.

In *Coventry v Lawrence* [2014] UKSC 13, the Supreme Court held that the application of the guidelines from *Shelfer* above must not be a fetter on the exercise of the court's discretion. It would normally be right to refuse an injunction if the four tests were satisfied and there were no additional relevant circumstances pointing the other way. However, the fact that those tests are not all satisfied does not mean that an injunction has to be granted. Furthermore, the public interest may be a relevant consideration (such as the employees of the defendant losing their jobs if an injunction is granted or whether other neighbours in addition to the claimant are badly affected by the nuisance). Also, where the nuisance complained of has previously been authorised in a planning permission, this may influence the court to conclude that it is in the public benefit that the claimant is awarded damages rather than an injunction.

12.2.10.3 Abatement (self-help)

The two principal remedies for private nuisance are damages and injunctions. A third remedy is abatement, which is considered briefly below.

Abatement involves the removal of the interference by the victim. The victim must, however, normally give prior notice to the wrongdoer, except in an emergency or where the nuisance can be abated (removed) without entering the wrongdoer's land.

🟊 Example

Samir and Terry are neighbours. The branches of a tree in Terry's garden overhang Samir's drive, making it difficult for Samir to get his car in and out of his garage. Rather than suing Terry for private nuisance, Samir would like to resolve the problem amicably.

He has therefore approached Terry, who has refused to do anything about the tree. Samir can cut down the overhanging branches himself, exercising the remedy of abatement (self-help). He does not need to notify Terry in advance because he does not need to enter Terry's land to remove the nuisance. However, the branches still belong to Terry and must be returned to him once they have been cut.

12.2.11 Differences between private nuisance and negligence

The principal differences between private nuisance and negligence include the following:

- Private nuisance is an interference with land. Consequently, only someone with a proprietary interest in the land affected by the interference can sue. The class of potential claimants in negligence is wider since it is not necessary to show that the use or enjoyment of the claimant's land has been affected.

- Private nuisance requires some continuity. Therefore, an isolated interference, unless it results from a state of affairs, will not constitute a private nuisance. Liability in negligence does not require any continuity – an isolated act or omission is enough.

- The concept of reasonableness has relevance for both torts. In deciding whether an interference is unlawful for the purposes of a nuisance claim, the relevant issue is whether the defendant's use of the land is unreasonable. In a negligence claim, on the other hand, the issue is whether the defendant's act is unreasonable, ie whether the defendant has fallen below the standard of the reasonable person in the defendant's position.

- Where a defendant is sued in private nuisance for a hazard which has arisen naturally on the land, the courts are willing to take into account the defendant's financial means. A defendant's financial resources are generally irrelevant, however, in deciding whether the duty of care has been breached in a negligence claim.

- A defendant can still be liable in private nuisance even if the defendant has exercised reasonable care. (The relevant issue is not whether the defendant's act is reasonable, but whether the use of the land is reasonable.) In negligence, on the other hand, the defendant will be liable only if they have fallen below the standard of the reasonable person.

- A claimant can sue in private nuisance for intangible damage (as well as tangible damage). Intangible damage is insufficient for a negligence claim. Personal discomfort caused by, for example, noise and smells, would not constitute 'damage' for the purposes of a negligence claim.

- Following *Hunter v Canary Wharf Ltd* [1997] 2 All ER 426, it would appear that personal injury no longer falls within the scope of private nuisance. (The same may also be true of damage to personal property.) This represents a major difference between claims in private nuisance and negligence.

- An injunction is a potential remedy if a claim in private nuisance succeeds. It is not a remedy in a negligence claim.

It is important to be aware of the possibility of a claimant having claims in both private nuisance and negligence. This would be the case only where a claimant has suffered actual (tangible) damage to their property. If a claimant has only suffered intangible damage (eg personal discomfort from smells or noise), a claim would lie only in private nuisance since this type of damage is insufficient for a claim in negligence.

12.3 The rule in *Rylands v Fletcher*

The rule in *Rylands v Fletcher* comes from the case of the same name (*Rylands v Fletcher* (1868) LR 3 HL 330). This case created a tort that covers the situation where there is an escape of something dangerous in the course of a non-natural use of land. The occupier of the land is liable for the damage caused as a result of the escape, irrespective of fault. The tort, therefore, imposes strict liability for the harm because it is not based upon the need to prove that the occupier failed to take reasonable care or that the defendant has been an unreasonable user of their land.

The rule in *Rylands v Fletcher* is a type of private nuisance that protects claimants from interferences due to isolated escapes from a neighbour's land. The rules on who can sue, who can be liable, the types of damage recoverable (eg personal injury is not a harm protected by the tort), the defences and the remedies available are essentially the same as those of private nuisance.

The elements of the tort are:

- The defendant brings onto their land for their own purposes something likely to do mischief
- if it escapes
- which represents a non-natural use of land
- it causes foreseeable damage of the relevant type.

Each of these elements is considered below.

12.3.1 The defendant brings onto their land for their own purposes something likely to do mischief

The thing or substance brought onto land need not be dangerous in itself but must be capable of causing damage if it escapes. The kinds of things that have been found to be likely to cause damage if they escape are water, cattle, sewage, fumes and electricity.

In Transco v Stockport Metropolitan Borough Council [2003] UKHL 61, water had escaped from a pipe belonging to the defendant local authority and supplying a block of flats of which it was the owner. The water caused the collapse of a nearby railway embankment which left a gas pipe belonging to the claimant unsupported and at risk of damage. The claimant claimed against the local authority for the cost of remedial measures to protect the gas pipe, arguing that the local authority was liable for damage caused by the escape of the water without proof of negligence. One of the issues to be decided was whether the local authority had brought onto its land something likely to cause danger or mischief if it escaped.

The House of Lords restricted the ability of claimants generally to satisfy this element of the tort. The court held that it must be shown that the defendant had done something which they recognised, or, judged by the standards appropriate at the relevant place and time, they ought reasonably to have recognised, as giving rise to an exceptionally high risk of danger or mischief *if there should be an escape however unlikely an escape may have been thought of. The requirement of a risk of mischief (ie damage) was, therefore, increased from 'likely' to 'exceptionally likely'. This was not satisfied on the facts of* Transco v Stockport Metropolitan Borough Council *and the claim failed.*

12.3.2 Escape

There must be an escape of a 'thing likely to do mischief'. In contrast to private nuisance, which requires continuity and frequency before an interference is unlawful, the rule in *Rylands v Fletcher* applies to isolated escapes from land.

The necessary requirement for an escape is that the substance or item causing damage must actually move from the defendant's premises to a place outside the defendant's occupation or control. This was confirmed by the Court of Appeal in *Stannard (t/a Wyvern Tyres) v Gore* [2012] EWCA Civ 1248. Tyres stored on the defendant's land caught fire and destroyed both the claimant's and the defendant's premises. The claim failed as, while fire had spread from the defendant's land to the claimant's land, the tyres themselves had not escaped. (The fire itself had not been brought onto the defendant's land and then escaped).

12.3.3 Non-natural use of land

The rule in *Rylands v Fletcher* only applies when the thing that causes damage by its escape is not 'naturally' on the defendant's land.

The leading case on the meaning of 'non-natural use' is *Transco v Stockport Metropolitan Borough Council* (considered above). The House of Lords held that the test was that the use of land must be extraordinary or unusual according to the standards of the day. This indicates that the use of land for normal industrial purposes is not generally a 'non-natural use' as it is regarded as a natural use of land. However, it is a question of fact in each case. For example, while a factory that produces bicycles is an ordinary use of land, it is likely that a producer of explosives would be deemed an extraordinary or unusual use of land.

12.3.4 Causes foreseeable damage of the relevant type

While the first three elements of requirements for the rule in *Rylands v Fletcher* come from the *Rylands* case itself, this fourth requirement was added by *Cambridge Water Co Ltd v Eastern Counties Leather Plc* (above). This case introduced the remoteness principle from negligence (*The Wagon Mound (No 1)* considered in **Chapter 3**) as an element of the rule in *Rylands v Fletcher*.

The claimant was ultimately unsuccessful in *Cambridge Water Co Ltd v Eastern Counties Leather Plc* because the damage they suffered was held not to be reasonably foreseeable, ie it was too remote.

12.3.5 Defences

12.3.5.1 Escape caused by the unforeseeable act of a stranger

The defendant will not be liable if they could not have reasonably foreseen the act of the stranger and therefore could not do anything to prevent the harm.

12.3.5.2 Escape caused by an 'act of God' which could not have been reasonably foreseen

The defendant will not be liable for an extraordinary act of nature, which could not have been reasonably foreseen.

12.3.5.3 Statutory authority

This is considered in the context of private nuisance above.

12.3.5.4 Consent (voluntary assumption of risk)

This is considered in **Chapter 7**.

12.3.5.5 Contributory negligence

This is considered in **Chapter 7**.

12.4 Public nuisance

Public nuisance is a crime that is defined as:

> as an act or an omission that endangers the life, health, property or comfort of the public, or obstructs the public in the exercise or enjoyment of rights common to all His Majesty's subjects (Archbold: Criminal Pleading, Evidence and Practice (2020)).

Public officers or bodies are primarily responsible for enforcement of public nuisance (eg the Attorney General, or local authorities).

However, public nuisance can also give rise to tortious liability in some circumstances as it may be used by individuals who have suffered particular harm to claim damages in the civil courts.

The elements of the tort of public nuisance are:

- conduct that materially affects the reasonable comfort and convenience of a 'class of Her Majesty's subjects'; and
- the claimant has suffered particular harm.

12.4.1 Unreasonable conduct that materially affects the reasonable comfort and convenience of a 'class of His Majesty's subjects'

A key difference between private and public nuisance is that a public nuisance affects 'His Majesty's subjects' generally, whereas a private nuisance only affects particular individuals. The number of people in a locality required to be affected by the nuisance, so as to constitute a class of the public, is a question of fact in each case. It is not necessary that every member of the class is affected but a representative cross-section must have been affected.

⭐ Example

A restaurant collects a large quantity of putrefying food waste on its land near a village. The householders nearest to the restaurant suffer the most from the smell, but everyone in the neighbourhood suffers too.

In this case the Attorney General could take proceedings for an injunction to restrain the nuisance. The Attorney General would do this in defence of the public right, not for any individual interests.

⭐ Example

A landowner collects a large quantity of putrefying rubbish on their land in a remote part of the countryside. Only three property owners are affected by the smell.

The affected property owners would not constitute a sufficiently large class of the public to give rise to an action for public nuisance. The affected property owners would need to take proceedings under private nuisance on their own account to stop the interference to their private rights.

12.4.2 The claimant has suffered particular harm

A claimant who wishes to bring a claim in the tort of public nuisance must have suffered 'particular' damage over and above that suffered by the public at large. This can include property damage and loss of profit. In contrast to private nuisance, and the rule in *Rylands v Fletcher*, the particular harm suffered by the claimant can also include personal injury.

⭐ Example

A car driver on the road next to the defendant's golf course is struck by a golf ball hit from the thirteenth tee. Evidence shows that balls from the golf course frequently go over the highway from the thirteenth tee.

The car driver could bring a claim for their personal injury under the tort of public nuisance. The class of persons affected are highway users and the public's right to use the highway has been affected. The claimant has suffered particular damage in the form of a personal injury. (This example is based upon the case of Castle v St Augustine's Links *(1922) 38 TLR 615.)*

12.4.3 Differences between public nuisance and private nuisance

Public nuisance is concerned with conduct that endangers the life, safety and health of the public. It therefore has a potentially greater scope of application than private nuisance as it is not limited to conduct interfering with the enjoyment of land.

In contrast to private nuisance, claimants in public nuisance do not need a proprietary interest in land affected by the nuisance and can be compensated for their personal injuries. Defendants can be liable for isolated events in public nuisance.

However, in many cases both types of nuisance will be relevant in that a public nuisance that causes the claimant particular harm may give rise to a claim in private nuisance as interfering with the individual's use and enjoyment of their land. The defences to private and public nuisance are essentially the same.

Summary

- To establish the elements of a claim in private nuisance, a person must have a proprietary interest in land, must show that the interference is 'unlawful' and that the defendant is a person who is liable for the interference. The defences available to a defendant and available remedies for the claimant must also be considered.

- The structure of private nuisance is very different to a claim in negligence, but it is important that private nuisance claims are approached in the structured way considered in this chapter.

- There are overlaps and differences between a claim in negligence and private nuisance. In essence, negligence requires a careless act by the defendant and will be relevant only where the claimant has suffered some tangible damage (injury or damage to property).

- The rule in *Rylands v Fletcher* is a type of private nuisance that covers the situation where there is an escape of something dangerous in the course of a non-natural use of land. This tort protects claimants from interferences due to isolated escapes from a neighbour's land.

- Public nuisance is a crime but it can also give rise to tortious liability in some circumstances as it may be used by individuals who have suffered particular harm due to an interference with the reasonable comfort and convenience of the public at large.

Summary flowcharts

Figure 12.1 Private nuisance flowchart

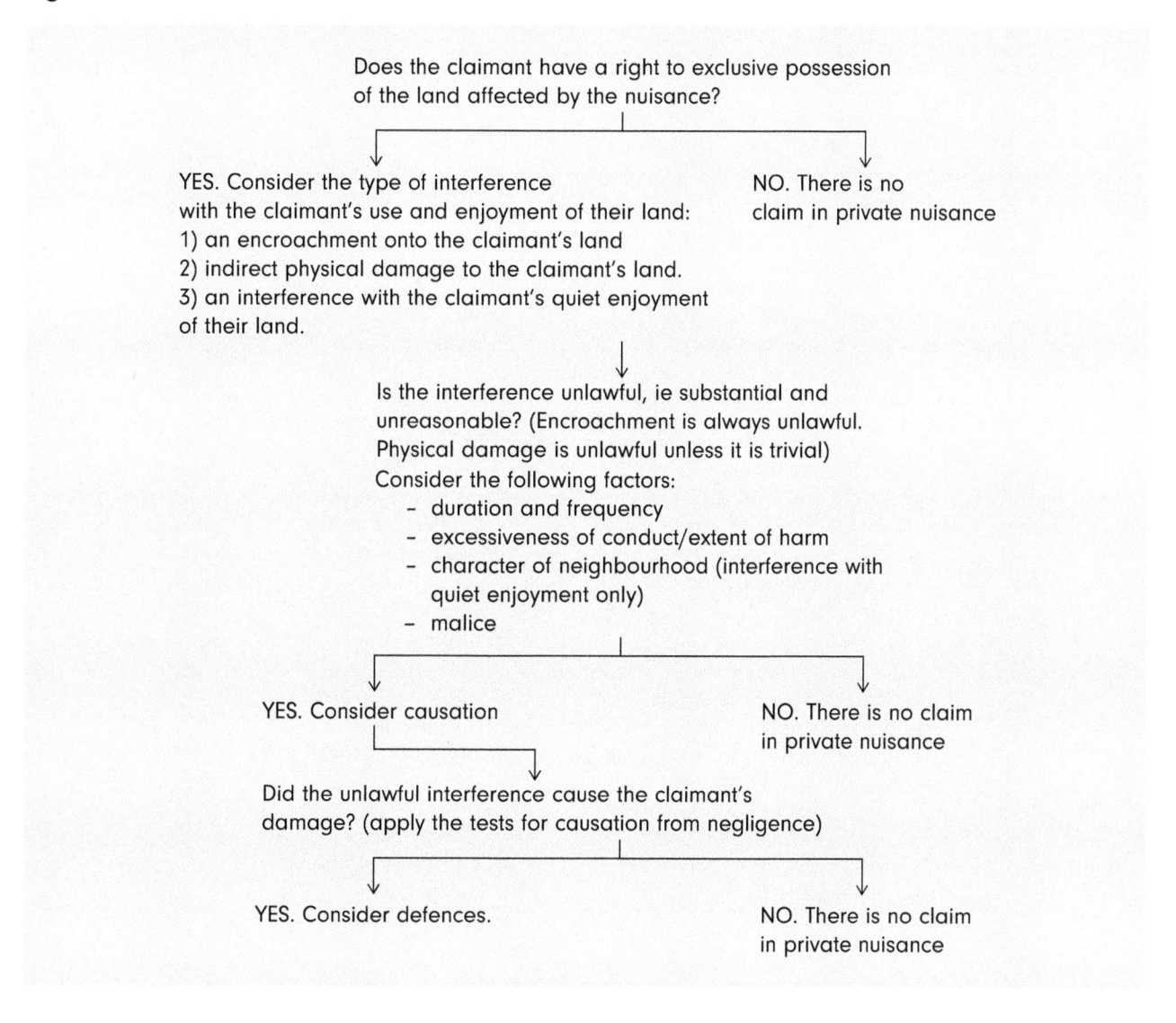

Does the claimant have a right to exclusive possession of the land affected by the nuisance?

YES. Consider the type of interference with the claimant's use and enjoyment of their land:
1) an encroachment onto the claimant's land
2) indirect physical damage to the claimant's land.
3) an interference with the claimant's quiet enjoyment of their land.

NO. There is no claim in private nuisance

Is the interference unlawful, ie substantial and unreasonable? (Encroachment is always unlawful. Physical damage is unlawful unless it is trivial) Consider the following factors:
- duration and frequency
- excessiveness of conduct/extent of harm
- character of neighbourhood (interference with quiet enjoyment only)
- malice

YES. Consider causation

NO. There is no claim in private nuisance

Did the unlawful interference cause the claimant's damage? (apply the tests for causation from negligence)

YES. Consider defences.

NO. There is no claim in private nuisance

Figure 12.2 The rule in *Rylands v Fletcher* flowchart

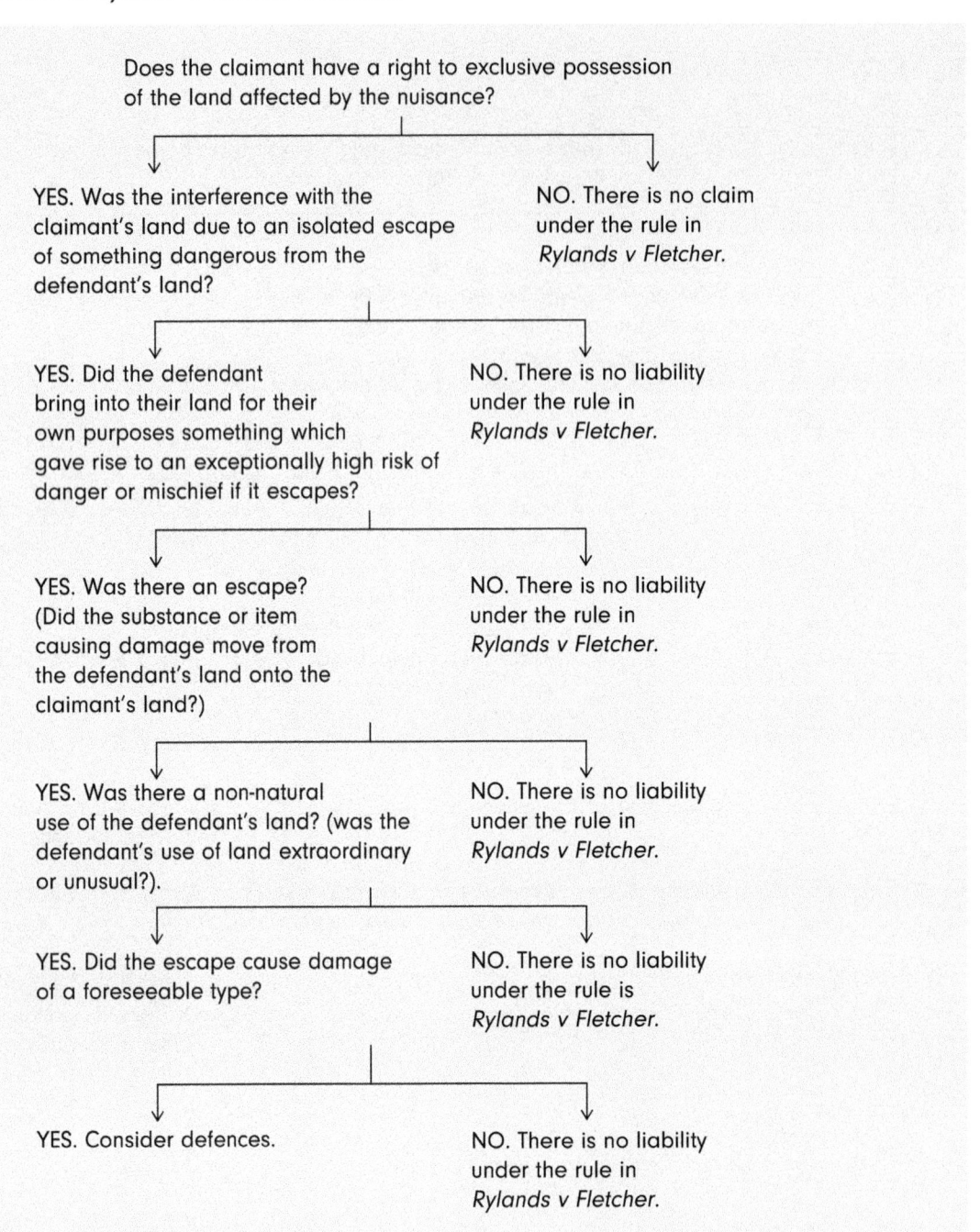

Does the claimant have a right to exclusive possession of the land affected by the nuisance?

YES. Was the interference with the claimant's land due to an isolated escape of something dangerous from the defendant's land?

NO. There is no claim under the rule in *Rylands v Fletcher*.

YES. Did the defendant bring into their land for their own purposes something which gave rise to an exceptionally high risk of danger or mischief if it escapes?

NO. There is no liability under the rule in *Rylands v Fletcher*.

YES. Was there an escape? (Did the substance or item causing damage move from the defendant's land onto the claimant's land?)

NO. There is no liability under the rule in *Rylands v Fletcher*.

YES. Was there a non-natural use of the defendant's land? (was the defendant's use of land extraordinary or unusual?).

NO. There is no liability under the rule in *Rylands v Fletcher*.

YES. Did the escape cause damage of a foreseeable type?

NO. There is no liability under the rule is *Rylands v Fletcher*.

YES. Consider defences.

NO. There is no liability under the rule in *Rylands v Fletcher*.

Nuisance

Figure 12.3 Public nuisance flowchart

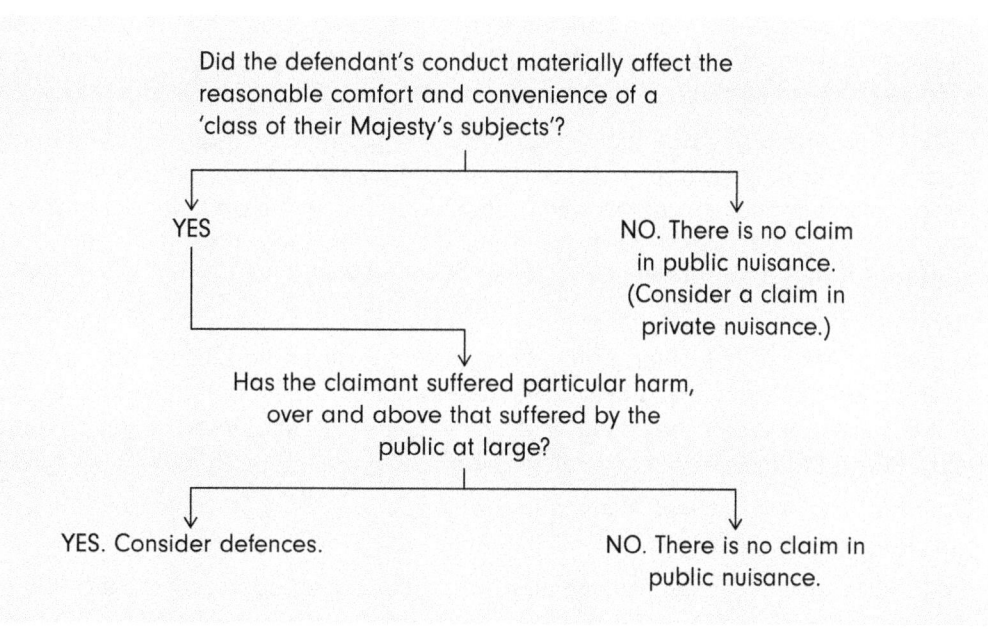

```
Did the defendant's conduct materially affect the
reasonable comfort and convenience of a
'class of their Majesty's subjects'?
         |
    ┌────┴────┐
    ▼         ▼
   YES      NO. There is no claim
    |       in public nuisance.
    |       (Consider a claim in
    |       private nuisance.)
    ▼
Has the claimant suffered particular harm,
over and above that suffered by the
public at large?
         |
    ┌────┴────┐
    ▼         ▼
YES. Consider defences.   NO. There is no claim in
                          public nuisance.
```

Sample questions

Question 1

A solicitor is instructed by a client who bought a house located in a rural location six months ago. A cement factory is near to the client's house. Heavy lorries regularly arrive and leave during the day and night via a public road, making it difficult for the client to sleep at night.

The client has complained to the factory owner. The factory owner has responded that the factory has been operating for 25 years in the same location and that the client should not have bought their house near a factory if they are a light sleeper. The factory owner has also confirmed that their lorries are fitted with the best noise reduction mechanisms that are available on the market.

Which of the following statements best explains whether the client may have a claim in tort against the factory owner?

A   Yes, because the client will be able to pursue a claim in public nuisance because the lorries are using a public road.

B   Yes, because the client will be able to pursue a claim in private nuisance because the noise from the lorries is substantial and unreasonable.

C   Yes, because the factory is a non-natural use of land in a rural location.

D   No, because the factory was already operating before the client moved to the area.

E   No, because the factory owner has taken reasonable care to ensure that the noise from the lorries is kept to a minimum level.

189

Tort

Answer

Option B is correct. The noise from the lorries may be a substantial and unreasonable interference with the claimant's use of their land. The fact that the noise is at night and in a rural location would indicate that the claimant would have a claim in private nuisance.

Option A is wrong because there is nothing to suggest that the noise from the lorries affects a 'class of Her Majesty's subjects', ie a sufficient number of members of the public. Public nuisance is primarily concerned with protecting public rights and the fact that the lorries are using a public road is only incidental to the interference with the client's private right to be able to use and enjoy their land.

Option C is wrong because a non-natural use of land is only one element of the rule in *Rylands v Fletcher*. The other requirements are not satisfied on these facts as there has not been an escape of anything likely to cause damage to the claimant's land. In fact, it is unlikely that this is a non-natural use of land in any event. A cement factory is not an extraordinary or unusual use of land, even in a rural location.

Option D is wrong because 'coming to the nuisance' is an ineffective defence to a claim in private nuisance.

Option E is wrong because private nuisance is not based upon proving that the defendant has not taken reasonable care. Private nuisance is concerned with whether the consequences of the defendant's use of their land is unlawful in that it causes a substantial and unreasonable interference with the claimant's use of their land.

Question 2

A solicitor is instructed by the manufacturer of explosives used in the mining industry. A relatively minor explosion at the client's factory scattered debris over the trading estate situated next door to their factory. Fortunately, no one was injured. However, the client has been contacted by one potential claimant. They are the owner of one of the businesses on the trading estate who are looking to claim for the cost of damage to the roof of their warehouse.

An expert has investigated the cause of the explosion and they have advised that the client was not to blame for the explosion.

Which of the following statements best explains whether the client may be liable in tort for the damage to the warehouse roof?

A   No, because the incident was an isolated event.

B   No, because the explosion was not the client's fault.

C   Yes, because the warehouse owner has suffered particular harm over and above the harm suffered by the public at large.

D   Yes, because the client's use of their land was non-natural and the debris caused foreseeable damage.

E   Yes, because property damage is always an unlawful interference with the use and enjoyment of land.

Answer

Option D is the correct answer. The manufacture of explosives is likely to do mischief and it is likely to be held to be a non-natural use of land. The debris from the explosives has 'escaped' and caused foreseeable harm to the warehouse owner. The rule in *Rylands v Fletcher* is, therefore, satisfied.

Option A is wrong because the torts of public nuisance and the rule in *Rylands v Fletcher* can be used by claimants where there have been 'one-off' or isolated events. It is correct, however, that private nuisance does not usually cover isolated events.

Option B is wrong because none of the torts of private nuisance, public nuisance and the rule in *Rylands v Fletcher* depend upon proving fault, ie that the defendant has not taken reasonable care.

Option C is wrong because, while it seems that the warehouse owner is the only person to have suffered harm, there is nothing to suggest that the public has been affected. A claim in public nuisance is not, therefore, appropriate on these facts.

Option E is wrong because property damage is not *always* an unlawful interference with the use and enjoyment of land. It is correct that an interference which causes physical damage to the claimant's land is likely to be considered excessive. However, this does not apply if the damage is only trivial. In any event, private nuisance is not the appropriate tort for isolated events.

Question 3

A solicitor is instructed by a client arising from the following incident. The client's next door neighbour employed a building contractor to dig into the foundations of their home to create a basement in their property. Despite carrying out all the normal surveys and investigations, the neighbour's building contractor disrupted a Roman sewer that was not shown on any charts or surveys. This caused the busy road outside the client's home to collapse. The road was closed for 12 weeks while remedial works were carried out, causing traffic to be diverted around the client's village.

The client was injured as she was crossing the road when the road collapsed. She fell into part of the hole in the road, breaking her leg.

Which of the following statements best explains whether the client may have a claim in tort against the building contractor?

A   Yes, because the building contractor has caused a substantial and unreasonable interference with the client's use and enjoyment of their land.

B   Yes, because the client owns their property and they have suffered particular harm over and above the harm suffered by the public as a whole.

C   Yes, because the client has suffered particular harm over and above the harm suffered by the public as a whole.

D   No, because the building contractor carried out all the normal surveys and investigations.

E   No, because the client suffered a personal injury.

Answer

Option C is correct. The public right to use the highway has been affected and the client has suffered particular harm, ie the personal injury.

Option A is wrong because there is nothing on the facts to suggest that the client's use and enjoyment of their land has been interfered with (the interference is with the use of a public road). In any event, the client's personal injury is not a type of harm that is recoverable in private nuisance.

Option B is wrong as an action in public nuisance does not depend upon the client having a proprietary interest in the land affected (it is a requirement for private nuisance and the rule in *Rylands v Fletcher*). In any event, the fact that the client owns their property is irrelevant as the land interfered with is a public road.

Option D is wrong because the fact that the building contractor used reasonable care is not relevant for the torts of private nuisance, the rule in *Rylands v Fletcher* and public nuisance.

Option E is wrong because, while personal injury is not a type of harm that is protected under private nuisance and the rule in *Rylands v Fletcher*, it is a type of harm protected under public nuisance.

Index

A

accepted trade practice, compliance with, 22
actions of claimant, chain of causation, 37
actions of third party, chain of causation, 36
    instinctive intervention, 36
    negligent intervention, 36
    reckless or intentional intervening conduct, 36-7
adequate plant and equipment, employer's common law duty, 82
already-settled claim, damages on death, 117
amenity, loss of, 107

B

bereavement, damages for, 119
breach of duty, 16, 24-5
    burden of proof, 23
        Civil Evidence Act 1968, 24
        res ipsa loquitur, 23-4
    employer's common law duty, 84-5
    flowchart, 25
    occupiers' liability to trespassers, 146
        children, 147
        warnings, 146
    occupiers' liability to visitor
        children, 139
    product liability, 157
    and pure economic loss, 55
    pure psychiatric harm, 72
    and standard of care, 16
        children, 19
        reasonable person test, 16
        skilled defendant, 17-18
        special standards, 17-19
        under-skilled defendant, 18-19
    standard of care, achievement determination, 19
        common practice, 22
        cost and practicability of precautions, 21-2
        current state of knowledge, 22-3
        defendant's purpose, 22
        risk magnitude, 20
'but for' test, 31

C

causation and remoteness of damage, 30, 37, 158
    basic rule, 37
    'but for' test, 31
    chain of causation, 31
    chain of causation, breaking of, 35-6
        actions of a third party, 36-7
        actions of the claimant, 37
    divisible injury, 34
    'egg-shell skull' rule, 39-40
    employer's common law duty, 85
    factual causation
        'all or nothing' approach, 31-2
        claimant injured more than once, 33
        material contribution approach, 32
        material increase in risk, 33
    indivisible injury, 34-5
    occupiers' liability to trespassers, 147
    private nuisance, 176
    product liability, 158
    and pure economic loss, 55
    pure psychiatric harm, 72
    'similar in type' rule, 39
    visitors, occupiers' liability to, 142
'caused by,' 159-60
children
    contributory negligence, 96-7
    and loss of earnings, 112
    occupiers' liability
        to trespassers, 147
        to visitors, 139
    standard of care, 19
Civil Evidence Act 1968, 24
claimants
    consent of, 92-3
    knowledge of the risk, 92
compensatory damages, 105
    general damages, 106
    measure of damages, 105
    mitigation of loss, 105
    one action rule, 105
    special damages, 106
competent staff, employer's common law duty, 81-2

Index

consent
  negligence defences, 92
    of claimant, 92–3
      claimant's knowledge of the risk, 92
      and employees, 93
      and rescuers, 93–4
  nuisance, 184
  occupiers' liability
    to trespassers, 147
    to visitors, 142–3
  private nuisance, 177
  product liability, 158
Consumer Protection Act 1987, 158
  'caused by,' 159–60
  criteria for suing, 158–9
  damage, 159
  defect, 160
  defences, 161–2
    contributory negligence, 162
    defect did not exist when the defendant supplied the product, 162
    defect was attributable to compliance with legal requirements, 161
    defendant did not supply the product to another, 161–2
    defendant supplied the product otherwise than in the course of business, 162
    'development risks' (or 'state of the art'), 162
    exclusion of liability, 162
    manufacturer of component parts is not liable for a defect in the finished product, 162
  liability, 160
    'forgetful supplier,' 161
    importer, 161
    nature of, 161
    'own-brander,' 161
    producer (manufacturer), 160–1
  product, 160
consumers, 155
contributory negligence, 94
  behaviour that may amount to, 96
    children, 96–7
    dilemma cases, 98
    employees, 97–8
    rescuers, 97
  effect of finding of, 94–5
  examples
    crash helmets, 96
    drunken drivers, 96
    seatbelts, 95–6
  occupiers' liability to trespassers, 147
  occupiers' liability to visitors, 144
  product liability, 158, 162
current state of knowledge, standard of care, 22–3

D

damages
  causation and remoteness (*see* causation and remoteness of damage)
  on death (*see* death, damages on)
  economic loss unconnected to physical damage, 49
    damage to the property of a third party, 50–1
    no physical damage, 51–5
  non-pecuniary damages, quantification on, 107–8
  pecuniary losses, 113–14
  personal injury (*see* personal injury, damages for)
  private nuisance, 176, 180
  product liability, 159
  to property of third party, 50–1
  proportionate damages, 34
death, damages on, 115
  dependency calculation, 118–19
  Fatal Accidents Act 1976, 117, 121
    damages for bereavement, 119
    funeral expenses, 119
    loss of dependency, 118–19
  flowchart, 121
  Law Reform (Miscellaneous Provisions) Act 1934, 115–16, 121
    already-settled claim, 117
    deceased claimant, 116
  terminologies, 115
deceased claimant, 116
defective item of property, economic loss caused by acquiring, 47–9
defects, 160
defences, 158, 161
  consent, 92–5, 158
  contributory negligence, 158
  employer's common law duty, 86
  exclusion of liability, 158
  occupiers' liability to trespassers, 147
    consent, 147
    contributory negligence, 147
    exclusion of liability, 147
    illegality, 147

occupiers' liability to visitors, 142
    consent, 142-3
    contributory negligence, 144
    exclusion of liability, 143-4
private nuisance, 176-9
    effective defences, 176
    ineffective defences, 178-9
product liability
    contributory negligence, 162
    defect did not exist when the defendant supplied the product, 162
    defect was attributable to compliance with legal requirements, 161
    defendant did not supply the product to another, 161-2
    defendant supplied the product otherwise than in the course of business, 162
    'development risks' (or 'state of the art'), 162
    exclusion of liability, 162
    manufacturer of component parts is not liable for a defect in the finished product, 162
see also negligence defences
defendant's purpose, standard of care, 22
dependency, loss of, 118-119
dilemma cases, contributory negligence, 98
divisible injury, 34
duty of care, 2-3, 9-10
    breach, occupiers' liability to visitors, 138
    children, 139
    escaping breach by warnings, 140-1
    independent contractors, 141-2
    skilled visitors, 139-40
    established duty situations, 3-4
    flowchart, 10
    limiting factors for, 65
    no liability for omissions, 7-8
    no liability for omissions, exceptions to, 8
    duty not to make the situation worse, 8
    occasions when there is a duty to act positively, 8-9
    novel duty situations, 4
    neighbour principle, 4-6
    policy factor, 6-7
    test for, 7
    product liability, 154
see also breach of duty

E

earning capacity, loss of, 113
earnings, loss of see loss of earnings
economic loss, 46-7, 57-8
    breach of duty, 55
    causation of damage, 55
    caused by acquiring a defective item of property, 47-9
    exclusion of liability, 56
    fair and reasonable requirements, 56
    unconnected to physical damage, 49
    damage to the property of a third party, 50-1
    no physical damage, 51-5
'egg-shell skull' rule, 39-40, 72-3
employees
    contributory negligence, 97-8
    course of employment, 128-9
    and independent contractor, distinction between, 126-8
    negligence defences, 93
employers
    acts expressly prohibited by, 129-30
    indemnity of, 131
employers' liability, 80, 86
    breach of duty, 84-5
    causation, 85
    common law duty, 80-1
    adequate plant and equipment, 82
    competent staff, 81-2
    safe system of work, 82-3
    safe workplace, 83
    tress at work, 83-4
    defences, 86
    flowchart, 86
established duty situations and novel duty situations, distinction between, 7
exclusion of liability
    economic loss, 56
    negligence defences, 99
    occupiers' liability
        to trespassers, 147
        to visitors, 143-4
    product liability, 158, 162
expert witnesses, 23

F

factual causation
    'all or nothing' approach, 31-2
    claimant injured more than once, 33
    material contribution approach, 32
    material increase in risk, 33

Index

Fatal Accidents Act 1976, 117, 121
    damages for bereavement, 119
    funeral expenses, 119
    loss of dependency, 118-19
'forgetful supplier,' 161
fraud, 129-30
'frolic' cases, 130-1
funeral expenses, 119

I

illegality
    negligence defences, 98-9
    occupiers' liability to trespassers, 147
importers, 161
indivisible injury, 34-5
instinctive intervention, for breaking chain of causation, 36
intentional torts, 129
intermediate examination, 155-6

L

Law Reform (Miscellaneous Provisions) Act 1934, 115-16, 121
    already-settled claim, 117
    deceased claimant, 116
liability see employers' liability; product liability; trespassers, occupiers' liability to; vicarious liability; visitors, occupiers' liability to
litigation friend, 19
loss of earnings
    after trial, 109-11
    and children, 112
    lost years, 111-12
    before trial, 109

M

manufacturers, 154-5, 160-1
medical expenses, pecuniary losses, 108-9

N

negligence see breach of duty; causation and remoteness of damage; duty of care; economic loss; employers' liability; product liability; pure psychiatric harm; trespassers, occupiers' liability to; vicarious liability; visitors, occupiers' liability to
negligence defences, 92, 99
    consent, 92
        of claimant, 92-3
        claimant's knowledge of the risk, 92
        and employees, 93
        and rescuers, 93-4
    contributory negligence (see contributory negligence)
    exclusion of liability, 99
    flowchart, 100
    illegality (ex turpi causa non oritur actio), 98-9
negligent intervention, for breaking chain of causation, 36
neighbour principle, 4-5, 4-6
    fair, just and reasonable, 5, 6
    proximity between parties, 5, 6
no physical damage, and economic loss, 51
    actions, 51
    statements, 51
        special relationships, 52-4
        special relationships, extension of, 54-5
non-pecuniary damages, quantification on, 107-8
non-pecuniary losses, 106-7
    amenity, loss of, 107
    deceased claimant, 116
    pain and suffering, 107
novel duty situations, and established duty situations, distinction between, 7
nuisance, 170, 186
    flowchart, 187
    private nuisance, 170
        abnormal sensitivity, 173
        causation and remoteness, 176
        creator of the nuisance, 174
        damage, 176
        damage recoverable, 176
        defences, 176-9
        definition of, 170
        duration and frequency, 171-2
        effective defences, 176
        excessiveness of conduct/extent of harm, 172
        ineffective defences, 178-9
        interferences, 170-1
        landlord, 175
        liability, 174-5
        malice, 173
        and negligence, differences between, 182
        neighbourhood character, 172
        occupier, 174-5

public benefit, 173
relevant factors, 171-3
remedies, 179-82
suing eligibility, 174
unlawful interference, 171
public nuisance, 185
claimant has suffered particular harm, 185-6
conduct that materially affects reasonable comfort and convenience of 'class of Her Majesty's subjects,' 185
and private nuisance, differences between, 186
Rylands v Fletcher, rule in, 183
causes foreseeable damage of relevant type, 184
consent, 184
contributory negligence, 184
defences, 184
defendant brings onto their land for their own purposes, 183
escape caused by an 'act of God,' 184
escape caused by the unforeseeable act of a stranger, 184
non-natural use of land, 184
statutory authority, 184

O

occupiers' liability, 136, 147
flowchart, 148
to trespassers (*see* trespassers, occupiers' liability to)
to visitors (*see* visitors, occupiers' liability to)
Ogden tables, 111
omissions, no liability for, 7-8
exceptions to, 8
duty not to make the situation worse, 8
occasions when there is a duty to act positively, 8-9
'own-brander,' 161

P

pain and suffering, non-pecuniary losses, 107
pecuniary losses, 108
deceased claimant, 116
deductions from damages and exceptions, 113-14
earning capacity, loss of, 113
earnings, loss of, 109-12

medical expenses, 108-9
other pecuniary expenses, 113
services provided to claimant, 112-13
personal injury, damages for, 104, 106
flowchart, 120
non-pecuniary damages, quantification on, 107-8
non-pecuniary losses, 106-7
amenity, loss of, 107
pain and suffering, 107
pecuniary losses (*see* pecuniary losses)
provisional damages and periodic payments, 114-15
physical damage, economic loss unconnected to, 49
damage to the property of a third party, 50-1
no physical damage, 51
actions, 51
statements, 51-5
precautions, cost and practicability of, 21-2
premises, occupiers' liability to visitors, 138
primary victims, of pure psychiatric harm, 66, 67
private nuisance, 170
abnormal sensitivity, 173
damage, 176
causation and remoteness, 176
types of damage recoverable, 176
defences, effective, 176
act of God or nature, 177
consent, 177
contributory negligence, 177
necessity, 178
prescription, 176-7
statutory authority, 177
defences, ineffective, 178
claimant 'came to the nuisance,' 178
contributory actions of others, 179
planning permission, 179
public benefit, 178
definition of, 170
interferences, 170-1
liability, 174
creator of the nuisance, 174
landlord, 175
occupier, 174-5
and negligence, differences between, 182
relevant factors, 171
duration and frequency, 171-2
excessiveness of conduct/extent of harm, 172
malice, 173

Index

private nuisance (*Continued*)
    neighbourhood character, 172
    public benefit, 173
  remedies, 179
    abatement (self-help), 181-2
    damages, 180
    injunctions, 180-2
    mandatory injunction, 180
    personal discomfort, 180
    physical damage to the claimant's land, 180
    prohibitory injunction, 180
    '*quia timet*' injunction, 180-1
    suing eligibility, 174
    unlawful interference, 171
producers (manufacturers), 154-5, 160-1
product liability, 154, 163
  Consumer Protection Act 1987, 158
    'caused by,' 159-60
    criteria for suing, 158-9
    'damage,' 159
    'defect,' 160
    defences, 161-2
    liability, 160-1
    'product,' 160
  flowchart, 163
  negligence, 154
    breach of duty, 157
    causation and remoteness, 158
    consumer, 155
    defences, 158
    duty of care, 154
    intermediate examination, 155-6
    manufacturer, 154-5
    product, 155
    proof of breach, 157
    scope of duty owed, 156-7
products, 155, 160
proof of breach, product liability, 157
proportionate damages, 34
provisional damages and periodic payments, 114-15
psychiatric harm, pure *see* pure psychiatric harm
public nuisance, 185
  claimant has suffered particular harm, 185-6
  conduct that materially affects the reasonable comfort and convenience of a 'class of Her Majesty's subjects,' 185
  and private nuisance, differences between, 186
pure psychiatric harm, 64-5, 73-4
  breach of duty, 72
  causation of damage, 72
  definition of, 65
  limiting factors for duty of care, 65
  primary victims, 66, 67
  rescuers, 71
  secondary victims, 66, 67-8
    foreseeability of psychiatric harm, 68, 69
    proximity in time and space, 69, 70
    proximity of perception, 69, 70-1
    proximity of relationship, 68-9
  victim types, 66

R

reasonable person test, 16
reckless or intentional intervening conduct, for breaking chain of causation, 36-7
remoteness of damage *see* causation and remoteness of damage
res ipsa loquitur, 23-4
rescuers, 71
  contributory negligence, 97
  negligence defences, 93-4
risk magnitude, standard of care, 20
  likelihood of an injury occurring, 20
  risk of greater injury, 20
Rylands v Fletcher, rule in, 183
  causes foreseeable damage of relevant type, 184
  defences, 184
    consent, 184
    contributory negligence, 184
    escape caused by an 'act of God,' 184
    escape caused by the unforeseeable act of a stranger, 184
    statutory authority, 184
  defendant brings onto their land for their own purposes, 183
  escape, 184
  non-natural use of land, 184

S

safe system of work, employer's common law duty, 82-3
safe workplace, employer's common law duty, 83
secondary victims, of pure psychiatric harm, 66, 67-8
  foreseeability of psychiatric harm, 68, 69
  proximity in time and space, 69, 70

proximity of perception, 69, 70-1
proximity of relationship, 68-9
services provided to claimant, pecuniary losses, 112-13
'similar in type' rule, for remoteness of damage, 39
skilled defendant, standard of care, 17-18
standard of care, 16
    achievement determination, 19
        common practice, 22
        cost and practicability of precautions, 21-2
        current state of knowledge, 22-3
        defendant's purpose, 22
        risk magnitude, 20
    reasonable person test, 16
    special standards, 17-19
        children, 19
        skilled defendant, 17-18
        under-skilled defendant, 18-19
stress at work, employer's common law duty, 83-4

T

tortfeasors
    contribution between, 34-5
    definition of, 2
trespassers, occupiers' liability to, 144
    breach of duty, 146
        children, 147
        warnings, 146
    causation and remoteness, 147
    defences, 147
        consent, 147
        contributory negligence, 147
        exclusion of liability, 147
        illegality, 147
    duty owed to people other than visitors, 144-5
    existence of duty, 145
    scope of the Occupiers' Liability Act 1984 duty, 145
    trespassers, definition of, 144

U

under-skilled defendant, standard of care, 18-19

V

vicarious liability, 126, 131
    employer's indemnity, 130
    flowchart, 131
    requirements for, 126
        acts expressly prohibited by the employer, 128
        employee and independent contractor, distinction between, 126-7
        employee must act 'in the course of employment,' 127-8
        'frolic' cases, 129-30
        intentional torts, 129
visitors, occupiers' liability to, 136
    causation and remoteness of damage, 142
    common duty of care, 138
    common duty of care, breach of, 138
        children, 139
        escaping breach by warnings, 140-1
        independent contractors, 141-2
        skilled visitors, 139-40
    defences, 142
        consent, 142-3
        contributory negligence, 144
        exclusion of liability, 143-4
    occupier, definition of, 136-7
    premises, 138
    visitor, definition of, 137-8
voluntary assumption of risk, 92, 142, 184

W

warnings, occupiers' liability to trespassers, 146
witness evidence, 23